Complete HSPT®!

High School Placement Test Study Guide & Practice Test Questions

Published by

Complete **TEST** ™
Preparation Inc.

We strongly recommend that students check with exam providers for up-to-date information regarding test content.

Published by
Complete Test Preparation Inc.
Victoria BC Canada
Visit us on the web at https://www.test-preparation.ca
Printed in the USA

About Complete Test Preparation Inc.

The Complete Test Preparation Team has been publishing high quality study materials since 2005. Over 1 million students visit our websites every year, and thousands of students, teachers and parents all over the world (over 100 countries) have purchased our teaching materials, curriculum, study guides and practice tests.

Complete Test Preparation is committed to providing students with the best study materials and practice tests available on the market. Members of our team combine years of teaching experience, with experienced writers and editors, all with advanced degrees.

ISBN-13: 978-1927358658

Version 7.5 April 2018

Feedback

We welcome your feedback. Email us at feedback@test-preparation.ca with your comments and suggestions. We carefully review all suggestions and often incorporate reader suggestions into upcoming versions. As a Print on Demand Publisher, we update our products frequently.

Find us on Facebook

WWW.FACEBOOK.COM/COMPLETETESTPREPARATION

Contents

Getting Started

CONGRATULATIONS! By deciding to take the High School Placement Test (HSPT®), you have taken the first step toward a great future! Of course, there is no point in taking this important examination unless you intend to do your best to earn the highest grade you possibly can. That means getting yourself organized and discovering the best approaches, methods and strategies to master the material. Yes, that will require real effort and dedication on your part, but if you are willing to focus your energy and devote the study time necessary, before you know it you will be on you way to a brighter future!

We know that taking on a new endeavour can be scary, and it is easy to feel unsure of where to begin. That's where we come in. This study guide is designed to help you improve your test-taking skills, show you a few tricks of the trade and increase both your competency and confidence.

The High School Placement Test

The HSPT® is composed of five sections, verbal skills, quantitative skills, reading, mathematics and language skills. The verbal skills section consists of analogies, synonyms and antonyms, logic and verbal classification. The quantitative skills section consists of number series, geometric and non geometric comparisons, and basic math. The reading section consists of reading comprehension and vocabulary questions. The mathematics section consists of problem solving questions or word problems. The language skills section consists of punctuation and capitalization, English usage, spelling and composition.

While we seek to make our guide as comprehensive as possible, note that like all exams, the HSPT® Exam might be adjusted at some future point. New material might be added, or content that is no longer relevant or applicable might be removed. It is always a good idea to give the materials you receive when you register to take the HSPT® a careful review.

How this study guide is organized

This study guide is divided into three sections. The first section, Self-Assessments, which will help you recognize your areas of strength and weaknesses. This will be a boon when it comes to managing your study time most efficiently; there is not much point of focusing on material you have already got firmly under control. Instead, taking the self-assessments will show you where that time could be much better spent. In this area you will begin with a few questions to quickly evaluate your understanding of material that is likely to appear on the HSPT®. If you do poorly in certain areas, simply work carefully through those sections in the tutorials and then try the self-assessment again.

The second section, Tutorials, offers information in each of the content areas, as well as strategies to help you master that material. The tutorials are not intended to be a complete course, but cover general principles. If you find that you do not understand the tutorials, it is recommended that you seek out additional instruction.

Third, we offer two sets of practice test questions, similar to those on the HSPT® Exam.

The HSPT® Study Plan

Now that you have made the decision to take the HSPT®, it is time to get started. Before you do another thing, you will need to figure out a plan of attack. The best study tip is to start early! The longer the time period you devote to regular study practice, the more likely you will be to retain the material and be able to access it quickly. If you thought that 1x20 is the same as 2x10, guess what? It really is not, when it comes to study time. Reviewing material for just an hour per day over the course of 20 days is far better than studying for two hours a day for only 10 days. The more often you revisit a particular piece of information, the better you will know it. Not only will your grasp and understanding be better, but your ability to reach into your brain and quickly and efficiently pull out the tidbit you need, will be greatly enhanced as well.

The great Chinese scholar and philosopher Confucius believed that true knowledge could be defined as knowing both what you know and what you do not know. The first step in preparing for the HSPT® is to assess your strengths and weaknesses. You may already have an idea of what you know and what you do not know, but evaluating yourself using our Self- Assessment modules for each of the three areas, Math, Writing and Quantitative skills, will clarify the details.

Making a Study Schedule

To make your study time the most productive you will need to develop a study plan. The purpose of the plan is to organize all the bits of pieces of information in such a way that you will not feel overwhelmed. Rome was not built in a day, and learning everything you will need to know to pass the HSPT® is going to take time, too. Arranging the material you need to learn into manageable chunks is the best way to go. Each study session should make you feel as though you have accomplished your goal, or at least are a little closer, and your goal is simply to learn what you planned to learn during that particular session. Try to organize the content in such a way that each study session builds on previous ones. That way, you will retain the information, be better able to access it, and review the previous bits and pieces at the same time.

Self-assessment

The Best Study Tip! The best study tip is to start early! The longer you study regularly, the more you will retain and 'learn' the material. Studying for 1 hour per day for 20 days is far better than studying for 2 hours for 10 days.

What don't you know?

The first step is to assess your strengths and weaknesses. You may already have an idea of where your weaknesses are, or you can take our Self-assessment modules for each of the content areas.

Exam Component	Rate 1 to 5
Verbal Skills	
Verbal Analogies	
Synonyms	
Logic	
Verbal Classifications	
Antonyms	
Quantitative Skills	
Number Series	
Geometric Comparison	
Non-geometric Comparison	
Number Manipulation	
Mathematics	
Mathematical Concepts	

Problem-Solving	
Language Skills	
Punctuation and Capitalization	
Usage	
Spelling	

Making a Study Schedule

The key to making a study plan is to divide the material you need to learn into manageable sized pieces and learn it, while at the same time reviewing the material that you already know.

Using the table above, any scores of 3 or below, you need to spend time learning, going over and practicing this subject area. A score of 4 means you need to review the material, but you don't have to spend time re-learning. A score of 5 and you are OK with just an occasional review before the exam. A score of 0 or 1 means you really need to work on this should allocate the most time and the highest priority. Some students prefer a 5-day plan and others a 10-day plan. It also depends on how much time you have until the exam.

Here is an example of a 5-day plan based on an example from the table above:

Verbal Analogies: 1- Study 1 hour everyday – review on last day

Vocabulary: 3 - Study 1 hour for 3 days then ½ hour a day, then review

Problem Solving (Word Problems): 4 - Review every second day

Geometric Comparisons: 5 - Review for ½ hour every other day

Usage: 5 - Review for ½ hour every other day

Using this example, Spelling and Grammar are good, and only need occasional review. Geometric Comparison is good and needs 'some' review. Vocabulary needs a bit of work, Word Problems need a lot of work and Verbal Analogies are very weak and need most of your time. Based on this, here is a sample study plan:

Day	Subject	Time
Monday		
Study	Verbal Analogies	1 hour
Study	Word Problems	1 hour
½ hour break		
Study	Vocabulary	1 hour
Review	Reading Comp.	½ hour
Tuesday		
Study	Verbal Analogies	1 hour
Study	Word Problems	½ hour
½ hour break		
Study	Vocabulary	½ hour
Review	Geometric Comparisons	½ hour
Review	Usage	½ hour
Wednesday		
Study	Verbal Analogies	1 hour
Study	Word Problems	½ hour
½ hour break		
Study	Vocabulary	½ hour
Review	Reading Comp.	½ hour
Thursday		
Study	Verbal Analogies	½ hour
Study	Word Problems	½ hour
Review	Vocabulary	½ hour
½ hour break		
Review	Usage	½ hour
Review	Geometric Comparisons	½ hour
Friday		
Review	Verbal Analogies	½ hour
Review	Word Problems	½ hour
Review	Vocabulary	½ hour
½ hour break		
Review	Geometric Comparisons	½ hour
Review	Usage	½ hour

Using this example, adapt the study plan to your own schedule. This schedule assumes 2 ½ - 3 hours available to study everyday for a 5 day period.

First, write out what you need to study and how much. Next figure out how many days you have before the test. Note, do NOT study on the last day before the test. On the last day before the test, you won't learn anything and will probably only confuse yourself.

Make a table with the days before the test and the number of hours you have available to study each day. We suggest working with 1 hour and ½ hour time slots.

Start filling in the blanks, with the subjects you need to study the most getting the most time and the most regular time slots (i.e. everyday) and the subjects that you know getting the least time (e.g. ½ hour every other day, or every 3rd day).

Tips for making a schedule

Once you make a schedule, stick with it! Make your study sessions reasonable. If you make a study schedule and don't stick with it, you set yourself up for failure. Instead, schedule study sessions that are a bit shorter and set yourself up for success! Make sure your study sessions are do-able. Studying is hard work but after you pass, you can party and take a break!

Schedule breaks. Breaks are just as important as study time. Work out a rotation of studying and breaks that works for you.

Build up study time. If you find it hard to sit still and study for 1 hour straight through, build up to it. Start with 20 minutes, and then take a break. Once you get used to 20-minute study sessions, increase the time to 30 minutes. Gradually work you way up to 1 hour.

40 minutes to 1 hour is optimal. Studying for longer than this is tiring and not productive. Studying for shorter isn't long enough to be productive.

Studying Math. Studying Math is different from studying other subjects because you use a different part of your brain. The best way to study math is to practice everyday. This will train your mind to think in a mathematical way. If you miss a day or days, the mathematical mind-set is gone, and you have to start all over again to build it up.

Study and practice math everyday for at least 5 days before the exam.

For additional information on getting organized to study, see our How to Study book at www.study-skills.ca.

Verbal Skills

THIS SECTION CONTAINS A SELF-ASSESSMENT AND VERBAL SKILLS TUTORIAL. The tutorials are designed to familiarize general principles and the self-assessment contains general questions similar to the verbal skills questions likely to be on the HSPT®, but are not intended to be identical to the exam questions. The tutorials are not designed to be a complete reading course, and it is assumed that students have some familiarity with verbal skills questions. If you do not understand parts of the tutorial, or find the tutorial difficult, it is recommended that you seek out additional instruction.

Tour of the HSPT Verbal Skills

The HSPT® verbal skills section has 60 questions. Below is a detailed list of the types of reading questions that generally appear on the HSPT®.

- Verbal Analogies

- Synonyms and antonyms

- Sentence logic

- Verbal Classification

The questions below are not the same as you will find on the HSPT® - that would be too easy! And nobody knows what the questions will be and they change all the time. Mostly the changes consist of substituting new questions for old, but the changes can be new question formats or styles, changes to the number of questions in each section, changes to the time limits for each section and combining sections. Below are general verbal skills questions that cover the same areas as the HSPT®. While the format and exact wording of the questions may differ slightly, and change from year to year, if you can answer the questions below, you will have no problem with the verbal skills section of the HSPT®.

Verbal Skills Self-Assessment

The purpose of the self-assessment is:

- Identify your strengths and weaknesses.

- Develop your personalized study plan (above)

- Get accustomed to the HSPT® format

- Extra practice – the self-assessments are almost a full 3rd practice test!

- Provide a baseline score for preparing your study schedule.

Since this is a Self-assessment, and depending on how confident you are with Verbal Skills, timing is optional. The HSPT® has 60 verbal skills questions to be answered in 16 minutes. The self-assessment has 50 questions, so allow about 12 minutes to complete this assessment.

Once complete, use the table below to assess your understanding of the content, and prepare your study schedule described in chapter 1.

80% - 100%	Excellent – you have mastered the content
60 – 79%	Good. You have a working knowledge. Even though you can just pass this section, you may want to review the tutorials and do some extra practice to see if you can improve your mark.
40% - 59%	Below Average. You do not understand verbal skills problems. Review the tutorials, and retake this quiz again in a few days, before proceeding to the Practice Test Questions.
Less than 40%	Poor. You have a very limited understanding of verbal skills problems. Please review the tutorials, and retake this quiz again in a few days, before proceeding to the Practice Test Questions.

Verbal Skills Self-Assessment Answer Sheet

1. Ⓐ Ⓑ Ⓒ Ⓓ	18. Ⓐ Ⓑ Ⓒ Ⓓ	35. Ⓐ Ⓑ Ⓒ Ⓓ
2. Ⓐ Ⓑ Ⓒ Ⓓ	19. Ⓐ Ⓑ Ⓒ Ⓓ	36. Ⓐ Ⓑ Ⓒ Ⓓ
3. Ⓐ Ⓑ Ⓒ Ⓓ	20. Ⓐ Ⓑ Ⓒ Ⓓ	37. Ⓐ Ⓑ Ⓒ Ⓓ
4. Ⓐ Ⓑ Ⓒ Ⓓ	21. Ⓐ Ⓑ Ⓒ Ⓓ	38. Ⓐ Ⓑ Ⓒ Ⓓ
5. Ⓐ Ⓑ Ⓒ Ⓓ	22. Ⓐ Ⓑ Ⓒ Ⓓ	39. Ⓐ Ⓑ Ⓒ Ⓓ
6. Ⓐ Ⓑ Ⓒ Ⓓ	23. Ⓐ Ⓑ Ⓒ Ⓓ	40. Ⓐ Ⓑ Ⓒ Ⓓ
7. Ⓐ Ⓑ Ⓒ Ⓓ	24. Ⓐ Ⓑ Ⓒ Ⓓ	41. Ⓐ Ⓑ Ⓒ Ⓓ
8. Ⓐ Ⓑ Ⓒ Ⓓ	25. Ⓐ Ⓑ Ⓒ Ⓓ	42. Ⓐ Ⓑ Ⓒ Ⓓ
9. Ⓐ Ⓑ Ⓒ Ⓓ	26. Ⓐ Ⓑ Ⓒ Ⓓ	43. Ⓐ Ⓑ Ⓒ Ⓓ
10. Ⓐ Ⓑ Ⓒ Ⓓ	27. Ⓐ Ⓑ Ⓒ Ⓓ	44. Ⓐ Ⓑ Ⓒ Ⓓ
11. Ⓐ Ⓑ Ⓒ Ⓓ	28. Ⓐ Ⓑ Ⓒ Ⓓ	45. Ⓐ Ⓑ Ⓒ Ⓓ
12. Ⓐ Ⓑ Ⓒ Ⓓ	29. Ⓐ Ⓑ Ⓒ Ⓓ	46. Ⓐ Ⓑ Ⓒ Ⓓ
13. Ⓐ Ⓑ Ⓒ Ⓓ	30. Ⓐ Ⓑ Ⓒ Ⓓ	47. Ⓐ Ⓑ Ⓒ Ⓓ
14. Ⓐ Ⓑ Ⓒ Ⓓ	31. Ⓐ Ⓑ Ⓒ Ⓓ	48. Ⓐ Ⓑ Ⓒ Ⓓ
15. Ⓐ Ⓑ Ⓒ Ⓓ	32. Ⓐ Ⓑ Ⓒ Ⓓ	49. Ⓐ Ⓑ Ⓒ Ⓓ
16. Ⓐ Ⓑ Ⓒ Ⓓ	33. Ⓐ Ⓑ Ⓒ Ⓓ	50. Ⓐ Ⓑ Ⓒ Ⓓ
17. Ⓐ Ⓑ Ⓒ Ⓓ	34. Ⓐ Ⓑ Ⓒ Ⓓ	

Part I – Verbal Analogies

Instructions: Select the pair with the same relationship.

1. Nest : Bird

    a. Cave : Bear
    b. Flower : Petal
    c. Window : House
    d. Dog : Basket

2. Teacher : School

    a. Businessman : Money
    b. Waitress : Coffee shop
    c. Dentist : Tooth
    d. Fish : Water

3. Pebble : Boulder

    a. Pond : Ocean
    b. River: Rapids
    c. Fish : Elephant
    d. Feather : Bird

4. Poodle : Dog

    a. Shark : Great White
    b. Dalmatian : Great Dane
    c. Money : Stock Market
    d. Horse : Pony

5. Fox : Chicken

    a. Rat : Mouse
    b. Cat : mouse
    c. Dog : cat
    d. Rabbit : hen

Part II – Synonyms

6. Select the synonym of conspicuous.

    a. Important
    b. Prominent
    c. Beautiful
    d. Convincing

7. Select the synonym of benevolence.

    a. Happiness
    b. Courage
    c. Kindness
    d. Loyalty

8. Select the synonym of boisterous.

    a. Loud
    b. Soft
    c. Gentle
    d. Warm

9. Select the synonym of fondle.

    a. Hold
    b. Caress
    c. Throw
    d. Keep

10. Select the synonym of momentous.

    a. Magical
    b. Memorable
    c. Extraordinary
    d. Very important

11. Select the synonym of antagonist.

    a. Supporter

    b. Fan

    c. Enemy

    d. Partner

12. Select the synonym of memento.

    a. Monument

    b. Remember

    c. Reminder

    d. Idea

13. Select the synonym of insidious.

    a. Wise

    b. Brave

    c. Helpful

    d. Deceitful

14. Select the synonym of itinerary.

    a. Schedule

    b. Guidebook

    c. Pass

    d. Diary

15. Select the synonym of illustrious.

    a. Rich

    b. Noble

    c. Gallant

    d. Poor

16. Select the synonym of succulent.

    a. Dull

    b. Adventurous

    c. Sweet

    d. Juicy

17. Select the synonym of construe.

    a. Decide

    b. Design

    c. Interpret

    d. Examine

18. Select the synonym of gregarious.

    a. Sad

    b. Sociable

    c. Loving

    d. Funny

19. Select the synonym of hesitant.

    a. Willing

    b. Doubtful

    c. Eager

    d. Happy

20. Select the synonym of lucid.

    a. Dark

    b. Clear

    c. Memorable

    d. Easy

Part III – Logic

21. The Silver fish can swim faster than the black fish. The gold fish can swim faster than the black fish. The gold fish can swim faster than the silver fish. If the first 2 statements are true, then the third statement is:

True   False   Uncertain

22. All rabbits have fur. Some rabbits are pets. Some pets have fur. If the first 2 statements are true, then the third statement is:

True   False   Uncertain

23. Deciduous trees drop their leaves in the fall. Confers keep their leaves all year round. Conifers are deciduous. If the first 2 statements are true, then the third statement is:

True   False   Uncertain

24. No homework is fun. Reading is homework. Reading is not fun. If the first 2 statements are true, then the third statement is:

True   False   Uncertain

25. All informative things are useful things. Some websites are not useful things. Some websites are not informative. If the first 2 statements are true, then the third statement is:

True   False   Uncertain

Part IV – Verbal Classification

26. Which word does not belong?

a. Jet

b. Float plane

c. Kite

d. Biplane

27. Which does not belong?

a. Number

b. Denominate

c. Numerate

d. Figure

28. Which does not belong?

a. Abc

b. bCD

c. Nmo

d. Pqr

29. Which does not belong?

a. CD

b. OP

c. LM

d. BD

30. Which does not belong?

a. 121212

b. 141414

c. 151415

d. 292929

31. Which does not belong?

a. 246
b. 123
c. 468
d. 024

32. Which does not belong?

a. QRS
b. LMN
c. ACF
d. RST

33. Which does not belong?

a. aBCd
b. lMNo
c. PQRs
d. tUVw

34. Which does not belong?

a. ABCD
b. JKLM
c. PQRS
d. WXYZ

35. Which does not belong?

a. BBCCDDEE
b. LLMMNNOO
c. HHIIJJKK
d. RRSSTTUU

36. Which does not belong?

a. 123
b. 246
c. 456
d. 789

37. Which does not belong?

a. def
b. nop
c. tuv
d. lmn

38. Which does not belong?

a. Argue
b. Talk
c. Dispute
d. Contest

39. Which does not belong?

a. ddeeffgg
b. ffgghhii
c. nnooppqq
d. ttuuvwww

40. Which does not belong?

a. 11223344
b. 33445566
c. 33455666
d. 44556677

41. Which does not belong?

a. mNo
b. pQr
c. Stu
d. xYz

Part V - Antonyms

42. Choose the antonym pair.

a. Abundant and Scarce
b. Several and Plenty
c. Analysis and Review
d. Obtrusive and Hierarchical

43. Choose the antonym pair.

a. Bully and Animal
b. Teary-eyed and Gentle
c. Tough and Weak
d. Strong and Massive

44. Choose the antonym pair.

a. Illuminate and Emphasize
b. Resonance and Significance
c. Resonate and Justify
d. Rationalize and Practice

45. Choose the antonym pair.

a. Simple and Complex
b. Plain and Plaid
c. Gradual and Precipitous
d. Vibrant and Cheery

46. Choose the antonym pair.

a. Elevate and Escalate
b. Exhibit and Conceal
c. Boast and Brood
d. Show and Contest

47. Choose the antonym pair.

a. Strict and Tight
b. Hurtful and Offensive
c. Unpleasant and Mean
d. Stingy and Generous

48. Choose the antonym pair.

a. New and Torn
b. Advance and Retreat
c. Next and Last
d. Followed and Continued

49. Choose the antonym pair.

a. Halt and Speed
b. Began and Amidst
c. Stop and Delay
d. Cease and Begin

50. Choose the antonym pair.

a. Scary and Horrific
b. Honor and Justice
c. Immense and Tiny
d. Vague and Loud

Answer Key
Part I – Verbal Analogies

1. A
This is a functional relationship. A bird lives in a nest, the way a bear lives in a cave.

2. B
This is a functional relationship. A teacher works in a school in the same way a waitress works in a coffee shop.

3. A
This is a degree relationship. A boulder is a very large pebble - both are rocks, in the same way an ocean is a very large pond - both are bodies of water.

4. A
This is a type relationship. A poodle is a type of dog in the same way a great white is a type of shark.

5. B
This is a predator/prey relationship. Foxes eat chickens in the same way as cats eat mice.

Part II – Synonyms

6. B
Conspicuous and prominent are synonyms.

7. C
Benevolence and Kindness are synonyms.

8. A
Boisterous and loud are synonyms.

9. B
Fondle and caress are synonyms.

10. D
Momentous and very important are synonyms.

11. C
Antagonist and enemy are synonyms.

12. C
Memento and reminder are synonyms.

A memento is an object kept as a reminder or souvenir of a person or event.

13. D
Insidious and deceitful are synonyms.

Insidious means treacherous or crafty.

14. A
Itinerary and schedule are synonyms.

Itinerary is a travel document recording a trip or journey.

15. B
Illustrious and noble are synonyms.

Illustrious means well known, respected, and admired for past achievements.

16. D
Succulent and juicy are synonyms.

Succulent means tender, juicy, and tasty.

17. C
Construe and interpret are synonyms.

To construe means to interpret (a word or action) in a particular way.

18. B
Gregarious and sociable are synonyms.

Gregarious means fond of company; sociable.

19. B
Hesitant and doubtful are synonyms.

Hesitant means, tentative, unsure, or slow in acting or speaking.

20. B
Lucid and clear are synonyms.

Lucid means expressed clearly; easy to understand.

Part III – Logic

21. Uncertain
We don't have enough information here to make a decision. Perhaps the gold fish can swim faster than the black fish AND the silver fish – we don't know.

22. True
This argument is a little sloppy, because the 2nd statement and the conclusion both use 'some.' However, it is a valid argument.

23. False
This is a clearly false argument.

24. True
This is a very strong argument. If the first two statement are true, then the third statement or conclusion must be true.

25. True
This is a strong argument since the first statement uses 'all,' and the second statement uses 'some.' And the conclusion uses 'some.'

Part IV – Verbal Classification

26. C
A kite is not a type of plane.

27. D
This is a relationship of words question. All the choices are synonyms of count, except figure.

28. B
This is a capital small letter relationship. All choices start with a capital letter.

29. D
BD is not a sequence of consecutive letters.

30. C
This is a repetition pattern. All the choices repeat a 2-letter sequence.

31. B
123 are consecutive, the others are obtained by adding 2.

32. C
ACF is not a sequence of consecutive letters.

33. C
This is a capital letter small letter relationship. All choices have the middle two letters capitalized except c.

34. A
This is a vowel and consonant relationship. All the choices are only consonants.

35. C
This is a vowel and consonant relationship. All the choices have 2 vowels at the end.

36. B
246 is not a sequence of consecutive numbers.

37. D
This is a vowel and consonant relationship. All the choices have one vowel in the middle position.

38. B
This is a word meaning relationship. Talk is not a synonym for any of the choices.

39. B
This is a vowel and consonant rela-

tionship. All the choices have vowels in positions 3 and 4.

40. C
This is a repetition pattern. All the choices have consecutive numbers repeated twice.

41. C
This is a capital letter small letter relationship. All choices have the middle letter capitalized.

Part V – Antonyms

42. A
Abundant and scarce are antonyms.

43. C
Tough and weak are antonyms.

44. B
Resonance and significance are antonyms.

45. A
Simple and complex are antonyms.

46. B
Exhibit and conceal are antonyms.

47. D
Stingy and generous are antonyms.

48. B
Advance and retreat are antonyms.

49. D
Cease and begin are antonyms.

50. C
Immense and tiny are antonyms.

Verbal Skills Tutorials

Verbal Analogies and Classification Tutorial

Verbal analogies can be tricky for anyone, which is why it is important to have strategies to have a better chance of choosing the correct answer. The following verbal analogies strategies will help you to excel with these types of tests and/ or problems:

1. The only way to become better at anything is to practice and the same is true for verbal analogies. There really is not any other way to study for verbal analogies than by practicing them. You can start up to a month in advance practicing an hour a day.

2. It does not matter how many relationships you can find between the words given in a verbal analogy, what is important is that you give the answer the test-maker is looking for. This strategy is to give the exact answer. Many times, the relationships you think you see are much more in depth than what the test maker is looking for. The following is an example of what this means:

Bigotry/Hatred

> a. sweetness: bitterness
> b. segregation: integration
> c. equality: government
> d. fanaticism: intolerance

You might automatically think that 'bigot' is to 'hate' or that 'bigots hate' is very similar to 'c,' as equality is normally associated with the government or 'd,' ad fanatics are often seen as intolerable. The problem is that this way of thinking is subjective or prejudiced and that not everyone thinks like this, so how can those choices be true. You will notice though, choices 'b,' and 'd,' are not a subjective thought but rather a social extreme, just as 'Bigotry/hatred' is. The way to narrow down the choices more is by looking at the words in accordance to one another, 'bigotry and hatred' are similar terms, but choice 'b,' is not, they are opposite words. 'd,' would be the correct choice because they are also similar terms.

3. Another strategy you can use with verbal analogies is to pick out a word or words that are similar to those in the analogy. This means to find a word that will name the relationship of the given words. The main relationships found in analogies and are listed below:

- **Purpose:** This means that 'A' is used for 'B' the same way that 'X' is used for 'Y'.

- **Cause and Effect:** This means that 'A' has an effect on 'B' the same way that 'X' has an effect on 'Y'.
- **Part to Whole** (individual to group): This means that 'A' is a part of 'B' the same way that 'X' is a part of 'Y'
- **Part to part:** 'A' and 'B' are both parts of something the way that 'X' and 'Y' are both parts of something
- **Action to object:** 'A' is done to 'B' the same way 'X' is done to 'Y'.
- **Object to action:** 'A' does something to 'B' just as 'X' does something to 'Y'.
- **Word meaning:** 'A' means about the same as 'B' and 'X' means about the same as 'Y'
- **Opposite word meaning:** 'A means about the opposite of 'B' and 'X' means about the opposite of 'Y'
- **Sequence:** 'A' comes before (or after) B" just as 'X' comes before (or after) 'Y'.
- **Place:** 'A' and 'B' are related places just as 'X' and 'Y' are related places.
- **Magnitude:** 'A' is greater than (or less than) 'B' and 'X' is greater than (or less than) 'Y'.
- **Grammatical:** 'A' and 'B' are parts of speech related to each other noun to noun, adjective to noun, etc. in the same way that parts of speech 'X' and 'Y' are related to each other.

4. The next strategy is to read the verbal analogies in sentences. If you take the example above, you could read it something like this 'Bigotry relates to hatred in the same way that'¦' and insert each of the choices at the end like 'equality relates to government', etc'. You can change how you word the sentence to whichever relationship is between the words.

5. Sometimes it is difficult to identify the relationship by just looking at the analogy in the order it is represented, so switch the words and try to find a relationship that way. Therefore, instead of considering how 'bigotry' relates to 'hatred' try to see how 'hatred' relates to 'bigotry'. If you are still stuck you can start finding relationships between the first and second word of the given analogy and the first and second word in the choices, respectively, of course. Compare all the first words to the original first word, and the second with the second word.

6. As with all types of tests, you can make an educated guess when all other strategies have failed. Follow your hunches, choose a letter that you have not chosen in a while, or maybe just mark the most complex relationship you see in the choices, if you are pressed for time.

Logic – A Quick Tutorial

Understanding syllogism can be tricky which is why it's important to understand the strategies involved in solving the problems. Here are some tips to guide you when reviewing for syllogism exam questions:

Logical syllogisms have three key components: the major premise, minor premise, and the conclusion. Practicing logic questions helps you identify these quickly and easily.

There are two terms used in each part, which can be understood through the form ""Some/all A is/are [not] B." Each premise has a common term with the conclusion as seen in the example below:

Premise: All birds are animals
Premise: All parrots are birds
Conclusion: All parrots are animals

In this example, "animal" is the major term and predicate of the conclusion, "parrot" is the minor term and subject of the conclusion, and "bird" is the middle term.

Clearly, this argument is rock-solid. If ALL birds are animals, AND all parrots are birds, then the conclusion must be true – All parrots must be animals.

To check on this, let's try a variation:

Some birds are animals.
All parrots are birds
All parrots are animals.

Clearly, this is not true. If only 'some' birds are animals, then there are some birds which are NOT animals, and we don't have any information about if the 'some' birds which are not animals. Perhaps the 'some birds that are not animals' are parrots, and perhaps not.

Here is another example:

This store only sells used textbooks.
My textbook is used.
My textbook came from that store.

This is clearly a not true. We do not know if the store is the only store in the world that sells textbooks, so clearly the textbook in question could have come from that store or any other store.

Structure

There are four possible variations to each "Some/all/no A is/are [not] B," structure.

All birds are animals.
All parrots are birds.

All parrots are animals.

Clearly a very solid argument – IF all birds are animals AND all parrots are birds, then the conclusion, all parrots are animals MUST be true.

Here is a variation that is NOT true:

Some birds are animals.
All parrots are birds.
All parrots are animals.

Here we don't know if the 'some' birds that are NOT animals includes parrots or not. They may be but we don't know.

Here is the negative example:

No birds are foxes.
All parrots are birds.
No parrots are foxes.

A very good argument where the conclusion, No parrots are foxes MUST be true if the premises are true.

Notice what happens if we substitute 'some' into the argument.

Some birds are foxes.
All parrots are birds.
No parrots are foxes.

No birds are foxes.
Some parrots are birds.
No parrots are foxes.

Both of these are clearly false.   The argument relies on the fact the absolute statements ALL and NONE.

Using some can give a very solid argument though. Consider these:

All dogs are animals.
Some mammals are dogs.
Some mammals are animals.

No dogs are birds.
Some mammals are dogs.
Some mammals are not birds.

No restaurant food is healthy.
Some recipes are healthy.
Some recipes are not restaurant foods.

All liars are evildoers.
Some doctors are not evildoers.
Some doctors are not liars.

All these are very good arguments where the conclusion MUST be true if the premises are true.

Below is a comprehensive list of all valid logic argument forms. Study these forms and make sure that you are familiar with them and understand why the conclusion must be true.

The Real World

Generally, exam questions are not exactly like the forms we have been discussing so far, but are similar. Understanding the correct forms is still very important and necessary to understanding the underlying structure. Here are some example logic questions:

1.
Practice makes perfect.
I am perfect.
I practiced a lot.

If the first 2 statements are true, then the third statement is:

True False Uncertain

The correct answer is - Uncertain. There are all sorts of reasons you could be perfect without practicing. For example, you could be perfect looking, or your hair could be perfect, or you could be perfect by a coincidence.

2.
People who smoke cigarettes have a 75% chance of getting cancer.

I have cancer.
I smoked a lot.

If the first 2 statements are true, then the third statement is:

True False Uncertain

The correct answer is - Uncertain. There are many reasons you could have cancer. In addition, you may be among the 25% of people who smoke and do NOT get cancer.

3.

Most car accidents happen in the morning.
I don't drive in the morning.
I am unlikely to have an accident.
If the first 2 statements are true, then the third statement is:

True False Uncertain
The correct answer is - Uncertain.

4.

Halibut are a large fish.
I caught a small fish.
I did not catch a halibut.
If the first 2 statements are true, then the third statement is:

True False Uncertain

The correct answer is – False. You could have caught a baby halibut. In order for this to be true, you would have to say,

All halibut are large fish.
I caught a small fish.
I did not catch a halibut.

Here, the first premise is ALL halibut are large, which would include baby halibut, so if the first two premises are true, the third statement MUST be true also.

A Different Style

Here is a different style of question.

1.

Angel gets the highest grades in all the subjects in school. She is also the president of the Student Council. Every year she gets the highest award given by the school.

   a. Angel is a slow learner.
   b. Everybody admires Angel.
   c. Other children are envious of Angel.
   d. Angel is at the top of her class.

Let's look at the choices. Choice A. is clearly false. Choice B, may be true but it also may not be true – no information is given. It is likely that everyone admires her, but we don't know that for sure. The same with choice C. Probably other students are envious of her, but we don't know that for sure and no information is given. She could, for example, have rigged the election for Student Council and cheated on all her exams and everyone hates her!

Choice D is correct – This we do now for sure.

2.
Students enjoy playing football after school. Sometimes, they play basketball with other kids. On weekends, they play baseball, badminton, or tennis.

    a. Students prefer playing indoors.
    b. Students enjoy different kinds of sports.
    c. Students hate playing.
    d. Playing is a form of exercise.

The correct answer is B. The only certain thing is children enjoy different kinds of sports. For choice A, no information is given if they are playing indoors or outdoors. Choice C is probably false, but we don't know. Choice D is true, but not related to the information given. Choice D is designed to confuse.

List of all Valid Logic Argument forms

All men are fallible.
All men are animals.
Some animals are fallible.

Some books are precious.
All books are perishable.
Some perishable things are precious.

All books are imperfect.
Some books are informative.
Some informative things are imperfect.

No snakes are good to eat.
All snakes are animals.
Some animals are not good to eat.

Some websites are not helpful.
All websites are internet resources.
Some internet resources are not helpful.

No lepers are allowed to enter the church.
All lepers are human.
Some humans are not allowed to enter the church.

All pigs are unclean.
All unclean things are best avoided.

Some things that are best avoided are pigs.

All trees are plants.
No plants are birds.
No birds are trees.

Some evil doers are lawyers.
All lawyers are human.
Some humans are evil doers.

No meals are free.
All free things are desirable.
Some desirable things are not meals.

No dogs are birds.
Some birds are pets.
Some pets are not dogs.

Verbal Classification Tutorial

Verbal classification is based on the similarity between things like objects, pictures, letters, ideas and words. Verbal Classification questions group items of the same kind together with one item being different in some way.

Your task is to identify the item that does NOT belong to the group. For instance take the group "apple, orange, fruit, banana." Of course they have many things in common but there is a fine distinction. While apple, orange and banana are specific, 'fruit' is a generic term: any fruit. Just as we say 'Toyota, Honda, Ford and Car.' The first three refer to car companies, or manufacturers, while the last is an umbrella term.

All possible relationships have to be explored when answering this type of question. Here are some relationships to watch for:

> 1. meanings and interpretations
> 2. characteristics
> 3. common prefixes/suffixes

For letter series questions, watch for,

> 1. position of letters in the alphabetical order
> 2. capital and small letter relationships
> 3. vowel-consonant relationships
> 4. frequency or omission of letters

How to solve Verbal Classification Questions:

1. Observe the possible relationship that exists between the words and letters.
2. Observe repetitions, omissions etc, if any
3. Identify and separate the unrelated one from the rest

Verbal Classification questions generally have two formats:

1. Series - In this type, four or five letters or words may be listed. All of them except for one are related in one way.

E.g.: apple, orange, fruit, banana.

Here fruit is the odd one. Fruit is a generic broad term and the others are types of fruit.

2. Series with a key word at the top - Here a key word may be given, followed by four or five alternatives with some letters or words. All of them other than one are related to the key word in one way or the other.

Consider the word, particular. Which does not belong?

a. part
b. pit
c. art
d. par

Here pit is the odd one as all other words in the series are formed without changing the order of letters in the given key word.

Consider the following group. Which does not belong?

a. banana
b. mango
c. apple
d. Guava

All words of this series are similar in the sense that they areal fruit and all are grown on trees. Looking closer, apple is the odd one, as its first letter is a vowel, and the first letters of the others are consonants. Here it is the letters, and not the meaning of the words is taken to be considered.

Consider the following group. Which does not belong?

    a. banana

    b. mango

    c. spinach

    d. Guava

Here spinach is the odd one as it is not a fruit.

Quantitative Skills

THIS SECTION CONTAINS A SELF-ASSESSMENT AND QUANTITATIVE SKILLS TUTORIAL. The tutorials are designed to familiarize general principles and the self-assessment contains general questions similar to the quantitative skills questions likely to be on the HSPT®, but are not intended to be identical to the exam questions. The tutorials are not designed to be a complete quantitative skills course, and it is assumed that students have some familiarity with quantitative skills questions. If you do not understand parts of the tutorial, or find the tutorial difficult, it is recommended that you seek out additional instruction.

Tour of the HSPT Quantitative Skills Content

The HSPT® quantitative skills section has 50 reading questions which include quantitative skills and vocabulary. Below is a detailed list of the types of quantitative skills questions that generally appear on the HSPT®.

- Drawing logical conclusions

- Identify the author's purpose to persuade, inform, entertain, or otherwise

- Make predictions

- Analyze and evaluate the use of text structure to solve problems or identify sequences

- Vocabulary - Give the definition of a word from context

- Summarize

The questions below are not the same as you will find on the HSPT® - that would be too easy! And nobody knows what the questions will be and they change all the time. Mostly the changes consist of substituting new questions for old, but the changes can be new question formats or styles, changes to the number of questions in each section, changes to the time limits for each section and combining sections. Below are general quantitative skills questions that cover the same areas as the HSPT®. So the format and exact wording of the questions may differ slightly, and change from year to year, if you can answer the questions below, you will have no problem with the quantitative skills section of the HSPT®.

Quantitative Skills Self-Assessment

The purpose of the self-assessment is:

- Identify your strengths and weaknesses.

- Develop your personalized study plan (above)

- Get accustomed to the HSPT® format

- Extra practice – the self-assessments are almost a full 3rd practice test!

- Provide a baseline score for preparing your study schedule.

Since this is a Self-assessment, and depending on how confident you are with quantitative skills, timing is optional. The HSPT® has 50 reading questions to be answered in 30 minutes. The self-assessment has 25 questions, so allow about 15 minutes to complete this assessment.

Once complete, use the table below to assess your understanding of the content, and prepare your study schedule described in chapter 1.

80% - 100%	Excellent – you have mastered the content
60 – 79%	Good. You have a working knowledge. Even though you can just pass this section, you may want to review the tutorials and do some extra practice to see if you can improve your mark.
40% - 59%	Below Average. You do not understand the quantitative skills problems. Review the tutorials , and retake this quiz again in a few days, before proceeding to the Practice Test Questions.
Less than 40%	Poor. You have a very limited understanding of the quantitative skills problems. Please review the tutorials , and retake this quiz again in a few days, before proceeding to the Practice Test Questions.

Quantitative skills Self-Assessment Answer Sheet

1. (A) (B) (C) (D)   11. (A) (B) (C) (D)   21. (A) (B) (C) (D)

2. (A) (B) (C) (D)   12. (A) (B) (C) (D)   22. (A) (B) (C) (D)

3. (A) (B) (C) (D)   13. (A) (B) (C) (D)   23. (A) (B) (C) (D)

4. (A) (B) (C) (D)   14. (A) (B) (C) (D)   24. (A) (B) (C) (D)

5. (A) (B) (C) (D)   15. (A) (B) (C) (D)   25. (A) (B) (C) (D)

6. (A) (B) (C) (D)   16. (A) (B) (C) (D)

7. (A) (B) (C) (D)   17. (A) (B) (C) (D)

8. (A) (B) (C) (D)   18. (A) (B) (C) (D)

9. (A) (B) (C) (D)   19. (A) (B) (C) (D)

10. (A) (B) (C) (D)   20. (A) (B) (C) (D)

Section 1 – Number Series

1. Consider the following series: 6, 12, 24, 48. What number should come next?

    a. 48

    b. 64

    c. 60

    d. 96

2. Consider the following series: 5, 6, 11, 17. What number should come next?

    a. 28

    b. 34

    c. 36

    d. 27

3. Consider the following series: 26, 21, ..., 11, 6. What is the missing number?

    a. 27

    b. 23

    c. 16

    d. 29

4. Consider the following series: 23, ..., 31, 37. What is the missing number?

    a. 19

    b. 27

    c. 29

    d. 30

5. Consider the following series: 3, 6, 11, 18. What number should come next?

    a. 30

    b. 27

    c. 22

    d. 29

6. Consider the following series: 26, 24, 20, 14. What number should come next?

    a. 6

    b. 18

    c. 12

    d. 8

7. Consider the following series: 6, 8, 4, 10, 18, 22. What number should come next?

    a. 34

    b. 32

    c. 24

    d. 26

8. Consider the following series: L, O, R, ..., X. What is the missing letter?

    a. S

    b. U

    c. T

    d. M

9. Consider the following series: X, Z, B, D. What number should come next?

    a. E
    b. F
    c. G
    d. H

10. Consider the following series: 25, 33, 41, 49. What number should come next?

    a. 51
    b. 55
    c. 59
    d. 57

Section II – Geometric Comparison

11. Examine (A), (B) and (C) and find the best answer.

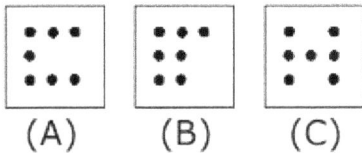

(A)   (B)   (C)

    a. (A) has more dots than (B)
    b. (A) has more than (C)
    c. (A) has more than (B) and (C)
    d. (A), (B) and (C) have an equal number of dots.

12. Examine (A), (B) and (C) and find the best answer.

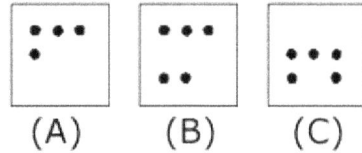

(A)   (B)   (C)

    a. (A) has more dots than (B)
    b. (B) has more than (A)
    c. (A) has more than (B) and (C)
    d. (A), (B) and (C) have an equal number of dots.

13. Examine (A), (B) and (C) and find the best answer.

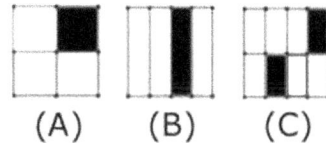

(A)   (B)   (C)

    a. The shaded area in (A) is equal to (B)
    b. The shaded area in (A) is greater than (B)
    c. The shaded area in (A) is greater than (C)
    d. The shaded area in (B) is greater than (C)

14. Examine (A), (B) and (C) and find the best answer.

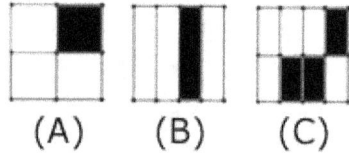

(A)   (B)   (C)

a. The shaded area in (A) is equal to (C)
b. The shaded area in (C) is greater than (B)
c. The shaded area in (A) is equal to (C)
d. The shaded area in (B) is equal to (C)

15. Examine (A), (B) and (C) and find the best answer.

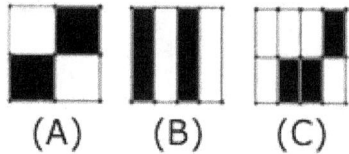

(A)   (B)   (C)

a. The shaded area in (A) is equal to (C)

b. The shaded area in (C) is greater than (B)

c. The shaded area in (A) is greater than (C)

d. The shaded area in (B) is equal to (C)

16. Examine (A), (B) and (C) and find the best answer.

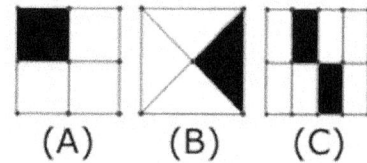

(A)   (B)   (C)

a. The shaded area in (A) is equal to (C)

b. The shaded area in (C) is greater than (B)

c. The shaded area in (A) is greater than (C)

d. The shaded area in (B) is less than (C)

Section III – Non-Geometric Comparison

17. Examine the following and find the best answer.

1. (3 X 4) - 7
2. (3 X 4) - 3
3. (3 X 5) – 10

a. 1 and 3 are equal

b. 1 and 3 are not equal

c. 1 and 2 are equal

d. 2 and 3 are equal

18. Examine the following and find the best answer.

1. (5 X 7) + 3

2. (5 X 6) + 9

3. (5 X 5) + 18

    a. 1 is less than 3 and greater than 2
    b. 3 is greater than 1 and 2
    c. 1 is less than 2 and 3
    d. 2 is greater than 3 and 1

19. Examine the following and find the best answer.

1. 23 - 15
2. 32 - 23
3. 42 - 26

    a. 1 < 2 < 3
    b. 2 > 3 > 1
    c. 3 > 1 > 2
    d. 1 < 2 > 3

20. Examine the following and find the best answer.

1. 4^2

2. 2^4

3. 2^3

4. 3^2

    a. 1 and 3 are equal
    b. 2 and 3 are equal
    c. 3 and 4 are equal
    d. None of the above

21. Examine the following and find the best answer.

A. (2 X 40) - 20
B. (3 X 14) + 15
C. (3 X 15) – 8

    a. A < B < C
    b. A > B > C
    c. B > C < A
    d. C > B < A

Section IV – Number Manipulation

22. What is 6 more than 1/3 of 25?

    a. 8.33
    b. 15
    c. 14.33
    d. 18

23. What number is the largest?

    a. 50% of 50
    b. 2/5 of 200
    c. 0.2 portion of 20
    d. 1/5th of 30

24. What is the smallest value?

    a. 0.4 portion of 200
    b. 50% of 100
    c. 0.06 portion of 2000
    d. 2% of 1000

25. What number is the largest?

    a. 5 % of 400
    b. 25% of 4000
    c. 2 % of 500
    d. 8% of 1000

Answer Key

Section I – Number Series

1. D
The numbers double each time.

2. A
Each number is the sum of the previous two numbers.

3. C
The numbers decrease by 5 each time.

4. C
The numbers are primes (divisible only by 1 and themselves).

5. B
The interval, beginning with 3, increases by 2 each time.

6. A
The interval, beginning with 2, increases by 2, and is subtracted each time.

7. B
Each number is the sum of the previous and the number 3 places to the left.

8. B
There are two letters missing between each one, so U is next.

9. B
Miss a letter each time and 'loop' back, so F is next.

10. D
The numbers increase by 8.

Section II – Geometric Comparison

11. D
12. B
13. A
14. B
15. C
16. A

Section III – Non-Geometric Comparisons

17. A
#1 = 5
#2 = 9
#3 = 5
1 and 3 are equal.

18. C
#1 = 38
#2 = 39
#3 = 43
1 is less than 2 and less than 3.

19. A
#1 = 8
#2 = 9
#3 = 16
1 < 2 < 3

20. D
#1 = 16
#2 = 16
#3 = 8
#4 = 9
None of the Above.

21. B
A = 60
B = 57
C = 37
A > B > C

Section IV – Number Manipulation

22. C
1/3 of 25 = 8.33 + 6 = 14.33

23. B
a. 50% of 50 = 25
b. 2/5 of 200 = 80
c. 0.2 portion of 20 = 4
d. 1/5 of 30 = 6
B is the largest.

24. D
a. 0.4 portion of 200 = 80
b. 50% of 100 = 50
c. 0.06 portion of 2000 = 120
d. 2% of 1000 = 20
D is the smallest

25. B
a. 5% of 400 = 20
b. 25% of 4000 = 1000
c. 2% of 500 = 10
d. 8% of 1000 = 80

Quantitative Skills Tutorials

Number Series Tutorial

Number series questions appear on most High School exams. An example is: Consider the following series: 26, 21, 0, 11, 6. What is the missing number?

    a. 27
    b. 23
    c. 16
    d. 29

Looking carefully at the sequence, we can see right away that each number is 5 less than the previous number, so the missing number is 16.

We can re-write this sequence in mathematical notation as, a_1, a_2, a_3, ... an, where n is an integer and an is called its nth term. And we can write the sequence in the form of a formula, where an integer is substituted in the place of the variable in the formula and the terms are obtained.

For example, let us consider the sequence 5,10,15,20,...

-   Here, a_n = 5n. The formula a_n = 5n.
-   The nth term of a sequence can be found by plugging n in the explicit formula for the sequence. So for example if we wanted to find the 100th number in this sequence, we would substitute n = 100 in the formula and get 500.

Type of Number Sequence problems

1. Simple addition or subtraction – each number in the sequence is obtained by adding a number to the previous number.

For example,   2, 5, 8, 11, 14
Each number in the sequence is obtained by adding 3 to the previous number, which we could write as, $a_{n+1} = a_n + 3$.

2. Simple multiplication - each number in the sequence is obtained by multiplying the previous number by a whole number or fraction.

For example,   3, 6, 18, 54

Or,

20, 10, 5, 2.5

Each number in the first sequence is obtained by multiplying the previous number by 3, which we could write as, $a_{n+1} = a_n \times 3$.

In the second example, each number in the series is the previous number divided by 2, or multiplied by 1/2, or $a_{n+1} = a_n \times 1/2$.

3. Prime Numbers – each number in the sequence is a prime number.

For example,

23, ..., 31, 37

Answer: 29

4. Operations on the previous two numbers. For example,

8, 14, 22, 36, 58

Here the sequence is created by adding the previous 2 numbers.

5. Exponents. The number sequence is created by each number squared or cubed.

For example,

3, 9, 81, 6561, where each number is squared.

6. Combining Sequences

2, 7, 13, 20, 28, 37

Here the sequence starts with 2, and each element is added to another sequence starting with 5. So, 2 + 5 = 7, 7 + 6 = 13, 13 + 7 = 20 and so on.

A variation is a sequence with a repeating element. For example,

1, 2, 3, 5, 7, 9, 12, 15

Here the sequence is, for each n, +1, +1, +1, +2, +2, +2, +3, +3,

7. Fractions

For example,

16/4, 4/2, 2/2, ½, 0

Fractions are often meant to confuse. If fractions don't have an obvious relationship, reduce them to lowest terms or to whole numbers. Reducing these to whole numbers, gives,

4, 2, 1, ½

Right away, we can see the numbers are half the previous number, so the next in the series is 1/4.

In this example, the answer is a fraction; however, you may have to reduce fractions to see the relation, and then convert back to get the answer in the correct form.

Strategy for Answering Number Series Questions

Answering number series questions is a skill of recognizing patterns, and the best way to improve is to familiarize yourself with the different types, and to practice.

Here is a quick method that will help you answer number series.

For example:

2, 5, 6, 7, 8, ...

Step 1 – glance at the series quickly and see if you can spot the pattern right away.

Step 2 – Start analyzing.

Take the different between the first 2 numbers and the different between the second 2 numbers.

2, (+3) 5, (+1)   6, (+1) 7, (+1)   8,

No clear pattern with a simple analysis. There is no addition, subtraction, multiplication, division, fractional or exponent relationship.

The relation must be a higher order or a second series.

Next look at the relation between the 1st number and the 2nd and the 1st and the 3rd.   We see that,
1st + 3 = 5, 1st + 4 = 6. That's it!   The number 2 is added to the sequence, 3, 4, 5, 6, so the next number will be 2 + 7 = 9.

Number Manipulation Tutorial

Here is an example of a number manipulation question:

What number divided by 5 is 1/4 of 100?

> a. 125
> b. 150
> c. 75
> d. 225

The answer is A – 125.

Number manipulation questions are 'double barrelled' questions, asking you to make 2 calculations – calculate 'something' of 'something else.' This increases the chance of error and forces you to think very carefully.

The best strategy for most math questions is to break them down into little pieces, solve the pieces, and then put them back together. Here is a systematic strategy for solving number manipulation problems.

Example #1

Step 1 – Break it down.

What number divided by 5

is

1/4 of 100?

Taking the example above, there are 2 parts:

Part 1 - A number, call it Z, divided by 5, so X/5
Part 2 – 1/4 of 100 = 25

The two parts are connected by 'is', which mean 'equals,' so we can re-write the problem:

Step 2 – Re-Write the problem

X/5 = 25

Step 3 - Solve
Then solve for X,

X = 5.

Example #2

What number subtracted from 50 is 1/5 of 40?

This example has 'subtracted from' instead of 'is.' The operator phrase, 'subtracted from' can also be, 'multiplied by,' 'added to,' or similar.

Step 1 – Break it down.

| **What number subtracted from 50** |

is

| **1/5 of 40?** |

Step 2 – Re-Write the problem

Let Z be the number, so we can write as:

50 – Z is 1/5 of 40   or

50 – Z = 1/5 of 40

Step 3 - Solve the Problem

50 – Z = 40/5
50 – Z = 8
Z = 42

Reading

THIS SECTION CONTAINS A SELF-ASSESSMENT AND READING TUTORIAL. The tutorials are designed to familiarize general principles and the self-assessment contains general questions similar to the reading questions likely to be on the HSPT®, but are not intended to be identical to the exam questions. The tutorials are not designed to be a complete reading course, and it is assumed that students have some familiarity with reading comprehension and vocabulary questions. If you do not understand parts of the tutorial, or find the tutorial difficult, it is recommended that you seek out additional instruction.

For addition practice and help with reading comprehension see our Multiple Choice Secrets books at www.multiple-choice.ca.

Tour of the Reading Content

Below is a detailed list of the types of reading questions that generally appear on your exam.

- Drawing logical conclusions

- Make predictions

- Analyze and evaluate the use of text structure to solve problems or identify sequences

- Vocabulary - Give the definition of a word from context

- Summarize

The questions below are not the same as you will find on the exam - that would be too easy! And nobody knows what the questions will be and they change all the time. Mostly the changes consist of substituting new questions for old, but the changes can be new question formats or styles, changes to the number of questions in each section, changes to the time limits for each section and combining sections. Below are general reading and vocabulary questions that cover the same areas as the exam. So the format and exact wording of the questions may differ slightly, and change from year to year, if you can answer the questions below, you will have no problem with the reading section.

Reading Self-Assessment

The purpose of the self-assessment is:

- Identify your strengths and weaknesses.

- Develop your personalized study plan (above)

- Get accustomed to the HSPT® format

- Extra practice – the self-assessments are almost a full 3rd practice test!

- Provide a baseline score for preparing your study schedule.

Since this is a self-assessment, and depending on how confident you are with reading comprehension and vocabulary, timing is optional. This self-assessment has 34 questions, so allow about 20 minutes to complete this assessment.

Once complete, use the table below to assess your understanding of the content, and prepare your study schedule described in chapter 1.

80% - 100%	Excellent – you have mastered the content
60 – 79%	Good. You have a working knowledge. Even though you can just pass this section, you may want to review the tutorials and do some extra practice to see if you can improve your mark.
40% - 59%	Below Average. You do not understand reading comprehension problems. Review the tutorials , and retake this quiz again in a few days, before proceeding to the Practice Test Questions.
Less than 40%	Poor. You have a very limited understanding of reading comprehension problems. Please review the tutorials , and retake this quiz again in a few days, before proceeding to the Practice Test Questions.

Reading and Vocabulary Self-Assessment Answer Sheet

1. Ⓐ Ⓑ Ⓒ Ⓓ   11. Ⓐ Ⓑ Ⓒ Ⓓ   21. Ⓐ Ⓑ Ⓒ Ⓓ   31. Ⓐ Ⓑ Ⓒ Ⓓ

2. Ⓐ Ⓑ Ⓒ Ⓓ   12. Ⓐ Ⓑ Ⓒ Ⓓ   22. Ⓐ Ⓑ Ⓒ Ⓓ   32. Ⓐ Ⓑ Ⓒ Ⓓ

3. Ⓐ Ⓑ Ⓒ Ⓓ   13. Ⓐ Ⓑ Ⓒ Ⓓ   23. Ⓐ Ⓑ Ⓒ Ⓓ   33. Ⓐ Ⓑ Ⓒ Ⓓ

4. Ⓐ Ⓑ Ⓒ Ⓓ   14. Ⓐ Ⓑ Ⓒ Ⓓ   24. Ⓐ Ⓑ Ⓒ Ⓓ   34. Ⓐ Ⓑ Ⓒ Ⓓ

5. Ⓐ Ⓑ Ⓒ Ⓓ   15. Ⓐ Ⓑ Ⓒ Ⓓ   25. Ⓐ Ⓑ Ⓒ Ⓓ

6. Ⓐ Ⓑ Ⓒ Ⓓ   16. Ⓐ Ⓑ Ⓒ Ⓓ   26. Ⓐ Ⓑ Ⓒ Ⓓ

7. Ⓐ Ⓑ Ⓒ Ⓓ   17. Ⓐ Ⓑ Ⓒ Ⓓ   27. Ⓐ Ⓑ Ⓒ Ⓓ

8. Ⓐ Ⓑ Ⓒ Ⓓ   18. Ⓐ Ⓑ Ⓒ Ⓓ   28. Ⓐ Ⓑ Ⓒ Ⓓ

9. Ⓐ Ⓑ Ⓒ Ⓓ   19. Ⓐ Ⓑ Ⓒ Ⓓ   29. Ⓐ Ⓑ Ⓒ Ⓓ

10. Ⓐ Ⓑ Ⓒ Ⓓ   20. Ⓐ Ⓑ Ⓒ Ⓓ   30. Ⓐ Ⓑ Ⓒ Ⓓ

Questions 1 – 4 refer to the following passage.

Passage 1 - Who Was Anne Frank?

You may have heard mention of the word Holocaust in your History or English classes. The Holocaust took place from 1939-1945. It was an attempt by the Nazi party to purify the human race, by eliminating Jews, Gypsies, Catholics, homosexuals and others they deemed inferior to their "perfect" Aryan race. The Nazis used Concentration Camps, which were sometimes used as Death Camps, to exterminate the people they held in the camps. The saddest fact about the Holocaust was the over one million children under the age of sixteen died in a Nazi concentration camp. Just a few weeks before World War II was over, Anne Frank was one of those children to die.

Before the Nazi party began its persecution of the Jews, Anne Frank had a happy live. She was born in June of 1929. In June of 1942, for her 13th birthday, she was given a simple present which would go onto impact the lives of millions of people around the world. That gift was a small red diary that she called Kitty. This diary was to become Anne's most treasured possession when she and her family hid from the Nazi's in a secret annex above her father's office building in Amsterdam.

For 25 months, Anne, her sister Margot, her parents, another family, and an elderly Jewish dentist hid from the Nazis in this tiny annex. They were never permitted to go outside and their food and supplies were brought to them by Miep Gies and her husband, who did not believe in the Nazi persecution of the Jews. It was a very difficult life for young Anne and she used Kitty as an outlet to describe her life in hiding.

After 2 years, Anne and her family were betrayed and arrested by the Nazis. To this day, nobody is exactly sure who betrayed the Frank family and the other annex residents. Anne, her mother, and her sister were separated from Otto Frank, Anne's father. Then, Anne and Margot were separated from their mother. In March of 1945, Margot Frank died of starvation in a Concentration Camp. A few days later, at the age of 15, Anne Frank died of typhus. Of all the people who hid in the Annex, only Otto Frank survived the Holocaust.

Otto Frank returned to the Annex after World War II. It was there that he found Kitty, filled with Anne's thoughts and feelings about being a persecuted Jewish girl. Otto Frank had Anne's diary published in 1947 and it has remained continuously in print ever since. Today, the diary has been published in over 55 languages and more than 24 million copies have been sold around the world. The Diary of Anne Frank tells the story of a brave young woman who tried to see the good in all people.

1. From the context clues in the passage, what does annex mean?

    a. Attic

    b. Bedroom

    c. Basement

    d. Kitchen

2. Why do you think Anne's diary has been published in 55 languages?

    a. So everyone could understand it.

    b. So people around the world could learn more about the horrors of the Holocaust.

    c. Because Anne was Jewish but hid in Amsterdam and died in Germany.

    d. Because Otto Frank spoke many languages.

3. From the description of Anne and Margot's deaths in the passage, what can we assume typhus is?

    a. The same as starving to death.

    b. An infection the Germans gave to Anne.

    c. A disease Anne caught in the concentration camp.

    d. Poison gas used by the Germans to kill Anne.

4. In the third paragraph, what does outlet mean?

    a. A place to plug things into the wall

    b. A store where Miep bought cheap supplies for the Frank family

    c. A hiding space similar to an Annex

    d. A place where Anne could express her private thoughts.

Questions 5 – 8 refer to the following passage.

Passage 2 - Was Dr. Seuss A Real Doctor?

A favorite author for over 100 years, Theodor Seuss Geisel was born on March 2, 1902. Today, we celebrate the birthday of the famous "Dr. Seuss" by hosting Read Across America events throughout the March. School children around the country celebrate the "Doctor's" birthday by making hats, giving presentations and holding read aloud circles featuring some of Dr. Seuss' most famous books.

But who was Dr. Seuss? Did he go to medical school? Where was his office?

You may be surprised to know that Theodor Seuss Geisel was not a medical doctor at all. He took on the nickname Dr. Seuss when he became a noted children's book author. He earned the nickname because people said his books were "as good as medicine." All these years later, his nickname has lasted and he is known as Dr. Seuss all across the world.

Think back to when you were a young child. Did you ever want to try "green eggs and ham?" Did you try to "Hop on Pop?" Do you remember learning about the environment from a creature called The Lorax? Of course, you must recall one of Seuss' most famous characters; that green Grinch who stole Christmas. These stories were all written by Dr. Seuss and featured his signature rhyming words and letters. They also featured made up words to enhance his rhyme scheme and even though many of his characters were made up, they sure seem real to us today.

And what of his "signature" book, The Cat in the Hat? You must remember that cat and Thing One and Thing Two from your childhood. Did you know that in the early 1950's there was a growing concern in America that children were not becoming avid readers? This was, book publishers thought, because children found books dull and uninteresting. An intelligent publisher sent Dr. Seuss a book of words that he thought all children should learn as young readers. Dr. Seuss wrote his famous story The Cat in the Hat, using those words. We can see, over the decades, just how much influence his writing has had on very young children. That is why we celebrate this doctor's birthday each March.

5. What does the word "avid" mean in the last paragraph?

    a. Good

    b. Interested

    c. Slow

    d. Fast

6. What can we infer from the statement " His books were like medicine?"

    a. His books made people feel better

    b. His books were in doctor's office waiting rooms

    c. His books took away fevers

    d. His books left a funny taste in readers' mouths.

7. Why is the publisher in the last paragraph referred to as "intelligent?"

    a. The publisher knew how to read.

    b. The publisher knew that kids did not like to read.

    c. The publisher knew Dr. Seuss would be able to create a book that sold well.

    d. The publisher knew that Dr. Seuss would be able to write a book that would get young children interested in reading.

8. The theme of this passage is

    a. Dr. Seuss was not a doctor.

    b. Dr. Seuss influenced the lives of generations of young children.

    c. Dr. Seuss wrote rhyming books.

    d. Dr. Suess' birthday is a good day to read a book.

Questions 10 - 12 refer to the following passage.

Keeping Tropical Fish

Keeping tropical fish at home or in your office used to be very popular. To-day, interest has declined, but it remains as rewarding and relaxing a hobby as ever. Ask any tropical fish hobbyist, and you will hear how soothing and relaxing watching colorful fish live their lives in the aquarium. If you are considering keeping tropical fish as pets, here is a list of the basic equipment you will need.

A filter is essential for keeping your aquarium clean and your fish alive and healthy. There are different types and sizes of filters and the right size for you depends on the size of the aquarium and the level of stocking. Generally, you need a filter with a 3 to 5 times turn over rate per hour. This means that the water in the tank should go through the filter about 3 to 5 times per hour.

Most tropical fish do well in water temperatures ranging between 24^0 C and 26^0 C, though each has its own ideal water temperature. A heater with a thermostat is necessary to regulate the water temperature. Some heaters are submersible and others are not, so check carefully before you buy.

Lights are also necessary, and come in a large variety of types, strengths and sizes. A light source is necessary for plants in the tank to photosynthesize and give the tank a more attractive appearance. Even if you plan to use plastic plants, the fish still require light, although here you can use a lower strength light source.

A hood is necessary to keep dust, dirt and unwanted materials out of the tank. Sometimes the hood can also help prevent evaporation. Another requirement is aquarium gravel. This will improve the aesthetics of the aquarium and is necessary if you plan to have real plants.

9. What is the general tone of this article?

    a. Formal

    b. Informal

    c. Technical

    d. Opinion

10. Which of the following cannot be inferred?

a. Gravel is good for aquarium plants.
b. Fewer people have aquariums in their office than at home.
c. The larger the tank, the larger the filter required.
d. None of the above.

11. What evidence does the author provide to support their claim that aquarium lights are necessary?

a. Plants require light.
b. Fish and plants require light.
c. The author does not provide evidence for this statement.
d. Aquarium lights make the aquarium more attractive.

12. Which of the following is an opinion?

a. Filter with a 3 to 5 times turn over rate per hour are required.
b. Aquarium gravel improves the aesthetics of the aquarium.
c. An aquarium hood keeps dust, dirt and unwanted materials out of the tank.
d. Each type of tropical fish has its own ideal water temperature.

Questions 13 - 14 refer to the following passage.

The Civil War

The Civil War began on April 12, 1861. The first shots of the Civil War were fired in Fort Sumter, South Carolina. Note that even though more American lives were lost in the Civil War than in any other war, not one person died on that first day. The war began because eleven Southern states seceded from the Union and tried to start their own government, The Confederate States of America.

Why did the states secede? The issue of slavery was a primary cause of the Civil War. The eleven southern states relied heavily on their slaves to foster their farming and plantation lifestyles. The northern states, many of whom had already abolished slavery, did not feel that the southern states should have slaves. The north wanted to free all the slaves and President Lincoln's goal was to both end slavery and preserve the Union. He had Congress declare war on the Confederacy on April 14, 1862. For four long, blood soaked years, the North and South fought.

From 1861 to mid 1863, it seemed as if the South would win this war. However, on July 1, 1863, an epic three day battle was waged on a field in Gettysburg, Pennsylvania. Gettysburg is remembered for being the bloodiest battle in American history. At the end of the three days, the North turned the tide of the war in their favor. The North then went on to dominate the South for the remainder of the war. Most well remembered might be General Sherman's "March to The Sea," where he famously led the Union Army through Georgia and the Carolinas, burning and destroying everything in their path.

In 1865, the Union army invaded and captured the Confederate capital of Richmond Virginia. Robert E. Lee, leader of the Confederacy surrendered to General Ulysses S. Grant, leader of the Union forces, on April 9, 1865. The Civil War was over and the Union was preserved.

13. What does secede mean?

   a. To break away from
   b. To accomplish
   c. To join
   d. To lose

14. Which of the following statements summarizes a FACT from the passage?

   a. Congress declared war and then the Battle of Fort Sumter began.
   b. Congress declared war after shots were fired at Fort Sumter.
   c. President Lincoln was pro slavery
   d. President Lincoln was at Fort Sumter with Congress

Part II - Vocabulary

15. Choose the noun that means, self evident or clear obvious truth.

   a. Truism
   b. Catharsis
   c. Libertine
   d. Tractable

16. Choose the best definition for: virago

   a. A loud domineering woman
   b. A quiet woman
   c. A load domineering Man
   d. A quiet man

17. When Joe broke his _____ in a skiing accident, his entire leg was in a cast.

   a. Ankle
   b. Humerus
   c. Wrist
   d. Femur

18. Select another word for the underlined word in the sentence below.

At first I thought she was very rude and boorish, but when I talked to her again she was very genteel.

   a. Chivalrous
   b. Hilarious
   c. Civilized
   d. Governance

19. Choose an adjective that means corrupted, impure.

   a. Adulterate
   b. Harbor
   c. Infuriate
   d. Inculcate

20. Select another word for the underlined word in the sentence below.

Her business success showed that she was very shrewd.

   a. Slow
   b. astute
   c. Ignorant
   d. Heinous

21. Choose an adjective that means, beyond what is obvious or evident.

   a. Ulterior
   b. Sybarite
   c. Torsion
   d. Trenchant

22. Choose a noun that means, homeless child or stray.

   a. Elegy
   b. Waif
   c. Martyr
   d. Palaver

23. Select another word for the underlined word in the sentence below.

His inheritance was very large - a princely sum!

a. Minor

b. Tolerable

c. Large

d. Pittance

24. What is the best definition of deprecate?

a. Approve

b. Indifference

c. Disapprove

d. None of the above

25. Choose the best definition for succor.

a. To suck on

b. To hate

c. To like

d. Give help of assistance

26. Select the synonym of conspicuous.

a. Important

b. Prominent

c. Beautiful

d. Convincing

27. Select the noun that means eagerness and enthusiasm.

a. Alacrity

b. Happiness

c. Donator

d. Marital

28. Fill in the blank.

After Lisa's aunt had her tenth child, Lisa found that she had more than twenty _____.

a. Uncles

b. Friends

c. Stepsisters

d. Cousins

29. Select the word that means benevolence.

a. Happiness

b. Courage

c. Kindness

d. Loyalty

30. Select the verb that means, to make less severe.

a. Suspense

b. Alleviate

c. Ingrate

d. Action

31. What is the name of one who gives a gift or who gives money to a charity organization?

a. Captain

b. Benefactor

c. Source

d. Teacher

32. What is another word for subordinate, or person of lesser rank or authority?

a. Palliate

b. Plebeian

c. Underling

d. Expiate

33. Choose the best definition of specious.

    a. Logical

    b. Illogical

    c. Emotional

    d. 2 species

34. Choose the best definition of proscribe.

    a. Welcome

    b. Write a prescription

    c. Banish

    d. Give a diagnosis

Answer Key

1. A

We know that an annex is like an attic because the text states the annex was above Otto Frank's building.

Choice B is incorrect because an office building doesn't have bedrooms. Choice C is incorrect because a basement would be below the office building. Choice D is incorrect because there would not be a kitchen in an office building.

2. B

The diary has been published in 55 languages so people all over the world can learn about Anne. That is why the passage says it has been continuously in print.

Choice A is incorrect because it is too vague. Choice C is incorrect because it was published after Anne died and she did not write in all three languages. Choice D is incorrect because the passage does not give us any information about what languages Otto Frank spoke.

3. C

Use the process of elimination to figure this out.

Choice A cannot be the correct answer because otherwise the passage would have simply said that Anne and Margot both died of starvation. Choices B and D cannot be correct because if the Germans had done something specifically to murder Anne, the passage would have stated that directly. By the process of elimination, choice C has to be the correct answer.

4. D

We can figure this out using context clues. The paragraph is talking about Anne's diary and so, outlet in this instance is a place where Anne can pour her feelings.

Choice A is incorrect answer. That is the literal meaning of the word outlet and the passage is using the figurative meaning. Choice B is incorrect because that is the secondary literal meaning of the word outlet, as in an outlet mall. Again, we are looking for figurative meaning. Choice C is incorrect because there are no clues in the text to support that answer.

5. B

When someone is avid about something that means they are highly interested in the subject. The context clues are dull and boring, because they define the opposite of avid.

6. A

The author is using a simile to compare the books to medicine. Medicine is what you take when you want to feel better. They are suggesting that if a person wants to feel good, they should read Dr. Seuss' books.

Choice B is incorrect because there is no mention of a doctor's office. Choice C is incorrect because it is using the literal meaning of medicine and the author is using medicine in a figurative way. Choice D is incorrect because it makes no sense. We know not to eat books.

7. D

The publisher is described as intelligent because he knew to get in touch with a famous author to develop a book that children would be interested in reading.

Choice A is incorrect because we can assume that all book publishers must know how to read. Choice B is incorrect because it says in the article that more than one publisher was concerned about whether or not children liked to read. Choice D is incorrect because there is no mention in the article about how well The Cat in the Hat sold when it was first published.

8. B

The passage describes in detail how Dr. Seuss had a great effect on the lives of children through his writing. It names several of his books, tells how he helped children become avid readers and explains his style of writing.

Choice A is incorrect because that is just one single fact about the passage. Choice C is incorrect because that is just one single fact about the passage. Choice D is incorrect because that is just one single fact about the passage. Again, choice B is correct because it encompasses ALL the facts in the passage, not just one single fact.

9. B

The general tone is informal.

10. B

The statement, "Fewer people have aquariums in their office than at home," cannot be inferred from this article.

11. B

Light is necessary for the fish and plants.

12. B

The following statement is an opinion, " Aquarium gravel improves the aesthetics of the aquarium."

13. A

Secede means to break away from because the 11 states wanted to leave the United States and form their own country.

Choice B is incorrect because the states were not accomplishing anything. Choice C is incorrect because the states were trying to leave the USA not join it. Choice D is incorrect because the states seceded before they lost the war.

14. B

Look at the dates in the passage. The shots were fired on April 12 and Congress declared war on April 14.

Choice C is incorrect because the passage states that Lincoln was against slavery. Choice D is incorrect because it never mentions who was or was not at Fort Sumter.

Part II - Vocabulary

15. A
Truism: n. self-evident or clear obvious truth.

16. A
Virago: Given to undue belligerence or ill manner at the slightest provocation; a shrew, a termagant.

17. D
Femur: n. The bone of the thigh or upper hind limb, articulating at the hip and the knee.

18. C
Genteel: Polite and well-mannered. Stylish or elegant. Aristocratic

19. A
Adulterate: v. To render (something) poorer in quality by adding another substance, typically an inferior one.

20. B
Shrewd: showing clever resourcefulness in practical matters, artful, tricky or cunning, streetwise, knowledgeable.

21. A
Ulterior: adj. beyond what is obvious or evident.

22. B
Waif: n. homeless child or stray.

23. C
Princely: adj. In the manner of a royal prince's conduct; large or grand.

24. C
Deprecate: v. To belittle or express disapproval of.

25. D
Succor: n. Aid, assistance or relief given to one in distress; ministration.

26. B
Prominent: adj. Important, famous.

27. A
Alacrity: adj. Eagerness; liveliness; enthusiasm.

28. D
Cousins

29. C
Benevolent: adj. Well meaning and kindly.

30. B
Alleviate: v. To make less severe, as a pain or difficulty.

31. B
Benefactor: n. Somebody who gives one a gift. Usually refers to someone who gives money to a charity or another form of organization.

32. C
Underling: n. subordinate of lesser rank or authority.

33. B
Specious: adj. Seemingly well-reasoned or factual, but actually fallacious or insincere; strongly held but false.

34. C
Proscribe: v. To forbid or denounce. To banish.

Help with Reading Comprehension

At first sight, reading comprehension tests look challenging especially if you are given long essays to answer only two to three questions. While reading, you might notice your attention wandering, or you may feel sleepy. Do not be discouraged because there are various tactics and long range strategies that make comprehending even long, boring essays easier.

Your friends before your foes. It is always best to start with essays or passages with familiar subjects rather than those with unfamiliar ones. This approach applies the same logic as tackling easy questions before hard ones. Skip passages that do not interest you and leave them for later.

Don't use 'special' reading techniques. This is not the time for speed-reading or anything like that – just plain ordinary reading – not too slow and not too fast.

Read through the entire passage and the questions before you do anything. Many students try reading the questions first and then looking for answers in the passage thinking this approach is more efficient. What these students do not realize is that it is often hard to navigate in unfamiliar roads. If you do not familiarize yourself with the passage first, looking for answers become not only time-consuming but also dangerous because you might miss the context of the answer you are looking for. If you read the questions first you will only confuse yourself and lose valuable time.

Familiarize yourself with reading comprehension questions. If you are familiar with the common types of reading questions, you are able to take note of important parts of the passage, saving time. There are six major kinds of reading questions.

- **Main Idea**- Questions that ask for the central thought or significance of the passage.

- **Specific Details** - Questions that asks for explicitly stated ideas.

- **Drawing Inferences** - Questions that ask for a statement's intended meaning.

- **Tone or Attitude** - Questions that test your ability to sense the emotional state of the author.

- **Context Meaning** – Questions that ask for the meaning of a word depending on the context.

- **Technique** – Questions that ask for the method of organization or the writing style of the author.

Read. Read. Read. The best preparation for reading comprehension tests is always to read, read and read. If you are not used to reading lengthy passages, you will probably lose concentration. Increase your attention span by making a habit out of reading.

Reading comprehension tests become less daunting when you have trained yourself to read and understand fast. Always remember that it is easier to understand passages you are interested in. Do not read through passages hastily. Make mental notes of ideas you may be asked.

Reading Strategy

When facing the reading comprehension section of a standardized test, you need a strategy to be successful. You want to keep several steps in mind:

- **First, make a note of the time and the number of sections**. Time your work accordingly. Typically, four to five minutes per section is sufficient. Second, read the directions for each selection thoroughly before beginning (and listen well to any additional verbal instructions, as they will often clarify obscure or confusing written guidelines). You must know exactly how to do what you're about to do!

- **Now you're ready to begin reading the selection**. Read the passage carefully, noting significant characters or events on a scratch sheet of paper or underlining on the test sheet. Many students find making a basic list in the margins helpful. Quickly jot down or underline one-word summaries of characters, notable happenings, numbers, or key ideas. This will help you better retain information and focus wandering thoughts. Remember, however, that your main goal in doing this is to find the information that answers the questions. Even if you find the passage interesting, remember your goal and work fast but stay on track.

- Now read the question and all the choices. Now you have read the passage, have a general idea of the main ideas, and have marked the important points. Read the question and all the choices. Never choose an answer without reading them all! Questions are often designed to confuse – stay focussed and clear. Usually the answer choices will focus on one or two facts or inferences from the passage. Keep these clear in your mind.

- **Search for the answer**. With a very general idea of what the different choices are, go back to the passage and scan for the relevant information. Watch for big words, unusual or unique words. These make your job easier as you can scan the text for the particular word.

- Mark the Answer. Now you have the key information the question is looking for. Go back to the question, quickly scan the choices and mark the correct one.

Understand and practice the different types of standardized reading comprehension tests. See the list above for the different types. Typically, there will be several questions dealing with facts from the selection, a couple more inference questions dealing with logical consequences of those facts, and periodically an application-oriented question surfaces to force you to make connections with what you already know. Some students prefer to answer the questions as listed, and feel classifying the question and then ordering is wasting precious time. Other students prefer to answer the different types of questions in order of how easy or difficult they are. The choice is yours and do whatever works for you. If you want to try answering in order of difficulty, here is a recommended order, answer fact questions first; they're easily found within the passage. Tackle inference problems next, after re-reading the question(s) as many times as you need to. Application or 'best guess' questions usually take the longest, so, save them for last.

Use the practice tests to try out both ways of answering and see what works for you.

For more help with reading comprehension, see Multiple Choice Secrets.

Main Idea and Supporting Details

Identifying the main idea, topic and supporting details in a passage can feel like an overwhelming task. The passages used for standardized tests can be boring and seem difficult - Test writers don't use interesting passages or ones that talk about things most people are familiar with. Despite these obstacles, all passages and paragraphs will have the information you need to answer the questions.

The topic of a passage or paragraph is its subject. It's the general idea and can be summed up in a word or short phrase. On some standardized tests, there is a short description of the passage if it's taken from a longer work. Make sure you read the description as it might state the topic of the passage. If not, read the passage and ask yourself, "Who or what is this about?" For example:

> Over the years, school uniforms have been hotly debated. Arguments are made that students have the right to show individuality and express themselves by choosing their own clothes. However, this brings up social and academic issues. Some kids cannot afford to wear the clothes they like and might be bullied by the "better dressed" students. With attention drawn to clothes and the individual, students will lose focus on class work and the reason they are in school. School uniforms should be mandatory.

Ask: What is this paragraph about?

Topic: school uniforms

Once you have the topic, it's easier to find the main idea. The main idea is a specific statement telling what the writer wants you to know about the topic. Writers usually state the main idea as a thesis statement. If you're looking for the main idea of a single paragraph, the main idea is called the topic sentence and will probably be the first or last sentence. If you're looking for the main idea of an entire passage, look for the thesis statement in either the first or last paragraph. The main idea is usually restated in the conclusion. To find the main idea of a passage or paragraph, follow these steps:

1. Find the topic.

2. Ask yourself, "What point is the author trying to make about the topic?"

3. Create your own sentence summarizing the author's point.

4. Look in the text for the sentence closest in meaning to yours.

Look at the example paragraph again. It's already established that the topic of the paragraph is school uniforms. What is the main idea/topic sentence?

Ask: "What point is the author trying to make about school uniforms?"

Summary: Students should wear school uniforms.

Topic sentence: School uniforms should be mandatory.

Main Idea: School uniforms should be mandatory.

Each paragraph offers supporting details to explain the main idea. The details could be facts or reasons, but they will always answer a question about the main idea. What? Where? Why? When? How? How much/many? Look at the example paragraph again. You'll notice that more than one sentence answers a question about the main idea. These are the supporting details.

Main Idea: School uniforms should be mandatory.

Ask: Why? Some kids cannot afford to wear clothes they like and could be bullied by the "better dressed" kids. Supporting Detail

With attention drawn to clothes and the individual, Students will lose focus on class work and the reason they are in school. Supporting Detail

What if the author doesn't state the main idea in a topic sentence? The passage will have an implied main idea. It's not as difficult to find as it might seem. Paragraphs are always organized around ideas. To find an implied main idea, you need to know the topic and then find the relationship between the supporting details. Ask yourself, "What is the point the author is making about the relationship between the details?."

Cocoa is what makes chocolate good for you. Chocolate comes in many varieties. These delectable flavors include milk chocolate, dark chocolate, semi-sweet, and white chocolate.

Ask: What is this paragraph about?

Topic: Chocolate

Ask: What? Where? Why? When? How? How much/many?

Supporting details: Chocolate is good for you because it is made of cocoa, Chocolate is delicious, Chocolate comes in different delicious flavors

Ask: What is the relationship between the details and what is the author's point?

Main Idea: Chocolate is good because it is healthy and it tastes good.

Testing Tips for Main Idea Questions

1. Skim the questions – not the answer choices - before reading the passage.

2. Questions about main idea might use the words "theme," "generalization," or "purpose."

3. Save questions about the main idea for last. Questions can often be found in order in the passage.

3. Underline topic sentences in the passage. Most tests allow you to write in your test booklet.

4. Answer the question in your own words before looking at the answer choices. Then match your answer with an answer choice.

5. Cross out incorrect answer choices immediately to prevent confusion.

6. If two of the answer choices mean the same thing but use different words, they are BOTH incorrect.

7. If a question asks about the whole passage, cross out the answer choices that apply only to part of it.

8. If only part of the information is correct, that answer choice is incorrect.

9. An answer choice that is too broad is incorrect. All information needs to be backed up by the passage.

10. Answer choices with extreme wording are usually incorrect.

Drawing Inferences And Conclusions

Drawing inferences and making conclusions happens all the time. In fact, you probably do it every time you read—sometimes without even realizing it! For example, remember the first time you saw the movie "The Lion King." When you meet Scar for the first time, he is trapping a helpless mouse with his sharp claws preparing to eat it. When you see this action you guess that Scar is going to be a bad character in the movie. Nothing appeared to tell you this. No caption came across the bottom of the screen that said "Bad Guy." No red arrow pointed to Scar and said "Evil Lion." No, you made an inference about his character based on the context clue you were given. You do the same thing when you read!

When you draw an inference or make a conclusion you are doing the same thing, you are making an educated guess based on the hints the author gives you. We call these hints "context clues." Scar trapping the innocent mouse is the context clue about Scar's character.

Usually you are making inferences and drawing conclusions the entire time that you are reading. Whether you realize it or not, you are constantly making educated guesses based on context clues. Think about a time you were reading a book and something happened that you were expecting to happen. You're not psychic! Actually, you were picking up on the context clues and making inferences about what was going to happen next!

Let's try an easy example. Read the following sentences and answer the questions at the end of the passage.

Shelly really likes to help people. She loves her job because she gets to help people every single day. However, Shelly has to work long hours and she can get called in the middle of the night for emergencies. She wears a white lab coat at work and usually she carries a stethoscope.

What is most likely Shelly's job?

a. Musician
b. Lawyer
c. Doctor
d. Teacher

This probably seemed easy. Drawing inferences isn't always this simple, but it is the same basic principle. How did you know Shelly was a doctor? She helps people, she works long hours, she wears a white lab coat, and she gets called in for emergencies at night. Context Clues! Nowhere in the paragraph did it say Shelly was a doctor, but you were able to draw that conclusion based on the information provided in the paragraph. This is how it's done!

There is a catch, though. Remember that when you draw inferences based on reading, you should only use the information given to you by the author. Sometimes it is easy for us to make conclusions based on knowledge that is already in our mind—but that can lead you to drawing an incorrect inference. For example, let's pretend there is a bully at your school named Brent. Now let's say you read a story and the main character's name is Brent. You could NOT infer that the character in the story is a bully just because his name is Brent. You should only use the information given to you by the author to avoid drawing the wrong conclusion.

Let's try another example. Read the passage below and answer the question.

Social media is an extremely popular new form of connecting and communicating over the internet. Since Facebook's original launch in 2004, millions of people have joined in the social media craze. In fact, it is estimated that almost 75% of all internet users aged 18 and older use some form of social media. Facebook started at Harvard University as a way to get students connected. However, it quickly grew into a worldwide phenomenon and today, the founder of Facebook, Mark Zuckerberg has an estimated net worth of 28.5 billion dollars.

Facebook is not the only social media platform, though. Other sites such as Twitter, Instagram, and Snapchat have since been invented and are quickly becoming just as popular! Many social media users actually use more than one type of social media. Furthermore, most social media sites have created mobile apps that allow people to connect via social media virtually anywhere in the world!

What is the most likely reason that other social media sites like Twitter and Instagram were created?

    a. Professors at Harvard University made it a class project.

    b. Facebook was extremely popular and other people thought they could also be successful by designing social media sites.

    c. Facebook was not connecting enough people.

    d. Mark Zuckerberg paid people to invent new social media sites because he wanted lots of competition.

Here, the correct answer is B. Facebook was extremely popular and other people thought they could also be successful by designing social media sites. How do we know this? What are the context clues? Take a look at the first paragraph. What do we know based on this paragraph? Well, one sentence refers to Facebook's original launch. This suggests that Facebook was one of the first social media sites. In addition, we know that the founder of Facebook has been extremely successful and is worth billions of dollars. From this we can infer that other people wanted to imitate Facebook's idea and become just as successful as Mark Zuckerberg.

Let's go through the other answers. If you chose A, it might be because Facebook started at Harvard University, so you drew the conclusion that all other social media sites were also started at Harvard University. However, there is no mention of class projects, professors, or students designing social media. So there doesn't seem to be enough support for choice A.

If you chose C, you might have been drawing your own conclusions based on outside information. Maybe none of your friends are on Facebook, so you made an inference that Facebook didn't connect enough people, so more sites were invented. Or maybe you think the people who connect on Facebook are too old, so you don't think Facebook connects enough people your age. This might be true, but remember inferences should be drawn from the information the author gives you!

If you chose D, you might be using the information that Mark Zuckerberg is worth over 28 billion dollars. It would be easy for him to pay others to design new sites, but remember, you need to use context clues! He is very wealthy, but that statement was giving you information about how successful Facebook was—not suggesting that he paid others to design more sites!

So remember, drawing inferences and conclusions is simply about using the information you are given to make an educated guess. You do this every single day so don't let this concept scare you. Look for the context clues, make sure they support your claim, and you'll be able to make accurate inferences and conclusions!

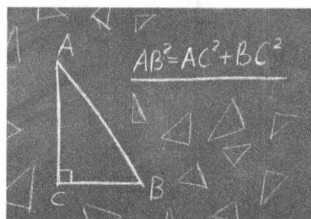

Mathematics

THIS SECTION CONTAINS A SELF-ASSESSMENT AND MATH TUTORIALS. The tutorials are designed to familiarize general principles and the self-assessment contains general questions similar to the math questions likely to be on the exam, but are not intended to be identical to the exam questions. The tutorials are not designed to be a complete math course, and it is assumed that students have some familiarity with math. If you do not understand parts of the tutorial, or find the tutorial difficult, it is recommended that you seek out additional instruction.

Tour of the HSPT Mathematics Content

Below is a detailed list of the mathematics topics likely to appear on the exam. Make sure that you understand these topics at the very minimum.

- Convert decimals, percent, roman numerals and fractions

- Solve word problems

- Calculate percent and ratio

- Operations using fractions, percent and fractions

- Analyze and interpret tables, graphs and charts

- Data and Statistics

- Geometry and measurement

- Understand and solve simple algebra problems

The questions in the self-assessment are not the same as you will find on the exam - that would be too easy! And nobody knows what the questions will be and they change all the time. Mostly, the changes consist of substituting new questions for old, but the changes also can be new question formats or styles, changes to the number of questions in each section, changes to the time limits for each section, and combining sections. So while the format and exact wording of the questions may differ slightly, and changes from year to year, if you can answer the questions below, you will have no problem with the mathematics section .

Mathematics Self-Assessment

The purpose of the self-assessment is:

- Identify your strengths and weaknesses.

- Develop your personalized study plan (above)

- Get accustomed to the format

- Extra practice – the self-assessments are almost a full 3rd practice test!

- Provide a baseline score for preparing your study schedule.

Since this is a Self-assessment, and depending on how confident you are with Math, timing yourself is optional.   This self-assessment has 60 questions, so allow about 60 minutes to complete.

Once complete, use the table below to assess your understanding of the content, and prepare your study schedule described in chapter 1.

80% - 100%	Excellent – you have mastered the content
60 – 79%	Good. You have a working knowledge. Even though you can just pass this section, you may want to review the tutorials and do some extra practice to see if you can improve your mark.
40% - 59%	Below Average. You do not understand the content. Review the tutorials , and retake this quiz again in a few days, bcforc proceeding to the Practice Test Questions.
Less than 40%	Poor. You have a very limited understanding. Please review the tutorials , and retake this quiz again in a few days, before proceeding to the Practice Test Questions.

Math Self-Assessment Answer Sheet

1. A B C D
2. A B C D
3. A B C D
4. A B C D
5. A B C D
6. A B C D
7. A B C D
8. A B C D
9. A B C D
10. A B C D
11. A B C D
12. A B C D
13. A B C D
14. A B C D
15. A B C D
16. A B C D
17. A B C D
18. A B C D
19. A B C D
20. A B C D
21. A B C D
22. A B C D
23. A B C D
24. A B C D
25. A B C D
26. A B C D
27. A B C D
28. A B C D
29. A B C D
30. A B C D
31. A B C D
32. A B C D
33. A B C D
34. A B C D
35. A B C D
36. A B C D
37. A B C D
38. A B C D
39. A B C D
40. A B C D
41. A B C D
42. A B C D
43. A B C D
44. A B C D
45. A B C D
46. A B C D
47. A B C D
48. A B C D
49. A B C D
50. A B C D
51. A B C D
52. A B C D
53. A B C D
54. A B C D
55. A B C D
56. A B C D
57. A B C D
58. A B C D
59. A B C D
60. A B C D

Math Self-Assessment

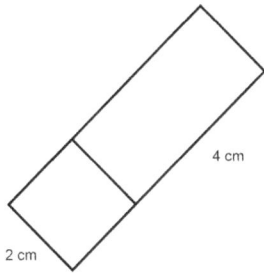

Note: Figure not drawn to scale

1. Assuming the figure with a 2 cm side is square, what is the perimeter of the above shape?

    a. 12 cm

    b. 16 cm

    c. 6 cm

    d. 20 cm

2. A boy has 5 red balls, 3 white balls and 2 yellow balls. What percent of the balls are yellow?

    a. 2%

    b. 8%

    c. 20%

    d. 12%

3. The length of a rectangle is twice its width and its area is equal to the area of a square of side 12 cm. What will be the perimeter of the rectangle to the nearest whole number?

    a. 36 cm

    b. 46 cm

    c. 51 cm

    d. 56 cm

4. There are 15 yellow and 35 orange balls in a basket. How many more yellow balls must be added to make yellow balls 65%?

    a. 35

    b. 50

    c. 65

    d. 70

5. $4^2 \times 4^7 =$

    a. 16^{-5}

    b. 4^9

    c. 16^{11}

    d. 4^{-5}

6. A man buys an item for $420 and has a balance of $3000.00. How much did he have before?

    a. $2,580

    b. $3420

    c. $2,420

    d. $342

7. At the beginning of 2009, Marilyn invested $5,000 in a savings account. The account pays 4% interest per year. At the end of the year, after the interest was paid, how much did Marilyn have in the account?

    a. $5,200

    b. $5,020

    c. $5,110

    d. $7,000

300°

d

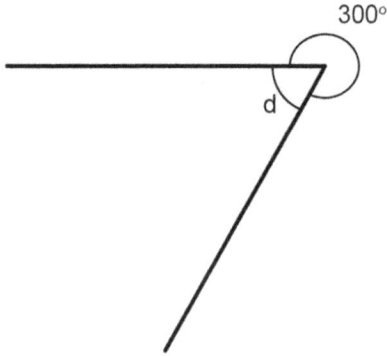

8. What is the measurement of the indicated angle?

     a. 45°

     b. 90°

     c. 60°

     d. 50°

9. The average weight of 13 students in a class of 15 (two were absent that day) is 42 kg. When the remaining 2 were weighed, the average became 42.7 kg. If one of the remaining students weighs 48, how much does the other weigh?

     a. 44.7 kg.

     b. 45.6 kg.

     c. 46.5 kg.

     d. 47.4 kg.

10. $10^{65} \div 10^{13}$

     a. 10^{52}

     b. 10^{78}

     c. 100^{62}

     d. 100^{78}

11. The total expense of building a fence around a square field is $2000 at a rate of $5 per meter. What is the length of one side?

     a. 40 meters

     b. 80 meters

     c. 100 meters

     d. 320 meters

12. Convert 23.67 to percent.

     a. 2.367%

     b 236.7%

     c. 23.67%

     d. 2367%

13. If 144 students need to go on a trip and the buses carry 36 students each, how many buses do they need?

     a. 6

     b. 5

     c. 4

     d. 3

14. A mother is making spaghetti for her son. The recipe calls for 500 grams of spaghetti, and 0.75 grams of salt. However, the mom just wants 125 grams of spaghetti. How much salt should she use?

     a. 0.38 grams

     b. 0.75 grams

     c. 0.19 grams

     d. 0.25 grams

15. A young student deposits $200 in a savings account hoping to buy a bicycle worth $245. If the bank offers a 15% interest rate, how long will the boy have to wait?

    a. 1½ years

    b. 2 ½ years

    c. 2 years

    d. 1 year

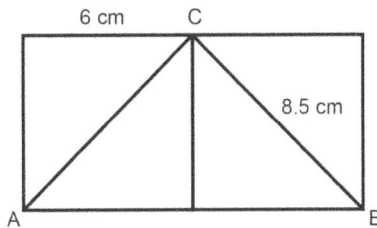

Note: Figure not drawn to scale

16. Assuming the quadrangles in the figure above are identical rectangles, what is the perimeter of △ABC?

    a. 25.5 cm

    b. 27 cm

    c. 30 cm

    d. 29 cm

17. A pet store had total sales of $19,304.56 for the month of June. If the wholesale cost was $5,284.34, the employees were paid $8,384.76, and the rent was $2,920.00, how much profit did the store make in June?

    a. $5,635.46

    b. $2,714.47

    c. $14,020.22

    d. $10,019.80

18. Tony bought 15 dozen eggs for $80. 16 eggs were broken during loading and unloading. He sold the remainder for $0.54 each. What will be his percentage profit? Provide answer in 2 significant digits.

    a. 11%

    b. 10%

    c. 13%

    d. 12%

19. The cost of waterproofing canvas is .50 per square yard. What's the total cost for waterproofing a canvas truck cover that is 15' x 24'?

    a. $18.00

    b. $6.67

    c. $180.00

    d. $20.00

20. John purchased a jacket at a 7% discount. He had a membership that gave him an additional 2% discount. If he paid $425, what is the retail price of the jacket?

    a. $448

    b. $460

    c. $466

    d. $472

21. In a certain game, players toss a coin and roll a dice. A player wins if the coin comes up heads, or the dice with a number greater than 4. In 20 games, how many times will a player win?

    a. 13

    b. 8

    c. 11

    d. 15

22. A square box measures 20 cm long and 20 cm wide and 20 cm high. What is the volume of the box?

    a. 60 cm³

    b. 20,000 cm³

    c. 4,000 cm³

    d. 8,000 cm³

23. 5/8 ÷ 2/3

    a. 15/16

    b. 10/24

    c. 5/12

    d. 1 2/5

24. 7.25 x 0.5

    a. 3.625

    b. 3.526

    c. 36.25

    d. 35.25

25. Employees of a discount appliance store receive an additional 20% off the lowest price on any item. If an employee purchases a dishwasher during a 15% off sale, how much will he pay if the dishwasher originally cost $450?

    a. $280.90

    b. $287

    c. $292.50

    d. $306

26. Mr. Brown bought 5 cheeseburgers, 3 drinks and 4 orders of fries for his family, plus a cookie pack for his dog. If the price of all single items is the same at $1.30, and a 3.5% tax is added, what was the total cost of dinner?

    a. $16.00

    b. $16.90

    c. $17.00

    d. $17.49

27. Solve √144

    a. 14

    b. 72

    c. 24

    d. 12

28. The sale price of a car is $12,590, which is 20% off the original price. What is the original price?

    a. $14,310.40

    b. $14,990.90

    c. $15,108.00

    d. $15,737.50

29. Estimate 16 x 230.

    a. 31,000

    b. 301,000

    c. 3,100

    d. 3,000,000

30. In a small village there are 9 families with 3 children, 8 families with 2 children, and 4 families having 5 children. What is the average number of children in a family?

a. 2.5
b. 2.8
c. 3
d. 3.5

31. A goat eats 214 kg. of hay in 60 days, while a cow eats the same amount in 15 days. How long will it take to eat this hay together?

a. 37.5
b. 75
c. 12
d. 15

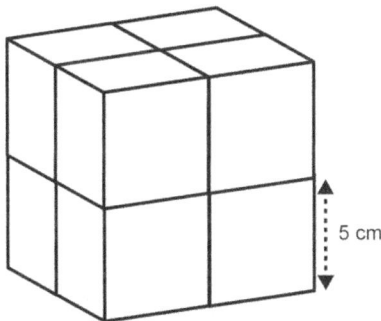

Note: Figure not drawn to scale

5 cm

32. If the figure above is composed of cubes, what is the volume?

a. 125 cm³
b. 875 cm³
c. 1000 cm³
d. 500 cm³

33. Sarah weighs 25 pounds more than Tony does. If together they weigh 205 pounds, how much does Sarah weigh approximately in kilograms? Assume 1 pound = 0.4535 kilograms

a. 41
b. 48
c. 50
d. 52

34. Ann went from point A to point B. At the same time, Peter went from point B to point A. In 6 hours, they met, and in 3 more hours, Peter reached B. How many hours did it take Ann to travel from A to B?

a. 18
b. 9
c. 15
d. 12

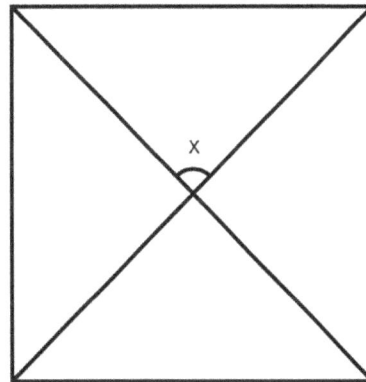

35. What is measurement of the indicated angle?

a. 45°
b. 90°
c. 60°
d. 30°

36. In a local election at polling station A, 945 voters cast their vote out of 1270 registered voters. At polling station B, 860 cast their vote out of 1050 registered voters and at station C, 1210 cast their vote out of 1440 registered voters. What is the total turnout including all three polling stations?

    a. 70%
    b. 74%
    c. 76%
    d. 80%

37. Mr. White wants to tile his rectangular backyard, which is 16 m × 11 m. The dimensions of each tile are 7 cm × 4 cm. If cost of each tile is $0.30 and 2.5% tiles break during handling, then what will be the total cost?

    a. $19,234
    b. $20,240
    c. $20,895
    d. $21,563

38. Find the mean of these set of numbers – 100, 1050, 320, 600 and 150

    a. 333
    b. 444
    c. 440
    d. 320

39. Translate the following into an equation: six times a number plus five.

    a. (6 * 5) + 5
    b. 6(X+5)
    c. 5X + 6
    d. None of the above

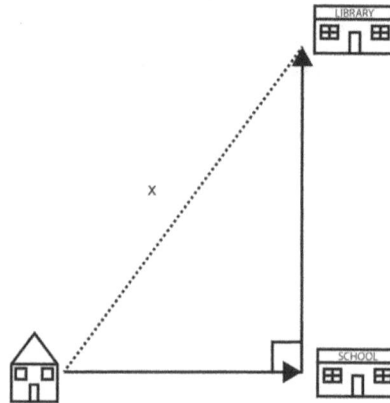

40. Every day starting from his home Peter travels due east 3 kilometers to the school. After school he travels due north 4 kilometers to the library. What is the distance between Peter's home and the library?

    a. 15 km
    b. 10 km
    c. 5 km
    d. 12 ½ km

41. In the Euro cup football game, England won gold, Spain won silver and Holland won bronze medals. The three winners share the total prize money of $605,500 in the ratio of 4:2:1. How much money did Spain win?

    a. $86,500
    b. $173,000
    c. $201,830
    d. $346,000

42. What is the least common multiple of 10 and 3?

    a. 35

    b. 30

    c. 15

    d. 60

43. Solve for b. 7 − 8b = 11 − 10b.

    a. 2

    b. 3

    c. 5

    d. 6

44. A building is 15 m long and 20 m wide and 10 m high. What is the volume of the building?

    a. 45 m³

    b. 3,000 m³

    c. 1500 m³

    d. 300 m³

45. Solve 3/4 + 2/4 + 1.2

    a. 1 1/7

    b. 2 3/4

    c. 2 9/20

    d. 3 1/4

46. 3 boys are asked to clean a surface that is 4 ft². If the portion is divided equally among the boys, what size will each of them clean?

    a. 1 ft 6 sq. inches²

    b. 14 sq. inches²

    c. 1 ft² sq. inches²

    d. 1 ft² 48 inches²

47. Great Britain has a Value Added Tax of 15%. A shop sells a camera for $545. If the VAT is included in the price, what is the actual cost of the camera?

    a. $490.40

    b. $473.91

    c. $505.00

    d. $503.15

48. In a train, 24 people are sitting while 8 people are standing. What is the ratio of people sitting to standing?

    a. 1:3

    b. 1:5

    c. 3:1

    d. 3:5

49. Simplify 0.12 + 1 2/5 − 1 3/5

    a. 1 1/25

    b. 1 3/25

    c. 1 2/5

    d. 2 3/5

50. A rectangular box measures 10 cm long and 8 cm wide and 10 cm high. What is the volume of the box?

    a. 28 cm³

    b. 2000 cm³

    c. 400 cm³

    d. 800 cm³

51. 5 men have to share a load weighing 10 kg 550 g equally among themselves. How much weight will each man have to carry?

  a. 900 g

  b. 1.5 kg

  c. 3 kg

  d. 2 kg 110 g

52. A worker's weekly salary was increased by 30%. If his new salary is $150, what was his old salary?

  a. $120.00

  b. $99.15

  c. $109.00

  d. $115.38

53. In a restaurant, 44 people ordered for coffee while 38 asked for tea. What is ratio of tea drinkers to coffee drinkers?

  a. 6:11

  b. 8:11

  c. 7:9

  d. 8:15

54. Simplify 0.25 + 1/3 + 2/3

  a. 1 1/4

  b. 2 1/4

  c. 1 1/3

  d. 2 1/4

55. Estimate 46,227 + 101,032.

  a. 14,700

  b. 147,000

  c. 14,700,000

  d. 104,700

56. 2/15 ÷ 4/5 =

  a. 6/65

  b. 6/75

  c. 5/12

  d. 1/6

57. If Tim deposits $5,500 in a savings account that offers a 5% interest, what will be the total amount in his savings account after 3 years?

  a. $6,225

  b. $6,0325

  c. $325

  d. $6,325

58. The price of a product was increased by 45%. If the initial cost of the product was $220, what is the new cost of the product?

  a. $230

  b. $300

  c. $319

  d. $245

59. A bag contains 38 black balls and 42 white balls. What is the ratio of black balls to white?

  a. 9:11

  b. 1:3

  c. 19:21

  d. 11:9

**60. A map uses a scale of 1:2,000
How much distance on the ground
is 5.2 inches on the map if the
scale is in inches?**

    a. 100,400

    b. 10, 500

    c. 10,400

    d. 10,440

Mathematics Self-Assessment Answer Key

1. B
We see that there is a square with side 2 cm and a rectangle adjacent to it, with one side 2 cm (common side with the square) and the other side 4 cm. The perimeter of a shape is found by summing up all sides surrounding the shape, not adding the ones inside the shape. Three 2 cm sides from the square, and two 4 cm sides and one 2 cm side from the rectangle contribute the perimeter.

So, the perimeter of the shape is: 2 + 2 + 2 + 4 + 2 + 4 = 16 cm.

2. C
Total no. of balls = 10, number of yellow balls = 2, so, 2/10 X 100 = 20%

3. C
Area of the square = 12 × 12 = 144 cm². Let x be the width so 2x will be the length of rectangle. The area will be 2 x 2 and the perimeter will be 2(2x + x) = 6x. According to the condition 2 x 2 = 144 then x = 8.48 cm. The perimeter will be 6 × 8.48 = 50.88 = 51 cm.

4. B
There are 50 balls in the basket now. Let x be the yellow balls that are to be added to make it 65%. So the equation becomes X + 15 /X + 50 = 65/100. X = 50.

5. B
When multiplying exponent, add the exponents. Therefore $4^{2+7} = 4^9$

6. B
(Amount Spent) $420 + $3000 (Balance) = $3420

7. A
5000 X 4% = 200
5000 + 200 = $5200

8. C
The sum of angles around a point is 360°
d + 300 = 360°
d = 60°

9. C
Total weight of 13 students with average 42 will be = 42 * 13 = 546 kg.

The total weight of the remaining 2 will be found by subtracting the total weight of 13 students from the total weight of 15 students: 640.5 - 546 = 94.5 kg.

94.5 = the total weight of two students. One of these students weigh 48 kg, so;

The weight of the other will be = 94.5 – 48 = 46.5 kg

10. A
When dividing exponents, subtract the exponents. $10^{65-13} = 10^{52}$

11. C
Total expense is $2000 and we are informed that $5 is spent per meter. Combining these two information, we know that the total length of the fence is 2000/5 = 400 meters.

The fence is built around a square-shaped field. If one side of the square is "a," the perimeter of the square is "4a." Here, the perimeter is equal to 400 meters. So,

400 = 4a

100 = a - this means that one side of the square is equal to 100 meters

12. D
To convert to percent, simply multiply the decimal by 100 or move the decimal point 2 places to the right. Therefore, 23.67 x 100 = 2367%

13. C
144 ÷ 36 = 4

14. C
125: 500 is the same as 25 : 100 or 1 : 4. So the amount of salt will be 0.75/4 = 0.1875, or about .19 grams.

15. A
$200 invested at 15% per year will yield $30 interest at the end of the first year. For the second year, the interest will be 34.50, so it will take about 1 1/2 years before he can buy the bike.

16. D
Perimeter of triangle ABC is asked.

Perimeter of a triangle = sum of three sides.

Here, Perimeter of ΔABC = |AC| + |CB| + |AB|.

Since the triangle is located in the middle of two adjacent and identical rectangles, we find the side lengths using these rectangles:

|AB| = 6 + 6 = 12 cm

|CB| = 8.5 cm

|AC| = |CB| = 8.5 cm

Perimeter = |AC| + |CB| + |AB| = 8.5 + 8.5 + 12 = 29 cm

17. A
19304.56 – 5284.34 – 8384.76 = 5635.46

18. A
Let us first mention the money Tony spent: $80

Now we need to find the money Tony earned:

He had 15 dozen eggs = 15 * 12 = 180 eggs. 16 eggs were broken. So,

Remaining number of eggs that Tony sold = 180 – 16 = 164.

Total amount he earned for selling 164 eggs = 164 * 0.54 = $88.56.

As a summary, he spent $80 and earned $88.56.

The profit is the difference: 88.56 - 80 = $8.56

Percentage profit is found by proportioning the profit to the money he spent:

8.56•100/80 = 10.7%

Checking the answers, we round 10.7 to the nearest whole number: 11%

19. D
First calculate total square feet, which is 15 * 24 = 360 ft². Next, convert this value to square yards, (1 yards² = 9 ft²) which is 360/9 = 40 yards². At $0.50 per square yard, the total cost is 40 * 0.50 = $20.

20. C
Let the original price be 100x.

At the rate of 7% discount, the discount will be (100x * 7)/100 = 7x. So, the discounted price will be = 100x - 7x = 93x.

Over this price, at the rate of 2% additional discount, the discount will be (93x * 2)/100 = 1.86x. So, the additionally discounted price will be = 93x - 1.86x = 91.14x.

This is the amount which John has paid for the jacket:

91.14x = 425

x = 425 / 91.14 = 4.6631

The jacket costs 100x. So, 100x = 100•4.6631 = $466.31.

When rounded to the nearest whole number, this is equal to $466.

21. A
The sample space of this event will be S = { (H,1),(H,2),(H,3),(H,4),(H,5),(H,6)(T,1),(T,2),(T,3),(T,4),(T,5),(T,6) } So there are a total of 12 outcomes and 8 winning outcomes. The probability of a win in a single event is P (W) =8/12=2/3. In 20 games the probability of a win = 2/3 × 20 = 13

22. D
Formula for volume of a shape is L x W x H = 20 x 20 x 20 = 8,000 cm³

23. A
To divide fractions, we multiply the first fraction with the inverse of the second fraction. Therefore we have 5/8 x 3/2, = 15/16

24. A
7.25 x 0.5 = 3.625

25. D
The cost of the dishwasher = $450

15% discount amount = (450 * 15)/100 = $67.5

The discounted price = 450 – 67.5 = $382.5

20% additional discount amount on lowest price = (382.5 * 20)/100 = $76.5

So, the final discounted price = 382.5 - 76.5 = $306.00

26. D
The total number of items is 5 + 3 + 4 + 1 = 13. 13 X 1.30 = 16.90 + 3.5% = $17.49

27.
$\sqrt{144}$ = 12

28. D
Original price = x,
80/100 = 12590/X,
80X = 1259000,
X = $15737.50.

29. C
16 X 230 = 3680, or about 3100.

30. C
Let X = total number of families
Y = total number of children
Y = 9 x 3 + 8 x 2 + 4 x 5 = 63 and
X = 9 + 8 + 4 = 21
Average number of children in a family = Y/X = 63/21 = 3

31. C
Total hay = 214 kg,
The goat eats at a rate of 214/60 days = 3.6 kg per day.
The cow eats at a rate of 214/15 = 14.3 kg per day,
Together they eat 3.6 + 14.3 = 17.9 per day.
At a rate of 17.9 kg per day, they will consume 214 kg in 214/17.9 = 11.96 or 12 days approx.

32. C
The large cube is made up of 8 smaller cubes with 5 cm sides. The volume of a cube is found by the third power of the length of one side.
Volume of the large cube = Volume of the small cube * 8

= (5³) * 8 = 125 * 8

= 1000 cm³

There is another solution for this question. Find the side length of the large cube. There are two cubes rows with 5 cm. length for each. So, one side of the large cube is 10 cm.

The volume of this large cube is equal to $10^3 = 1000$ cm³

33. D
Let us denote Sarah's weight by "x." Then, since she weighs 25 pounds more than Tony, Tony will be x-25. They together weigh 205 pounds which means that the sum of the two representations will be equal to 205:

Sarah : x

Tony : x - 25

x + (x - 25) = 205 ... by arranging this equation we have:

x + x - 25 = 205

2x - 25 = 205 ... we add 25 to each side to have x term alone:

2x - 25 + 25 = 205 + 25

2x = 230

x = 230/2

x = 115 pounds - Sarah weighs 115 pounds. Since 1 pound is 0.4535 kilograms, we need to multiply 115 by 0.4535 to have her weight in kilograms:

x = 115 * 0.4535 = 52.1525 kilograms - this is equal to 52 when rounded to the nearest whole number.

34. D
It took peter 3 hours to cover the distance Ann traveled in 6 hours (from point of meeting to point A, where Ann started). This means Peter is traveling at twice the speed of Ann. If it took peter 6 hours to reach the point of meeting, it will take Ann twice that long to get to Peter's point of origin = 6 x 2 = 12

35. A
The diagonals of a square intersect at right angles, so each angle measures 90° Half of that angle will be 45°

36. D
To find the total turnout in all three polling stations, we need to proportion the number of voters to the number of all registered voters.

Number of total voters = 945 + 860 + 1210 = 3015

Number of total registered voters = 1270 + 1050 + 1440 = 3760

Percentage turnout over all three polling stations = 3015•100/3760 = 80.19%

Checking the answers, we round 80.19 to the nearest whole number: 80%

37. A
The area of each tile is 7 cm X 4 cm = 28 cm². The area of the yard is 16 m X 11 m = 176 m² = 1760000 cm². The number of tiles required is 1760000/28 = 62858. 2% of the tiles break during handling, so 1.02 X 62858 = 64115. Total cost will be 64115 X 0.3 = $19234.55.

38. B
First add all the numbers 100 + 1050 + 320 + 600 + 150 = 2220. Then divide by 5 (the number of data provided) = 2220/5 = 444

39. A
Six times a number plus five is the same as saying six times (a number plus five). Or, 6 * (a number plus five). Let X be the number so, 6(X+5). Note that six times a number plus 5 could also be 6X + 5, depending on

how you look at it, however that is not a choice.

40. C
We see that two legs of a right triangle form by Peter's movements and we are asked to find the length of the hypotenuse. We use the Pythagorean Theorem:

(Hypotenuse)^2 = (Adjacent side)^2 + (Opposite side)^2

Given: $3^2 + 4^2 = h^2$
$h^2 = 9 + 16$
$h = \sqrt{25}$
$h = 5$

41. B
Spain won second prize so their ratio is 2/7
2/7 * 60550 = $173,000

42. B
The multiples of 10 are 10, 20, 30, 40 and the multiples of 3 are 3, 6, 9. 12, 15....24, 27, 30. The least common multiple is 30.

43. A
$7 - 8b = 11 - 10b$. Bring same terms to same side of the equation by changing the negative or positive signs when they cross over, therefore $-8b + 10b = 11 - 7$, $2b = 4$, $b = 4/2 = 2$

44. B
Formula for volume of a shape is L x W x H = 15 x 20 x 10 = 3,000 m^3

45. C
3/4 + 2/4 + 1.2, first convert the decimal to fraction, = 3/4 + 2/4 + 1 1/5 = ¾ + 2/4 + 6/5 = (find common denominator) (15 + 10 + 24)/20 = 49/20 = 2 9/20

46. D
1 foot is equal to 12 inches. So 1 ft^2 = 12 * 12 in^2
4 ft^2 = 4 * 12 * 12 in^2 = 576 in^2

The total surface area is divided equally among 3 boys.

Each boy will clean 576/3 = 192 in^2

192 in^2 = 144 in^2 + 48 in^2; 144 in^2 = 1 ft^2

So, each boy will clean 1 ft^2 and 48 in^2

47. B
Actual cost = X, therefore, 545 = x + 0.15x, 545 = 1x + 0.15x, 545 = 1.15x, x = 545/1.15 = 473.9

48. C
Ratio of people sitting to standing is 24:8, reduce to lowest terms = 3:1

49. B
0.12 + 2/5 + 3/5, Convert decimal to fraction to get 3/25 + 2/5 + 3/5, = (3 + 10 + 15)/25, = 28/25 = 1 3/25

50. D
Formula for volume of a shape is L x W x H = 10 x 8 x 10 = 800 cm^3

51. D
First, we need to convert all units to grams. Since 1000 g = 1 kg:

10 kg 550 g = 10 * 1000 g + 550 g = 10,000 g + 550 g = 10,550 g.

10,550 g is shared between 5 men. So each man will have to carry 10,550/5 = 2,110 g

2,110 g = 2,000 g + 110 g = 2 kg 110 g

52. D
Let old salary = X, therefore $150 = x + 0.30x, 150 = 1x + 0.30x, 150 = 1.30x, x = 150/1.30 = 115.38

53. B
Ratio of tea drinkers to coffee is 38:44, reduce to lowest terms = 8:11

54. A
0.25 + 2 1/3 + 2/3, first convert decimal to fraction, 1/4 + 1/3 + 2/3, (3 + 4 + 8)/12, = 15/12 = 5/4 = 1 1/4

55. B
46,227 + 101,032 is approximately 147,000. The actual total is 147,259.

56. D
To divide fractions, multiply the first fraction with the inverse of the second fraction. 2/15 x 5/4, (cancel out) = 1/3 x 1/2 = 1/6

57. D
P = $5,500, t = 3 years, r = 5%, I = ? convert rate to decimal and 5% = 0.05 I = 5,500 x 0.05 x 3 = 825. Total amount in the account = principal + interest or 5,500 + 825 = $6,325

58. C
Initial cost was $220. new cost = 220 + 45% of 220, 45/100 x 220 = 99, therefore new price is 220 + 99 = $319.

59. C
The ratio of black balls to white is 38:42. Reduce to lowest terms = 19:21

60. C
1 inch on map = 2,000 inches on ground. So, 5.2 inches on map = 5.2 * 2,000 = 10,400 inches on ground.

How to Solve Word Problems

Most students find math word problems difficult. Solving word problems is much easier if you have a systematic approach which we outline below.

Here is the biggest tip for studying word problems.

Practice regularly and systematically. Sounds simple and easy right? Yes it is, and yes it really does work.

Word problems are a way of thinking and require you to translate a real world problem into mathematical terms.

Some math instructors go so far as to say that learning how to think mathematically is the main reason for teaching word problems.

So what do we mean by practice regularly and systematically? Studying word problems and math in general requires a logical and mathematical frame of mind. The only way that you can get this is by practicing regularly, which means everyday.

It is critical that you practice word problems everyday for the 5 days before the exam as a bare minimum.

If you practice and miss a day, you have lost the mathematical frame of mind and the benefit of your previous practice is pretty much gone. Anyone who has done math will agree – you have to practice everyday.

Everything is important. The other critical point about word problems is that all the information given in the problem has some purpose. There is no unnecessary information! Word problems are typically around 50 words in 1 to 3 sentences. If the sometimes complicated relationships are to be explained in that short an explanation, every word has to count. Make sure that you use every piece of information.

Here are 9 simple steps to solving word problems.

Step 1 – Read through the problem at least three times. The first reading should be a quick scan, and the next two readings should be done slowly to find answers to these questions:

What does the problem ask? (Usually located towards the end of the problem)

What does the problem imply? (This is usually a point you were asked to remember).

Mark all information, and underline all important words or phrases.

Step 2 – Try to make a pictorial representation of the problem such as a circle and an arrow to show travel. This makes the problem a bit more real and sensible to you.

A favorite word problem is something like, 1 train leaves Station A traveling at 100 km/hr and another train leaves Station B traveling at 60 km/hr. ...

Draw a line, the two stations, and the two trains at either end. This will clarify the problem.

Step 3 – Use the information you have to make a table with a blank portion to indicate information you do not know.

Step 4 – Assign a single letter to represent each unknown data in your table. You can write down the unknown that each letter represents, so you do not assign answers for the wrong unknown, because a word problem may have multiple unknowns and you will need to create equations for each unknown.

Step 5 – Translate the English terms in the word problem into a mathematical algebraic equation. Remember that the main problem with word problems is that they are not expressed in regular math equations. You ability to identify correctly the variables and translate the word problem into an equation determines your ability to solve the problem.

Step 6 – Check the equation to see if it looks like regular equations that you are used to seeing and whether it looks sensible. Does the equation appear to represent the information in the question? Take note that you may need to re-write some formulas needed to solve the word problem equation. For example, word distance problems may need you rewriting the distance formula, which is Distance = Time x Rate. If the word problem requires that you solve for time you will need to use Distance/Rate and Distance/Time to solve for Rate. If you understand the distance word problem you should be able to identify the variable you need to solve for.

Step 7 – Use algebra rules to solve the derived equation. Take note that the laws of equation demands that what is done on this side of the equation has to also be done on the other side. You have to solve the equation so that the unknown ends alone on one side. Where there are multiple unknowns you will need to use elimination or substitution methods to resolve all the equations.

Step 8 – Check your final answers to see if they make sense with the information given in the problem. For example if the word problem involves a discount, the final price should be less or if a product was taxed then the final answer has to cost more.

Step 9 – Cross check your answers by placing the answer or answers in the first equation to replace the unknown or unknowns. If your answer is correct then both side of the equation must equate or equal. If your answer is not correct then you may have derived a wrong equation or solved the equation wrongly. Repeat the necessary steps to correct.

Types of Word Problems

Word problems can be classified into 12 types. Below are examples of each type with a complete solution. Some types of word problems can be solved quickly using multiple choice strategies and some cannot. Always look for ways to estimate the answer and then eliminate choices.

1. Age

A girl is 10 years older than her brother. By next year, she will be twice the age of her brother. What are their ages now?

   a. 25, 15
   b. 19, 9
   c. 21, 11
   d. 29, 19

Solution: B

We will assume that the girl's age is "a" and her brother's is "b." This means that based on the information in the first sentence,
a = 10 + b

Next year, she will be twice her brother's age, which gives
a + 1 = 2(b + 1)

We need to solve for one unknown factor and then use the answer to solve for the other. To do this we substitute the value of "a" from the first equation into the second equation. This gives

10 + b + 1 = 2b + 2
11 + b = 2b + 2
11 – 2 = 2b – b
b = 9

9 = b this means that her brother is 9 years old. Solving for the girl's age in the first equation gives a = 10 + 9. a = 19 the girl is aged 19. So, the girl is aged 19 and the boy is 9

2. Distance or speed

Two boats travel down a river towards the same destination, starting at the same time. One boat is traveling at 52 km/hr, and the other boat at 43 km/hr. How far apart will they be after 40 minutes?

   a. 46.67 km
   b. 19.23 km
   c. 6.0 km
   d. 14.39 km

Solution: C

After 40 minutes, the first boat will have traveled = 52 km/hr x 40 minutes/60 minutes = 34.66 km. After 40 minutes, the second boat will have traveled = 43 km/hr x 40/60 minutes = 28.66 km. Difference between the two boats will be 34.66 km – 28.66 km = 6 km.

Multiple Choice Strategy

First estimate the answer. The first boat is traveling 9 km. faster than the second, for 40 minutes, which is 2/3 of an hour. 2/3 of 9 = 6, as a rough guess of the distance apart.

Choices A, B and D can be eliminated right away.

3. Ratio

The instructions in a cookbook states that 700 grams of flour must be mixed in 100 ml of water, and 0.90 grams of salt added. A cook however has just 325 grams of flour. What is the quantity of water and salt that he should use?

    a. 0.41 grams and 46.4 ml
    b. 0.45 grams and 49.3 ml
    c. 0.39 grams and 39.8 ml
    d. 0.25 grams and 40.1 ml

Solution: A

The Cookbook states 700 grams of flour, but the cook only has 325. The first step is to determine the percentage of flour he has 325/700 x 100 = 46.4% That means that 46.4% of all other items must also be used.
46.4% of 100 = 46.4 ml of water
46.4% of 0.90 = 0.41 grams of salt.

Multiple Choice Strategy

The recipe calls for 700 grams of flour but the cook only has 325, which is just less than half, the amount of water and salt are going to be about half.

Choices C and D can be eliminated right away. Choice B is very close so be careful. Looking closely at Choice B, it is exactly half, and since 325 is slightly less than half of 700, it can't be correct.

Choice A is correct.

4. Percent

An agent received $6,685 as his commission for selling a property. If his commission was 13% of the selling price, how much was the property?

    a. $68,825
    b. $121,850
    c. $49,025
    d. $51,423

Solution: D

Let's assume that the property price is x
That means from the information given, 13% of x = 6,685
Solve for x,
x = 6685 x 100/13 = $51,423

Multiple Choice Strategy

The commission,13%, is just over 10%, which is easier to work with. Round up $6685 to $6700, and multiple by 10 for an approximate answer. 10 X 6700 = $67,000. You can do this in your head. Choice B is much too big and can be eliminated. Choice C is too small and can be eliminated. Choices A and D are left and good possibilities.

Do the calculations to make the final choice.

5. Sales & Profit

A store owner buys merchandise for $21,045. He transports them for $3,905 and pays his staff $1,450 to stock the merchandise on his shelves. If he does not incur further costs, how much does he need to sell the items to make $5,000 profit?

    a. $32,500
    b. $29,350
    c. $32,400
    d. $31,400

Solution: D

Total cost of the items is $21,045 + $3,905 + $1,450 = $26,400
Total cost is now $26,400 + $5000 profit = $31,400

Multiple Choice Strategy

Round off and add the numbers up in your head quickly.
21,000 + 4,000 + 1500 = 26500. Add in 5000 profit for a total of 31500.

Choice B is too small and can be eliminated. Choice C and Choice A are too large and can be eliminated.

6. Tax/Income

A woman earns $42,000 per month and pays 5% tax on her monthly income. If the Government increases her monthly taxes by $1,500, what is her income after tax?

    a. $38,400
    b. $36,050
    c. $40,500
    d. $39, 500

Solution: A

Initial tax on income was 5/100 x 42,000 = $2,100
$1,500 was added to the tax to give $2,100 + 1,500 = $3,600
Income after tax left is $42,000 - $3,600 = $38,400

7. Interest

A man invests $3000 in a 2-year term deposit that pays 3% interest per year. How much will he have at the end of the 2-year term?

    a. $5,200
    b. $3,020
    c. $3,182.7
    d. $3,000

Solution: C

This is a compound interest problem. The funds are invested for 2 years and interest is paid yearly, so in the second year, he will earn interest on the interest paid in the first year.

3% interest in the first year = 3/100 x 3,000 = $90
At end of first year, total amount = 3,000 + 90 = $3,090
Second year = 3/100 x 3,090 = 92.7.
At end of second year, total amount = $3090 + $92.7 = $3,182.7

8. Averaging

The average weight of 10 books is 54 grams. 2 more books were added and the average weight became 55.4. If one of the 2 new books added weighed 62.8 g, what is the weight of the other?

    a. 44.7 g
    b. 67.4 g
    c. 62 g
    d. 52 g

Solution: C

Total weight of 10 books with average 54 grams will be = 10 × 54 = 540 g
Total weight of 12 books with average 55.4 will be = 55.4 × 12 = 664.8 g
So total weight of the remaining 2 will be= 664.8 – 540 = 124.8 g
If one weighs 62.8, the weight of the other will be= 124.8 g – 62.8 g = 62 g

Multiple Choice Strategy

Averaging problems can be estimated by looking at which direction the average goes. If additional items are added and the average goes up, the new items much be greater than the average. If the average goes down after new items are added, the new items must be less than the average.

In this case, the average is 54 grams and 2 books are added which increases the average to 55.4, so the new books must weight more than 54 grams.

Choices A and D can be eliminated right away.

9. Probability

A bag contains 15 marbles of various colors. If 3 marbles are white, 5 are red and the rest are black, what is the probability of randomly picking out a black marble from the bag?

    a. 7/15
    b. 3/15
    c. 1/5
    d. 4/15

Solution: A

Total marbles = 15
Number of black marbles = 15 – (3 + 5) = 7
Probability of picking out a black marble = 7/15

10. Two Variables

A company paid a total of $2850 to book for 6 single rooms and 4 double rooms in a hotel for one night. Another company paid $3185 to book for 13 single rooms for one night in the same hotel. What is the cost for single and double rooms in that hotel?

    a. single= $250 and double = $345
    b. single= $254 and double = $350
    c. single = $245 and double = $305
    d. single = $245 and double = $345

Solution: D

We can determine the price of single rooms from the information given of the second company. 13 single rooms = 3185.
One single room = 3185 / 13 = 245
The first company paid for 6 single rooms at $245. 245 x 6 = $1470
Total amount paid for 4 double rooms by first company = $2850 - $1470 = $1380
Cost per double room = 1380 / 4 = $345

11. Geometry

The length of a rectangle is 5 in. more than its width. The perimeter of the rectangle is 26 in. What is the width and length of the rectangle?

    a. width = 6 inches, Length = 9 inches
    b. width = 4 inches, Length = 9 inches
    c. width =4 inches, Length = 5 inches
    d. width = 6 inches, Length = 11 inches

Solution: B

Formula for perimeter of a rectangle is 2(L + W)
p=26, so 2(L+W) = p
The length is 5 inches more than the width, so
2(w+5) + 2w = 26
2w + 10 + 2w = 26
2w + 2w = 26 - 10
4w = 18

W = 16/4 = 4 inches

L is 5 inches more than w, so L = 5 + 4 = 9 inches.

12. Totals and fractions

A basket contains 125 oranges, mangos and apples. If 3/5 of the fruits in the basket are mangos and only 2/5 of the mangos are ripe, how many ripe mangos are there in the basket?

    a. 30
    b. 68
    c. 55
    d. 47

Solution: A
Number of mangos in the basket is 3/5 x 125 = 75
Number of ripe mangos = 2/5 x 75 = 30

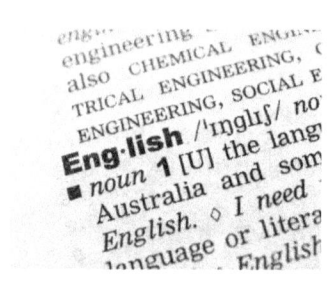

Language Arts

THIS SECTION CONTAINS AN ENGLISH LANGUAGE ARTS SELF-ASSESSMENT. The tutorials are designed to familiarize general principles and the self-assessment contains general questions similar to the language arts questions likely to be on the exam, but are not intended to be identical to the exam questions. The tutorials are not designed to be a complete course, and it is assumed that students have some familiarity with English grammar and usage. If you do not understand parts of the tutorial, or find the tutorial difficult, it is recommended that you seek out additional instruction.

Tour of the English Language Arts Content

Below is a detailed list of the topics likely to appear on the exam.

- Capitalization

- Spelling

- Punctuation

- English usage

- English grammar

- Sentence structure

The questions in the self-assessment are not the same as you will find on the exam - that would be too easy! And nobody knows what the questions will be and they change all the time. Mostly, the changes consist of substituting new questions for old, but the changes also can be new question formats or styles, changes to the number of questions in each section, changes to the time limits for each section, and combining sections. So the format and exact wording of the questions may differ slightly, and changes from year to year, if you can answer the questions below, you will have no problem with the Language Arts section.

Language Arts Self-Assessment

The purpose of the self-assessment is:

- Identify your strengths and weaknesses.

- Develop your personalized study plan (above)

- Get accustomed to the format

- Extra practice – the self-assessments are almost a full 3rd practice test!

- Provide a baseline score for preparing your study schedule.

Since this is a Self-assessment, and depending on how confident you are with language arts, timing yourself is optional. This self-assessment has 60 questions, so allow 30 minutes to complete.

Language Arts Self-Assessment Answer Sheet

1. Ⓐ Ⓑ Ⓒ Ⓓ   21. Ⓐ Ⓑ Ⓒ Ⓓ   41. Ⓐ Ⓑ Ⓒ Ⓓ
2. Ⓐ Ⓑ Ⓒ Ⓓ   22. Ⓐ Ⓑ Ⓒ Ⓓ   42. Ⓐ Ⓑ Ⓒ Ⓓ
3. Ⓐ Ⓑ Ⓒ Ⓓ   23. Ⓐ Ⓑ Ⓒ Ⓓ   43. Ⓐ Ⓑ Ⓒ Ⓓ
4. Ⓐ Ⓑ Ⓒ Ⓓ   24. Ⓐ Ⓑ Ⓒ Ⓓ   44. Ⓐ Ⓑ Ⓒ Ⓓ
5. Ⓐ Ⓑ Ⓒ Ⓓ   25. Ⓐ Ⓑ Ⓒ Ⓓ   45. Ⓐ Ⓑ Ⓒ Ⓓ
6. Ⓐ Ⓑ Ⓒ Ⓓ   26. Ⓐ Ⓑ Ⓒ Ⓓ   46. Ⓐ Ⓑ Ⓒ Ⓓ
7. Ⓐ Ⓑ Ⓒ Ⓓ   27. Ⓐ Ⓑ Ⓒ Ⓓ   47. Ⓐ Ⓑ Ⓒ Ⓓ
8. Ⓐ Ⓑ Ⓒ Ⓓ   28. Ⓐ Ⓑ Ⓒ Ⓓ   48. Ⓐ Ⓑ Ⓒ Ⓓ
9. Ⓐ Ⓑ Ⓒ Ⓓ   29. Ⓐ Ⓑ Ⓒ Ⓓ   49. Ⓐ Ⓑ Ⓒ Ⓓ
10. Ⓐ Ⓑ Ⓒ Ⓓ   30. Ⓐ Ⓑ Ⓒ Ⓓ   50. Ⓐ Ⓑ Ⓒ Ⓓ
11. Ⓐ Ⓑ Ⓒ Ⓓ   31. Ⓐ Ⓑ Ⓒ Ⓓ   51. Ⓐ Ⓑ Ⓒ Ⓓ
12. Ⓐ Ⓑ Ⓒ Ⓓ   32. Ⓐ Ⓑ Ⓒ Ⓓ   52. Ⓐ Ⓑ Ⓒ Ⓓ
13. Ⓐ Ⓑ Ⓒ Ⓓ   33. Ⓐ Ⓑ Ⓒ Ⓓ   53. Ⓐ Ⓑ Ⓒ Ⓓ
14. Ⓐ Ⓑ Ⓒ Ⓓ   34. Ⓐ Ⓑ Ⓒ Ⓓ   54. Ⓐ Ⓑ Ⓒ Ⓓ
15. Ⓐ Ⓑ Ⓒ Ⓓ   35. Ⓐ Ⓑ Ⓒ Ⓓ   55. Ⓐ Ⓑ Ⓒ Ⓓ
16. Ⓐ Ⓑ Ⓒ Ⓓ   36. Ⓐ Ⓑ Ⓒ Ⓓ   56. Ⓐ Ⓑ Ⓒ Ⓓ
17. Ⓐ Ⓑ Ⓒ Ⓓ   37. Ⓐ Ⓑ Ⓒ Ⓓ   57. Ⓐ Ⓑ Ⓒ Ⓓ
18. Ⓐ Ⓑ Ⓒ Ⓓ   38. Ⓐ Ⓑ Ⓒ Ⓓ   58. Ⓐ Ⓑ Ⓒ Ⓓ
19. Ⓐ Ⓑ Ⓒ Ⓓ   39. Ⓐ Ⓑ Ⓒ Ⓓ   59. Ⓐ Ⓑ Ⓒ Ⓓ
20. Ⓐ Ⓑ Ⓒ Ⓓ   40. Ⓐ Ⓑ Ⓒ Ⓓ   60. Ⓐ Ⓑ Ⓒ Ⓓ

Part 1 - Punctuation and Capitalization

1. Ted and Janice <u>who had been friends for years went on vacation to-gether</u> every summer.

    a. Ted and Janice, who had been friends for years, went on vacation to-gether every summer.

    b. Ted and Janice who had been friends for years, went on vacation to-gether every summer.

    c. Ted, and Janice who had been friends for years, went on vacation to-gether every summer.

    d. None of the choices are correct.

2. None of us want to go to the <u>party not even</u> if there will be live music.

    a. None of us want to go to the party not even, if there will be live music.

    b. None of us want to go to the party, not even if there will be live music.

    c. None of us want to go to the party; not even if there will be live music.

    d. None of the choice are correct.

3. <u>John, Maurice, and Thomas,</u> quit school two months before gradua-tion.

    a. John, Maurice, and Thomas quit school two months before graduation.

    b. John, Maurice and Thomas quit school two months before graduation.

    c. John Maurice and Thomas, quit school two months before graduation.

    d. None of the choice are correct.

4. "My father said that he would be there on <u>Sunday," Lee</u> explained.

    a. "My father said that he would be there on Sunday" Lee explained.

    b. None of the choices are correct.

    c. "My father said that he would be there on Sunday," Lee explained.

    d. "My father said that he would be there on Sunday." Lee explained.

5. I own two <u>dogs, a cat, named Jeffrey and Henry, the goldfish.</u>

    a. I own two dogs, a cat named Jeffrey, and Henry, the goldfish.

    b. I own two dogs a cat, named Jeffrey, and Henry, the goldfish.

    c. I own two dogs, a cat named Jeffrey; and Henry, the goldfish.

    d. None of the choices are correct.

6. Choose the sentence below with the correct punctuation.

    a. Marcus who won the debate tournament, is the best speaker that I know.

    b. Marcus, who won the debate tournament, is the best speaker that I know.

    c. Marcus who won the debate tournament is the best speaker that I know.

    d. Marcus who won the debate tournament is the best speaker, that I know.

7. Choose the sentence with the correct capitalization.

    a. "stop! I forgot to bring my wallet," said Carl.

    b. "please wait for me," shouted Stacy.

    c. "what is your name?" asked the teacher.

    d. "I will submit my project tomorrow," said Mary.

8. Choose the sentence with the correct capitalization.

    a. Our family will visit china next year.

    b. The Children are happy to see Santa claus.

    c. We have relatives in Mexico.

    d. The great barrier reef in Australia can be seen in outer space.

9. Choose the sentence with the correct capitalization.

    a. Coach Wilkins called a meeting.

    b. Ms. Tracy, Chairperson of the English Club called a meeting.

    c. The brave soldiers will see president Obama.

    d. secretary Rogers recorded the meeting.

10. Choose the sentence with the correct capitalization.

    a. How's my health, doctor?

    b. Is anything wrong, mister?

    c. Will you handle the case, Attorney?

    d. Can I see you now, ma'am?

11. Choose the sentence with the correct capitalization.

    a. Dear stacy,

    b. All The Best,

    c. Very truly yours,

    d. Dear Mr. carson,

12. Choose the sentence with the correct capitalization.

a. Are you taking Art and Music?

b. I'm enrolled in geometry II.

c. We will take Calculus I.

d. History and American literature aren't offered this semester.

Part II - Sentence Structure and Grammar

Combine the sentences below into one sentence with the same meaning.

13. I hate needles. I want to give blood. I can't give blood.

a. Although I hate needles, I couldn't give blood even if I wanted to.

b. Because I hate needles, I can't give blood, although I want to give blood.

c. Whenever I hate needles, I give blood although I can't give blood.

d. Whenever I can't give blood, I give blood anyway, although I hate needles.

14. The doctor was not looking forward to meeting Mrs. Lucas. The doctor would have to tell Mrs. Lucas that she has cancer. The doctor hates giving bad news to patients.

a. The doctor hates giving bad news, so he was not looking forward to meeting Mrs. Lucas and telling her she has cancer.

b. The doctor has cancer and was not looking forward to meeting Mrs. Lucas and telling her the bad news.

c. Before the doctor met Mrs. Lucas, he had to give his the patients the bad news that Mrs. Lucas has cancer.

d. The doctor was not looking forward to giving the bad news to his patients that he had to tell Mrs. Lucas that his patients have cancer.

15. Mom hates shopping. We were out of bread, milk and eggs. Mom went to the supermarket.

a. Because we were out of bread, milk and eggs, Mom hated shopping at the supermarket.

b. Although she hates shopping, Mom went to the supermarket since we were out of bread, milk and eggs.

c. Although we were out of bread, milk and eggs, Mom still hated shopping at the supermarket and went there anyway.

d. Because Mom hated shopping at the supermarket, she went to there to buy her bread, milk and eggs.

16. The ceremony had an emotional <u>affect</u> on the groom, but the bride was not <u>affected</u>.

    a. The ceremony had an emotional effect on the groom, but the bride was not affected.

    b. The ceremony had an emotional affect on the groom, but the bride was not affected.

    c. The ceremony had an emotional effect on the groom, but the bride was not effected.

17. Anna was taller <u>than Luis, but then</u> he grew four inches in three months.

    a. None of the choices are correct.
    b. Anna was taller then Luis, but than he grew four inches in three months.
    c. Anna was taller than Luis, but than he grew four inches, in three months.
    d. Anna was taller than Luis, but then he grew four inches in three months.

18. <u>There</u> second home is in Boca Raton, but <u>they're</u> not <u>there</u> for most of the year.

    a. Their second home is in Boca Raton, but there not their for most of the year.

    b. They're second home is in Boca Raton, but they're not there for most of the year.

    c. Their second home is in Boca Raton, but they're not there for most of the year.

    d. None of the choices are correct.

19. <u>Their</u> going to graduate in June; after that, <u>their</u> best option will be to go <u>there.</u>

    a. They're going to graduate in June; after that, their best option will be to go there.

    b. There going to graduate in June; after that, their best option will be to go there.

    c. They're going to graduate in June; after that, there best option will be to go their.

    d. None of the choices are correct.

20. Your mistaken; that is not you're book.

    a. You're mistaken; that is not you're book.

    b. Your mistaken; that is not your book.

    c. You're mistaken; that is not your book.

    d. None of the choices are correct.

21. <u>You're</u> classes are on the west side of campus, but <u>you're</u> living on the east side.

    a. You're classes are on the west side of campus, but you're living on the east side.

    b. Your classes are on the west side of campus, but your living on the east side.

    c. Your classes are on the west side of campus, but you're living on the east side.

    d. None of the choices are correct.

22. The Chinese lives in one of the world's most populous nations, while a citizen of Bermuda lives in one of the least populous.

    a. The Chinese live in one of the world's most populous nations, while a citizen of Bermuda lives in one of the least populous.

    b. The Chinese lives in one of the world's most populous nations, while a citizen of Bermuda live in one of the least populous.

    c. The Chinese live in one of the world's most populous nations, while a citizen of Bermuda live in one of the least populous.

    d. None of the choices are correct.

23. You shouldn't <u>sit</u> in that chair wearing black pants; I <u>sit</u> the white cat there just a moment ago.

    a. You shouldn't sit in that chair wearing black pants; I set the white cat there just a moment ago.

    b. You shouldn't set in that chair wearing black pants; I sit the white cat there just a moment ago.

    c. You shouldn't set in that chair wearing black pants; I set the white cat there just a moment ago.

    d. None of the choices are correct.

24. We saw the <u>golden gate Bridge in San Francisco.</u>

    a. Golden Gate Bridge in San Francisco
    b. golden gate bridge in San Francisco
    c. Golden gate bridge in San Francisco
    d. None of the choice are correct.

25. The teacher told us yesterday the sun was bigger than Earth.

    a. is the
    b. is
    c. was the
    d. none of the above

26. Please <u>die</u> this cloth.

    a. died
    b. dye
    c. dyed
    d. none of the above

Fill in the Blanks.

27. Our _____ to New York by train was very comfortable.

    a. voyage
    b. travel
    c. journey
    d. none of the above

28. We will _____ to New York by train.

    a. journey
    b. voyage
    c. travel
    d. none of the above

29. Our _____ to America by sea was not very comfortable.

    a. journey

    b. voyage

    c. travel

    d. none of the above

30. I do not want to _____ a friend like you.

    a. lose

    b. loose

    c. lost

    d. none of the above

31. This pain killer will _____ your pain.

    a. lesson

    b. lessen

    c. lesen

    d. leson

32. Our office is a four _____ building.

    a. storey

    b. storys

    c. story

    d. none of the above

33. The government didn't have the _____ idea what to do.

    a. finest

    b. faintest

    c. fairest

    d. none of the above.

34. His father is _____.

    a. a poet and novelist

    b. poet and novelist

    c. a poet and a novelist

    d. none of the above

Part III - Sentence Completion and Correction

35. Collecting stamps, _____ and listening to shortwave radio were Rick's main hobbies.

    a. building models

    b. to build models

    c. having built models

    d. build models

36. Every morning, _____, and before the sun comes up, my mother makes herself a cup of cocoa.

    a. after the kids left for school

    b. after the kids leave for school

    c. after the kids have left for school

    d. after the kids will leave for school

37. Elaine promised to bring the camera _____ at the mall yesterday.

    a. by me

    b. with me

    c. at me

    d. to me

38. Following the tornado, telephone poles _____ all over the street.

    a. laid

    b. lied

    c. were lying

    d. were laying

Part IV - Grammar – Sentence Correction

39. She is the <u>most cleverest</u> girl in the class.

    a. She is the most clever girl in the class.

    b. She is the cleverest girl in the class.

    c. She is the most cleverer girl in the class.

    d. None of the above.

40. He <u>lived</u> in California since 1995.

    a. He had lived in California since 1995.

    b. He has been living in California since 1995.

    c. He has living in California since 1995.

    d. None of the above.

41. Please excuse <u>me being</u> late.

    a. Please excuse me for late.

    b. Please excuse my being late.

    c. Please excuse my being lateness.

    d. None of the above.

42. Politics <u>are</u> his chief interest.

    a. Politics is his chief interest.

    b. Politics are his chief interests.

    c. Politics is his chief interests.

    d. The sentence is correct.

43. He is a <u>cowered</u> person.

a. He is a cowardest person.

b. He is a cowardly person.

c. He is a coward person.

d. The sentence is correct.

44. Choose the sentence with the correct grammar.

a. The man was asked to come with his daughter and her test results.

b. The man was asked to come with her daughter and her test results.

c. The man was asked to come with her daughter and our test results.

d. None of the above.

45. Choose the sentence with the correct grammar.

a. Neither of them came with their bicycle.

b. Neither of them came with his bicycle.

c. Neither of them came with our bicycle.

d. None of the above.

46. Choose the sentence with the correct grammar.

a. Each boy and girl were given a toy.

b. Each boy and girl was given a toy.

c. Each boy and girl is given a toy.

d. None of the above.

47. Choose the sentence with the correct grammar.

a. His measles is getting better

b. His measles are getting better

c. Both of the above

d. None of the above

48. Choose the sentence with the correct grammar.

a. The teachers and the student are standing in the hall

b. The teachers and the student is standing in the hall

c. Both of the above

d. None of the above

49. Choose the sentence with the correct grammar.

a. The sad news were delivered this morning

b. The sad news are delivered this morning

c. The sad news was delivered this morning

d. None of that above

50. Choose the sentence with the correct grammar.

a. The World Health Organization (WHO) were meeting by January.

b. The World Health Organization (WHO) are meeting by January.

c. The World Health Organization (WHO) is meeting by January.

d. None of the above.

51. Choose the correct spelling.

a. arguemint
b. arguement
c. argument
d. arguemant

52. Choose the correct spelling.

a. occurrence
b. ocurrence
c. ocurence
d. occurence

53. Choose the correct spelling.

a. desparate
b. desperete
c. desperate
d. despirate

54. Choose the correct spelling.

a. Wedesday
b. Wendesday
c. Wenesday
d. Wednesday

55. Choose the correct spelling.

a. kechup
b. ketcup
c. kechsup
d. ketchup

56. Choose the correct spelling.

a. correspondence
b. corespodence
c. correspodence
d. correspomdence

57. Choose the correct spelling.

a. henmorrhage
b. hemmorrhage
c. hemorrhage
d. hemorhage

58. Choose the correct spelling.

a. enviromnment
b. environment
c. environiment
d. enviromment

59. Choose the correct spelling.

a. govermment
b. goverment
c. govenment
d. government

60. Choose the correct spelling.

a. inucolate
b. inocculate
c. inoculate
d. innoculate

Answer Key

1. A
Use a comma to separate phrases.

2. B
Use a comma separates independent clauses. None of us wants to go to the party, not even if there will be live music.

3. B
Don't use a comma before 'and' in a list.

4. C
Commas always go with a quote and the use of said, explained etc.

5. A
This is an example if a comma which appears before 'and,' but is disambiguating. Without the comma, the sentence would be "I own two dogs, a cat named Jeffrey and Henry, the goldfish." This means there is a cat named Jeffrey and Henry, and a goldfish with no name mentioned. The comma appears to show the distinction.

I own two dogs, a cat named Jeffrey, and Henry, the goldfish.

6. B
Use a comma to separate phrases.

7. D
Capitalize the first word of a quoted sentence.

8. C
Always capitalize a proper noun.

9. C
Capitalize a person's title when it precedes the name. Do not capitalize when the title is acting as a description following the name.

10. C
Capitalize any title when used as a direct address.

11. C
Capitalize the first word of a salutation and the first word of a complimentary close.

12. C
Capitalize the names of specific course titles.

13. A
These three sentences can be combined using 'although,' and 'even if.'

14. A
These two sentences can be combined into one sentence with two clauses separated by a comma.

15. B
These three sentences can be combined using 'although,' and 'since.'

English Usage

16. A
Affect vs. Effect - Affect is a verb (action) and effect is a noun (thing).

17. D
Than vs. Then – Than is used for comparison, as in, taller than, and then is used for time, as in, but then...

18. C
There vs. their vs. they're. There indicates existence as in, "there are." Their is to indicate possession, as in, "their book." They're is the contraction form of "they are."

19. A
There vs. their vs. they're. There indicates existence as in, "there are." Their is to indicate possession, as in, "their book." They're is the contraction form of "they are."

20. C
Your vs. you're. Your is the possessive form of you. You're is the contraction form of you are.

21. C
Your vs. you're. Your is the possessive form of you. You're is the contraction form of you are.

22. A
Singular subjects. "The Chinese" is plural, and "a citizen of Bermuda" is singular.

23. A
Sit vs. Set. Set requires an object – something to set down. Sit is something that you do, like sit on the chair.

24. A
Always capitalize proper nouns.

25. B
Even though the conversation occurred in the past, "is" is correct since it refers to an unchanging state of being.

26. B
"Dye" mean to change the color of something by means of a stain or chemical process; "die" means to pass away.

27. C
"Travel" is a verb meaning to go from one place to another. A "journey" is a noun that refers to the travel event.

28. C
"Travel" is a verb meaning to go from one place to another. A "journey" is a noun that refers to the travel event.

29. B
"Travel" is a verb meaning to go from one place to another. A "journey" is a noun that refers to the travel event. A "voyage" is a journey by sea.

30. A
"Lose" is a verb meaning to misplace something or to fail at a competition. "Loose" is an adjective meaning untied or able to move freely.

31. B
"Lessen" means to reduce in size or intensity. "Lesson" refers to a formal time period in which particular information is taught or learned.

32. C
"Story," when used as an adjective modifying a building, is singular.

33. B
"Faintest" means least. "Finest" means the best. "Fairest" is the most fair.

34. A
There is no need to repeat the article, "a," a second time.

Grammar

35. A
Present progressive "building models" is correct in this sentence.

36. C
Past Perfect tense describes a completed action in the past, before another action in the past.

37. D
The preposition 'to' in this sentence means give.

38. C
"Lie" means to recline, and does not take an object. 'Lay' means to place and does take an object. Peter lay the books on the table, or the telephone poles were lying on the road.

39. B
Cleverest is the proper form to express 'most clever.'

40. B
Past perfect continuous, has been living, is proper because the time element, since 1995, and he is still living there now.

41. B
The correct form is, "please excuse me for being late," or, "please excuse my being late."

42. A
Despite 's' ending, "politics" is a singular noun.

43. B
"Cowardly" is an adjective used to modify a person.

44. A
A Pronoun should conform to its antecedent in gender, number and person.

45. B
Words such as neither, each, many, either, every, everyone, everybody and any should take a singular pronoun. Here we are assuming that the subject is male, and so use "his." The subject could be female, in which case we would use "her," however that is not one of the choices in this case.

46. B
Use the singular verb form when nouns are qualified with "every" or "each," even if they are joined by 'and.'

47. B
Use a plural verb for nouns like measles, tongs, trousers, riches, scissors etc.

48. A
When two subjects are linked with "with" or "as well," use the verb form that matches the first subject.

49. C
Always use the singular verb form for nouns like politics, wages, mathematics, innings, news, advice, summons, furniture, information, poetry, machinery, vacation, scenery etc.

50. C
Use a singular verb with a proper noun in plural form that refers to a single entity. Here the World Health Organization is a single entity, although it is made up on many members.

51. C
The correct spelling is argument.

52. A
The correct spelling is occurrence.

53. C
The correct spelling is desperate.

54. D
The correct spelling is Wednesday.

55. D
The correct spelling is ketchup.

56. A
The correct spelling is correspondence.

57. C
The correct spelling is hemorrhage.

58. B
The correct spelling is environment.

59. D
The correct spelling is government.

60. C
The correct spelling is inoculate.

English Grammar and Punctuation Tutorials

Capitalization

Although many of the rules for capitalization are pretty straight forward, there are several tricky points that are important to review.

Starting a Sentence

Everyone knows that you need to capitalize the first letter of the first word in a sentence, but is it really all that easy to figure out where one sentence starts and another stops? Take these three examples:

That was the moment it really sunk in: There would be no hockey this year.

It was April and that could mean only one thing: baseball.

We played for hours before heading home; everyone felt tired and happy.

In the first example, the first letter after the colon is capitalized while in the second example it is not. That is because everything after the first example's colon is a complete sentence, while after example two's colon there is only one word. In example three you have what could be a complete sentence ("everyone felt tired and happy"), but which is not because it follows a semicolon, making it just another clause instead.

Within a sentence you can have an additional complete sentence if the sentence follows a colon. However, if what could be a complete sentence follows a semicolon, it is a clause and does not get capitalized.

Remember that the same rules apply for quotation marks that apply for colons: A complete sentence inside quotation marks is capitalized, but a single word or phrase is not.

Proper Nouns

The first letter of all proper nouns needs to be capitalized. There are many categories of proper noun. The most common proper nouns are the specific names of people (such as Bill), places (such as Germany) or things (such as Honda Civic). However, there are several less obvious categories of words that should be capitalized as proper nouns.

Historical events such as World War II or the California Gold Rush need to be capitalized.

The names of celestial bodies such as Orion's Belt need to be capitalized.

The names of ethnicities such as African-American or Hispanic need to be capitalized.

Relationship words that replace a person's name such as Mom, Doctor and Mister need to be capitalized. However, this only happens when you use the word to replace the person's name. In the sentence, "My mom went to the store," you do not capitalize it, while in the sentence, "Hey Mom, did you get toothpaste at the store?" you do capitalize it.

Geographical locations are capitalized. This can be tricky because capitalized geographical locations and non-capitalized directions are easy to confuse. Saying, "We drove south for hours," is a direction, so the word "south" should not be capitalized. However, when saying, "While in the United States, we drove to the South to look at Civil War battle fields," you do capitalize the word "South." The difference is that in the first sentence "south" is just the direction you drove. In the second sentence "the South" is a specific region of the United States that formed itself into the Confederacy during the US Civil War.

Proper Adjectives

Proper adjectives are the adjective forms of proper nouns. People from Germany are German; people from Canada are Canadian. German and Canadian are proper adjectives because they are forms of proper nouns that are used to describe other nouns.

Titles of Works

Titles of works are generally capitalized following a specific pattern. Capitalize all the important words in a sentence. Do not capitalize unimportant words such as prepositions and articles.

For example: Alien Spaceship Spotted over Many of the World's Capitals

Notice that the prepositions "over" and "of," and the article "the" are the only non-capitalized words in the sentence.

Colons and Semicolons

Within a sentence there are several different types of punctuation marks that can denote a pause. Each of these punctuation marks has different rules when it comes to its structure and usage, so we will look at each one in turn.

Colons

The colon is used primarily to introduce information. It can start lists such as in the sentence, "There were several things Susan had to get at the store: bread, cereal, lettuce and tomatoes." Or acolon points specific information, such as in the sentence, "It was only then that the group fully realized what had happened: The Martian invasion had begun."

Note that if the information after the colon is a complete sentence, you capitalize and punctuate it exactly like you would a sentence. If, however, it does not constitute a complete sentence, you don't have to capitalize anything. ("Peering out the window Meredith saw them: zombies.")

Semicolons

Semicolons are super commas. They denote a stronger stop than a comma does, but they are still weaker than a period, not quite capable of ending a sentence. Semicolons are primarily used to separate independent clauses that are not being separated by a coordinating conjunction. ("Chris went to the store; he bought chips and salsa.") Semicolons can only do this, however, when the ideas in each clause are related. For instance, the sentence, "It's raining outside; my sister went to the movies," is not a proper usage of the semicolon since those clauses have nothing to do with each other.

Semicolons can also be used in lists if one or more element in the list is itself made up of a smaller list. If you want to write a list of things you plan to bring to a picnic, and those things only include a Frisbee, a chair and some pasta salad, you would not need to use a semicolon. But if you also wanted to bring plastic knives, forks and spoons, you would need to write your sentence like this: "For our picnic I am bringing a Frisbee; a chair; plastic knives, forks and spoons; and some pasta salad."

Using semicolons like this preserves the smaller list that you have in your larger list.

Commas

Commas are probably the most commonly used punctuation mark in English. Commas can break the flow of writing to give it a more natural sounding style, and they are the main punctuation mark used to separate ideas. Commas also separate lists, introductory adverbs, introductory prepositional phrases, dates and addresses.

The most rigid way that commas are used is when separating clauses. There are two primary types of clauses in a sentence, independent and subordinate (sometimes called dependent). Independent clauses are clauses that express a complete thought, such as, "Tim went to the store." Subordinate clauses, on the other hand, only express partial thoughts that expand on an independent clause, such as, "after the game ended," which you can see is clearly not a complete sentence. (You will learn more about clauses in different lessons.)

The rule for commas with clauses is that a comma must separate the clauses when a subordinate clause comes first in a sentence: "After the game ended,

Tim went to the store." But there should not be a comma when a subordinate clause follows an independent clause: "Tim went to the store after the game ended." If you leave the comma out of the first example, you have a run-on sentence. If you add one into the second example, you have a comma-splice error. Also, when you have two independent clauses joined with a coordinating conjunction, you need to separate them with a comma. "Tim went to the store, and Beth went home."

Commas are also used to separate items in a list. This area of English is unfortunately less clear than it should be, with two separate rules depending on what standard you are following. To understand the two different rules, let's pretend you are having a party at your house, and you are making a list of refreshments your friends will want. You may decide to serve three things: 1) pizza 2) chips 3) drinks. There are two different rules governing how you should punctuate this. According to many grammar books, you would write this as, "At the store I will buy pizza, chips, and drinks." This variation puts a comma after each item in the list. It is the version that the style books used in most college English and history courses will prefer, so it is probably the one you should follow. However, the Associated Press style guide, which is used in college journalism classes and at newspapers and magazines, says the sentence should be written like this: "At the store I will buy pizza, chips and drinks." Here you only use a comma between the first two words, letting the word "and" act as the separator between the last two.

Another important place to use commas is when you have a modifier that describes an element of a sentence, but that does not directly follow the thing it describes. Look at the sentence: "Tim went over to visit Beth, watching the full moon along the way." In this sentence there is no confusion about who is "watching the full moon"; it is Tim, probably as he walks to Beth's house. If you remove the comma, however, you get this: "Tim went over to visit Beth watching the full moon along the way." Now it sounds as though Beth is watching the full moon, and we are forced to wonder what "way" the moon is traveling along.

Commas are also used when adding introductory prepositional phrases and introductory adverbs to sentences. A comma is always needed following an introductory adverb. ("Quickly, Jody ran to the car.") Commas are even necessary when you have an adverb introducing a clause within a sentence, even if the clause not the first clause of the sentence. ("Amanda wanted to go to the movie; however, she knew her homework was more important.")

With introductory prepositional phrases you only add a comma if the phrase (or if a group of introductory phrases) is five or more words long. Thus, the sentence you just read did not have a comma following its introductory

prepositional phrase ("With introductory prepositional phrases") because it was only four words. Compare that to this sentence with a five word introductory phrase: "After the ridiculously long class, the friends needed to relax."

The last main way that commas are used in sentences is to separate out information that does not need to be there. For instance, "My cousin Hector, who wore a blue hat at the party, thought you were funny." The fact that Hector wore a blue hat is interesting, but it is not vital to the sentence; it could be removed and not changed the sentence's meaning. Therefore, it gets commas around it. Along these lines you should remember that any clause introduced by the word that is considered to provide essential information to the sentence and should not get commas around it. Conversely, any clause starting with the word which is considered nonessential and should not get commas around it.

Quotation Marks

Quotation marks are used in English in a variety of different ways. The most common use of quotation marks is to show quotations either as dialogue or when directly quoting a source in an essay or news article. Fortunately, both of these uses follow the same basic rules.

When you have a quote written as the second part of a sentence, you need to put a comma before the quotation marks and a period inside the quotation marks at the end. (Franklin said, "Let's go to the store.") Conversely, when you have quote as the first part of the sentence with information describing it second, a comma replaces the period at the end of the sentence inside the quotes. ("Let's go to the store," Franklin said.)

If the information in a quote is not a complete sentence, you do not need to capitalize it or put commas around it, if it is not dialogue. (No one thought the idea of "going to the store" sounded very fun.)

Note that when the last word in a sentence has both a quotation mark and a period attached to it, the period is always inside the quotes. This is the case when you have a complete sentence inside a quote ("Let's go to the store."), and when the last word in a sentence just happens to have quote marks around it (Kerri said I was "mean.") You also need to do the same thing with commas. (Kerri said I was "mean," and it made me feel bad.) However, other punctuation marks such as colons, semicolons and dashes do not follow this rule and should come outside the quotes. (Kerri said I was "mean"; it made me feel bad.)

When you want to use a quote inside a quote, you use the standard double-quotation marks for the outer quote and single-quotation marks for the inner quote. ("The sign on the door said 'no soliciting,' so we went to the next house.")

Quotation marks are also used around certain types of titles. To figure out which ones, it helps to look at which titles are not put in quotes as well.

Titles have two categories: large works and small works. Large works are things such as newspapers, magazines, CDs, books and television shows. The defining characteristic of a large work is that it is able to hold small works in it. Small works are the articles inside newspapers and magazines, the songs on a CD, the chapters in a book and the episodes of a television show. It is small works that get quotation marks around them. (Large works, meanwhile, are either underlined or italicized.)

Using quotation marks correctly in a title looks something like this: The two-page article entitled "San Francisco Giants Win World Series" appeared in yesterday's New York Times. The article title is in quotes, and the newspaper title is in italics.

Common English Usage Mistakes - A Quick Review

Like some parts of English grammar, usage is definitely going to be on the exam and there isn't any tricky strategies or shortcuts to help you get through this section.

Here is a quick review of common usage mistakes.

1. May and Might

'May' can act as a principal verb, which can express permission or possibility.

Examples:

Lets wait, the meeting may have started.
May I begin now?

'May' can act as an auxiliary verb, which an expresses a purpose or wish

Examples:

May you find favour in the sight of your employer.

May your wishes come true.
People go to school so that they may be educated.

The past tense of may is might.

Examples:

I asked if I might begin

'Might' can be used to signify a weak or slim possibility or polite suggestion.

Examples:

You might find him in his office, but I doubt it.
You might offer to help if you want to.

2. Lie and Lay

The verb lay should always take an object. The three forms of the verb lay are: laid, lay and laid.

The verb lie (recline) should not take any object. The three forms of the verb lie are: lay, lie and lain.

Examples:

Lay on the bed.
The tables were laid by the students.
Let the little kid lie.
The patient lay on the table.

The dog has lain there for 30 minutes.

Note: The verb lie can also mean "to tell a falsehood." This verb can appear in three forms: lied, lie, and lied. This is different from the verb lie (recline) mentioned above.

Examples:

The accused is fond of telling lies.
Did she lie?

3. Would and should

The past tense of shall is 'should', and so "should" generally follows the same principles as "shall."

The past tense of will is "would," and so "would" generally follows the same principles as "will."

The two verbs 'would and should' can be correctly used interchangeably to signify obligation. The two verbs also have some unique uses too. Should is used in three persons to signify obligation.

Examples:

I should go after work.
People should exercise everyday.
You should be generous.

"Would" is specially used in any of the three persons, to signify willingness, determination and habitual action.

Examples:

They would go for a test run every Saturday.
They would not ignore their duties.
She would try to be punctual.

4. Principle and Auxiliary Verbs

Two principal verbs can be used along with one auxiliary verb as long as the auxiliary verb form suits the two principal verbs.

Examples:

Several people have been employed and some promoted.

A new tree has been planted and the old has been cut down.
Again note the difference in the verb form.

5. Can and Could

A. Can is used to express capacity or ability.

Examples:

I can complete the assignment today
He can meet his target.

B. Can is also used to express permission.

Examples:

Yes, you can begin

In the sentence below, "can" was used to mean the same thing as "may." However, the difference is that the word "can" is used for negative or interrogative sentences, while "may" is used in affirmative sentences to express possibility.

Examples:

They may be correct.   Positive sentence - use may.
Can this statement be correct? A question using "can."
It cannot be correct. Negative sentence using "can."

The past tense of can is could. It can serve as a principal verb when it is used to express its own meaning.

Examples:

Despite the difficulty of the test, he could still perform well.
"Could" here is used to express ability.

6. Ought

The verb ought should normally be followed by the word to.

Examples:

I *ought to* close shop now.

The verb 'ought' expresses:
A. Desirability

You ought to wash your hands before eating.   It is desirable to wash your hands.

B. Probability

She ought to be on her way back by now.   She is probably on her way.

C. Moral obligation or duty

The government ought to protect the oppressed.   It is the government's duty to protect the oppressed.

7. Raise and Rise

Rise

The verb rise means to go up, or to ascend.

The verb rise can appear in three forms, rose, rise, and risen. The verb should not take an object.

Examples:

The bird rose very slowly.
The trees rise above the house.
My aunt has risen in her career.

Raise

The verb raise means to increase, to lift up.
The verb raise can appear in three forms, raised, raise and raised.

Examples:

He raised his hand.
The workers requested a raise.
Do not raise that subject.

8. Past Tense and Past Participle

Pay attention to the proper use of these verbs: sing, show, ring, awake, fly, flow, begin, hang and sink.
Mistakes usually occur when using the past participle and past tense of these verbs as they are often mixed up.

Each of these verbs can appear in three forms:

Sing, Sang, Sung.
Show, Showed, Showed/Shown.
Ring, Rang, Rung.
Awake, awoke, awaken
Fly, Flew, Flown.

Flow, Flowed, Flowed.
Begin, Began, Begun.
Hang, Hanged, Hanged (a criminal)
Hang, Hung, Hung (a picture)
Sink, Sank, Sunk.

Examples:

The stranger rang the door bell. (simple past tense)
I have rung the door bell already. (past participle - an action completed in the past)

The stone sank in the river. (simple past tense)
The stone had already sunk. (past participle - an action completed in the past)

The meeting began at 4:00.
The meeting has begun.

9. Shall and Will

When speaking informally, the two can be used interchangeably. In formal writing, they must be used correctly.

"Will" is used in the second or third person, while "shall" is used in the first person. Both verbs are used to express a time or even in the future.

Examples:

I shall, We shall (First Person)
You will (Second Person)
They will (Third Person)

This principle however reverses when the verbs are to be used to express threats, determination, command, willingness, promise or compulsion. In these instances, will is now used in first person and shall in the second and third person.

Examples:

I will be there next week, no matter what.
This is a promise, so the first person "I" takes "will."

You shall ensure that the work is completed.
This is a command, so the second person "you" takes "shall."

I will try to make payments as promised.
This is a promise, so the first person "I" takes "will."

They shall have arrived by the end of the day.
This is a determination, so the third person "they" takes shall.

Note

A. The two verbs, shall and will should not occur twice in the same sentence when the same future is being referred to

Example:

I shall arrive early if my driver is here on time.

B. Will should not be used in the first person when questions are being asked

Examples:

Shall I go?
Shall we go?

Subject Verb Agreement

Verbs in any sentence must agree with the subject of the sentence in person and number. Problems usually occur when the verb doesn't correspond with the right subject or the verb fails to match the noun close to it.

Unfortunately, there is no easy way around these principals - no tricky strategy or easy rule. You just have to memorize them.

Here is a quick review:

The verb to be, present (past)

Person	**Singular**	**Plural**
First	I am (was)	we are (were)
Second	you are (were)	you are (were)
Third	he, she, it is (was)	they are (were)

The verb to have, present (past)

Person	Singular	Plural
First	I have (had)	we have (had)
Second	you have (had)	you have (had)
Third	he, she, it has (had)	they have (had)

Regular verbs, e.g. to walk, present (past)

Person	Singular	Plural
First	I walk (walked)	we walk (walked)
Second	you walk (walked)	you walk (walked)
Third	he, she, it walks (walked)	they work (walked)

1. Every and Each

When nouns are qualified by "every" or "each," they take a singular verb even if they are joined by 'and'

Examples:

Each mother and daughter was a given separate test.
Every teacher and student was properly welcomed.

2. Plural Nouns

Nouns like measles, tongs, trousers, riches, scissors etc. are all plural.

Examples:

The trousers are dirty.
My scissors have gone missing.
The tongs are on the table.

3. With and As Well

Two subjects linked by "with" or "as well" should have a verb that matches the first subject.

Examples:

The pencil, with the papers and equipment, is on the desk.
David as well as Louis is coming.

4. Plural Nouns

The following nouns take a singular verb:

> politics, mathematics, innings, news, advice, summons, furniture, information, poetry, machinery, vacation, scenery

Examples:

The machinery is difficult to assemble
The furniture has been delivered
The scenery was beautiful

5. Single Entities

A proper noun in plural form that refers to a single entity requires a singular verb. This is a complicated way of saying; some things appear to be plural, but are really singular, or some nouns refer to a collection of things but the collection is really singular.

Examples:

The United Nations Organization is the decision maker in the matter.

Here the "United Nations Organization" is really only one "thing" or noun, but is made up of many "nations."

The book, "The Seven Virgins" was not available in the library.
Here there is only one book, although the title of the book is plural.

6. Specific Amounts are always singular

A plural noun that refers to a specific amount or quantity that is considered as a whole (dozen, hundred, score etc) requires a singular verb.

Examples:

60 minutes is quite a long time.
Here "60 minutes" is considered a whole, and therefore one item (singular noun).

The first million is the most difficult.

7. Either, Neither and Each are always singular

The verb is always singular when used with: either, each, neither, every one and many.

Examples:

Either of the boys is lying.
Each of the employees has been well compensated
Many a police officer has been found to be courageous
Every one of the teachers is responsible

8. Linking with Either, Or, and Neither match the second subject

Two subjects linked by "either," "or,""nor" or "neither" should have a verb that matches the second subject.

Examples:

Neither David nor Paul will be coming.
Either Mary or Tina is paying.

Note
If one of the subjects linked by "either," "or,""nor" or "neither" is in plural form, then the verb should also be in plural, and the verb should be close to the plural subject.

Examples:
Neither the mother nor her kids have eaten.
Either Mary or her friends are paying.

9. Collective Nouns are Plural

Some collective nouns such as poultry, gentry, cattle, vermin etc. are considered plural and require a plural verb.

Examples:

The poultry are sick.
The cattle are well fed.

Note
Collective nouns involving people can work with both plural and singular verbs.

Examples:

Nigerians are known to be hard working
Europeans live in Africa

10. Nouns that are Singular and Plural

Nouns like deer, sheep, swine, salmon etc. can be singular or plural and require the same verb form.

Examples:

The swine is feeding. (singular)
The swine are feeding. (plural)

The salmon is on the table. (singular)
The salmon are running upstream. (plural)

11. Collective Nouns are Singular

Collective nouns such as Army, Jury, Assembly, Committee, Team etc should carry a singular verb when they subscribe to one idea. If the ideas or views are more than one, then the verb used should be plural.

Examples:

The committee is in agreement in their decision.

The committee were in disagreement in their decision.
The jury has agreed on a verdict.
The jury were unable to agree on a verdict.

12. Subjects links by "and" are plural.

Two subjects linked by "and" always require a plural verb

Examples:

David and John are students.

Note

If the subjects linked by "and" are used as one phrase, or constitute one idea, then the verb must be singular

The color of his socks and shoe is black.
Here "socks and shoe" are two nouns, however the subject is "color" which is singular.

Practice Test Questions Set 1

THE QUESTIONS BELOW ARE NOT THE SAME AS YOU WILL FIND ON THE HSPT® - THAT WOULD BE TOO EASY! And nobody knows what the questions will be and they change all the time. Below are general questions that cover the same subject areas as the HSPT®. So, while the format and exact wording of the questions may differ slightly, and change from year to year, if you can answer the questions below, you will have no problem with the HSPT®.

For the best results, take these practice test questions as if it were the real exam. Set aside time when you will not be disturbed, and a location that is quiet and free of distractions. Read the instructions carefully, read each question carefully, and answer to the best of your ability.

Use the bubble answer sheets provided. When you have completed the practice questions, check your answer against the Answer Key and read the explanation provided.

Do not attempt more than one set of practice test questions in one day. After completing the first practice test, wait two or three days before attempting the second set of questions.

Section I – Verbal Skills

Questions: 50
Time: 16 Minutes

Section II – Quantitative Skills

Questions: 50
Time: 30 Minutes

Section III – Reading & Vocabulary

Questions: 60
Time: 25 Minutes

Section IV – Mathematics

Questions: 60
Time: 45 Minutes

Section V – English and Language Arts

Questions: 60
Time: 25 Minutes

Verbal Skills

1. (A) (B) (C) (D)
2. (A) (B) (C) (D)
3. (A) (B) (C) (D)
4. (A) (B) (C) (D)
5. (A) (B) (C) (D)
6. (A) (B) (C) (D)
7. (A) (B) (C) (D)
8. (A) (B) (C) (D)
9. (A) (B) (C) (D)
10. (A) (B) (C) (D)
11. (A) (B) (C) (D)
12. (A) (B) (C) (D)
13. (A) (B) (C) (D)
14. (A) (B) (C) (D)
15. (A) (B) (C) (D)
16. (A) (B) (C) (D)
17. (A) (B) (C) (D)

18. (A) (B) (C) (D)
19. (A) (B) (C) (D)
20. (A) (B) (C) (D)
21. (A) (B) (C) (D)
22. (A) (B) (C) (D)
23. (A) (B) (C) (D)
24. (A) (B) (C) (D)
25. (A) (B) (C) (D)
26. (A) (B) (C) (D)
27. (A) (B) (C) (D)
28. (A) (B) (C) (D)
29. (A) (B) (C) (D)
30. (A) (B) (C) (D)
31. (A) (B) (C) (D)
32. (A) (B) (C) (D)
33. (A) (B) (C) (D)
34. (A) (B) (C) (D)

35. (A) (B) (C) (D)
36. (A) (B) (C) (D)
37. (A) (B) (C) (D)
38. (A) (B) (C) (D)
39. (A) (B) (C) (D)
40. (A) (B) (C) (D)
41. (A) (B) (C) (D)
42. (A) (B) (C) (D)
43. (A) (B) (C) (D)
44. (A) (B) (C) (D)
45. (A) (B) (C) (D)
46. (A) (B) (C) (D)
47. (A) (B) (C) (D)
48. (A) (B) (C) (D)
49. (A) (B) (C) (D)
50. (A) (B) (C) (D)

Quantitative Skills

1. (A) (B) (C) (D)   18. (A) (B) (C) (D)   35. (A) (B) (C) (D)

2. (A) (B) (C) (D)   19. (A) (B) (C) (D)   36. (A) (B) (C) (D)

3. (A) (B) (C) (D)   20. (A) (B) (C) (D)   37. (A) (B) (C) (D)

4. (A) (B) (C) (D)   21. (A) (B) (C) (D)   38. (A) (B) (C) (D)

5. (A) (B) (C) (D)   22. (A) (B) (C) (D)   39. (A) (B) (C) (D)

6. (A) (B) (C) (D)   23. (A) (B) (C) (D)   40. (A) (B) (C) (D)

7. (A) (B) (C) (D)   24. (A) (B) (C) (D)   41. (A) (B) (C) (D)

8. (A) (B) (C) (D)   25. (A) (B) (C) (D)   42. (A) (B) (C) (D)

9. (A) (B) (C) (D)   26. (A) (B) (C) (D)   43. (A) (B) (C) (D)

10. (A) (B) (C) (D)   27. (A) (B) (C) (D)   44. (A) (B) (C) (D)

11. (A) (B) (C) (D)   28. (A) (B) (C) (D)   45. (A) (B) (C) (D)

12. (A) (B) (C) (D)   29. (A) (B) (C) (D)   46. (A) (B) (C) (D)

13. (A) (B) (C) (D)   30. (A) (B) (C) (D)   47. (A) (B) (C) (D)

14. (A) (B) (C) (D)   31. (A) (B) (C) (D)   48. (A) (B) (C) (D)

15. (A) (B) (C) (D)   32. (A) (B) (C) (D)   49. (A) (B) (C) (D)

16. (A) (B) (C) (D)   33. (A) (B) (C) (D)   50. (A) (B) (C) (D)

17. (A) (B) (C) (D)   34. (A) (B) (C) (D)

Reading Comprehension and Vocabulary

1. Ⓐ Ⓑ Ⓒ Ⓓ   21. Ⓐ Ⓑ Ⓒ Ⓓ   41. Ⓐ Ⓑ Ⓒ Ⓓ

2. Ⓐ Ⓑ Ⓒ Ⓓ   22. Ⓐ Ⓑ Ⓒ Ⓓ   42. Ⓐ Ⓑ Ⓒ Ⓓ

3. Ⓐ Ⓑ Ⓒ Ⓓ   23. Ⓐ Ⓑ Ⓒ Ⓓ   43. Ⓐ Ⓑ Ⓒ Ⓓ

4. Ⓐ Ⓑ Ⓒ Ⓓ   24. Ⓐ Ⓑ Ⓒ Ⓓ   44. Ⓐ Ⓑ Ⓒ Ⓓ

5. Ⓐ Ⓑ Ⓒ Ⓓ   25. Ⓐ Ⓑ Ⓒ Ⓓ   45. Ⓐ Ⓑ Ⓒ Ⓓ

6. Ⓐ Ⓑ Ⓒ Ⓓ   26. Ⓐ Ⓑ Ⓒ Ⓓ   46. Ⓐ Ⓑ Ⓒ Ⓓ

7. Ⓐ Ⓑ Ⓒ Ⓓ   27. Ⓐ Ⓑ Ⓒ Ⓓ   47. Ⓐ Ⓑ Ⓒ Ⓓ

8. Ⓐ Ⓑ Ⓒ Ⓓ   28. Ⓐ Ⓑ Ⓒ Ⓓ   48. Ⓐ Ⓑ Ⓒ Ⓓ

9. Ⓐ Ⓑ Ⓒ Ⓓ   29. Ⓐ Ⓑ Ⓒ Ⓓ   49. Ⓐ Ⓑ Ⓒ Ⓓ

10. Ⓐ Ⓑ Ⓒ Ⓓ   30. Ⓐ Ⓑ Ⓒ Ⓓ   50. Ⓐ Ⓑ Ⓒ Ⓓ

11. Ⓐ Ⓑ Ⓒ Ⓓ   31. Ⓐ Ⓑ Ⓒ Ⓓ   51. Ⓐ Ⓑ Ⓒ Ⓓ

12. Ⓐ Ⓑ Ⓒ Ⓓ   32. Ⓐ Ⓑ Ⓒ Ⓓ   52. Ⓐ Ⓑ Ⓒ Ⓓ

13. Ⓐ Ⓑ Ⓒ Ⓓ   33. Ⓐ Ⓑ Ⓒ Ⓓ   53. Ⓐ Ⓑ Ⓒ Ⓓ

14. Ⓐ Ⓑ Ⓒ Ⓓ   34. Ⓐ Ⓑ Ⓒ Ⓓ   54. Ⓐ Ⓑ Ⓒ Ⓓ

15. Ⓐ Ⓑ Ⓒ Ⓓ   35. Ⓐ Ⓑ Ⓒ Ⓓ   55. Ⓐ Ⓑ Ⓒ Ⓓ

16. Ⓐ Ⓑ Ⓒ Ⓓ   36. Ⓐ Ⓑ Ⓒ Ⓓ   56. Ⓐ Ⓑ Ⓒ Ⓓ

17. Ⓐ Ⓑ Ⓒ Ⓓ   37. Ⓐ Ⓑ Ⓒ Ⓓ   57. Ⓐ Ⓑ Ⓒ Ⓓ

18. Ⓐ Ⓑ Ⓒ Ⓓ   38. Ⓐ Ⓑ Ⓒ Ⓓ   58. Ⓐ Ⓑ Ⓒ Ⓓ

19. Ⓐ Ⓑ Ⓒ Ⓓ   39. Ⓐ Ⓑ Ⓒ Ⓓ   59. Ⓐ Ⓑ Ⓒ Ⓓ

20. Ⓐ Ⓑ Ⓒ Ⓓ   40. Ⓐ Ⓑ Ⓒ Ⓓ   60. Ⓐ Ⓑ Ⓒ Ⓓ

Mathematics

1. (A) (B) (C) (D)	21. (A) (B) (C) (D)	41. (A) (B) (C) (D)
2. (A) (B) (C) (D)	22. (A) (B) (C) (D)	42. (A) (B) (C) (D)
3. (A) (B) (C) (D)	23. (A) (B) (C) (D)	43. (A) (B) (C) (D)
4. (A) (B) (C) (D)	24. (A) (B) (C) (D)	44. (A) (B) (C) (D)
5. (A) (B) (C) (D)	25. (A) (B) (C) (D)	45. (A) (B) (C) (D)
6. (A) (B) (C) (D)	26. (A) (B) (C) (D)	46. (A) (B) (C) (D)
7. (A) (B) (C) (D)	27. (A) (B) (C) (D)	47. (A) (B) (C) (D)
8. (A) (B) (C) (D)	28. (A) (B) (C) (D)	48. (A) (B) (C) (D)
9. (A) (B) (C) (D)	29. (A) (B) (C) (D)	49. (A) (B) (C) (D)
10. (A) (B) (C) (D)	30. (A) (B) (C) (D)	50. (A) (B) (C) (D)
11. (A) (B) (C) (D)	31. (A) (B) (C) (D)	51. (A) (B) (C) (D)
12. (A) (B) (C) (D)	32. (A) (B) (C) (D)	52. (A) (B) (C) (D)
13. (A) (B) (C) (D)	33. (A) (B) (C) (D)	53. (A) (B) (C) (D)
14. (A) (B) (C) (D)	34. (A) (B) (C) (D)	54. (A) (B) (C) (D)
15. (A) (B) (C) (D)	35. (A) (B) (C) (D)	55. (A) (B) (C) (D)
16. (A) (B) (C) (D)	36. (A) (B) (C) (D)	56. (A) (B) (C) (D)
17. (A) (B) (C) (D)	37. (A) (B) (C) (D)	57. (A) (B) (C) (D)
18. (A) (B) (C) (D)	38. (A) (B) (C) (D)	58. (A) (B) (C) (D)
19. (A) (B) (C) (D)	39. (A) (B) (C) (D)	59. (A) (B) (C) (D)
20. (A) (B) (C) (D)	40. (A) (B) (C) (D)	60. (A) (B) (C) (D)

Language Arts

1. Ⓐ Ⓑ Ⓒ Ⓓ	21. Ⓐ Ⓑ Ⓒ Ⓓ	41. Ⓐ Ⓑ Ⓒ Ⓓ
2. Ⓐ Ⓑ Ⓒ Ⓓ	22. Ⓐ Ⓑ Ⓒ Ⓓ	42. Ⓐ Ⓑ Ⓒ Ⓓ
3. Ⓐ Ⓑ Ⓒ Ⓓ	23. Ⓐ Ⓑ Ⓒ Ⓓ	43. Ⓐ Ⓑ Ⓒ Ⓓ
4. Ⓐ Ⓑ Ⓒ Ⓓ	24. Ⓐ Ⓑ Ⓒ Ⓓ	44. Ⓐ Ⓑ Ⓒ Ⓓ
5. Ⓐ Ⓑ Ⓒ Ⓓ	25. Ⓐ Ⓑ Ⓒ Ⓓ	45. Ⓐ Ⓑ Ⓒ Ⓓ
6. Ⓐ Ⓑ Ⓒ Ⓓ	26. Ⓐ Ⓑ Ⓒ Ⓓ	46. Ⓐ Ⓑ Ⓒ Ⓓ
7. Ⓐ Ⓑ Ⓒ Ⓓ	27. Ⓐ Ⓑ Ⓒ Ⓓ	47. Ⓐ Ⓑ Ⓒ Ⓓ
8. Ⓐ Ⓑ Ⓒ Ⓓ	28. Ⓐ Ⓑ Ⓒ Ⓓ	48. Ⓐ Ⓑ Ⓒ Ⓓ
9. Ⓐ Ⓑ Ⓒ Ⓓ	29. Ⓐ Ⓑ Ⓒ Ⓓ	49. Ⓐ Ⓑ Ⓒ Ⓓ
10. Ⓐ Ⓑ Ⓒ Ⓓ	30. Ⓐ Ⓑ Ⓒ Ⓓ	50. Ⓐ Ⓑ Ⓒ Ⓓ
11. Ⓐ Ⓑ Ⓒ Ⓓ	31. Ⓐ Ⓑ Ⓒ Ⓓ	51. Ⓐ Ⓑ Ⓒ Ⓓ
12. Ⓐ Ⓑ Ⓒ Ⓓ	32. Ⓐ Ⓑ Ⓒ Ⓓ	52. Ⓐ Ⓑ Ⓒ Ⓓ
13. Ⓐ Ⓑ Ⓒ Ⓓ	33. Ⓐ Ⓑ Ⓒ Ⓓ	53. Ⓐ Ⓑ Ⓒ Ⓓ
14. Ⓐ Ⓑ Ⓒ Ⓓ	34. Ⓐ Ⓑ Ⓒ Ⓓ	54. Ⓐ Ⓑ Ⓒ Ⓓ
15. Ⓐ Ⓑ Ⓒ Ⓓ	35. Ⓐ Ⓑ Ⓒ Ⓓ	55. Ⓐ Ⓑ Ⓒ Ⓓ
16. Ⓐ Ⓑ Ⓒ Ⓓ	36. Ⓐ Ⓑ Ⓒ Ⓓ	56. Ⓐ Ⓑ Ⓒ Ⓓ
17. Ⓐ Ⓑ Ⓒ Ⓓ	37. Ⓐ Ⓑ Ⓒ Ⓓ	57. Ⓐ Ⓑ Ⓒ Ⓓ
18. Ⓐ Ⓑ Ⓒ Ⓓ	38. Ⓐ Ⓑ Ⓒ Ⓓ	58. Ⓐ Ⓑ Ⓒ Ⓓ
19. Ⓐ Ⓑ Ⓒ Ⓓ	39. Ⓐ Ⓑ Ⓒ Ⓓ	59. Ⓐ Ⓑ Ⓒ Ⓓ
20. Ⓐ Ⓑ Ⓒ Ⓓ	40. Ⓐ Ⓑ Ⓒ Ⓓ	60. Ⓐ Ⓑ Ⓒ Ⓓ

Section I – Verbal Skills

Choose the option with the same relationship.

1. Lawyer : Trial

a. Plumber : Pipe
b. Businessman : Secretary
c. Doctor : Operation
d. Hairdresser : Blow Dryer

2. Fat : Eat

a. Swim : Water
b. Live : Breathe
c. Walk : Run
d. Sing : Song

3. Dog : Canine

a. Elephant : Large
b. Tree : Flower
c. Cat : Mouse
d. Porpoise : Mammal

4. Turntable : MP3 player

a. Horse Drawn Carriage : Vehicle
b. Radio : Telephone
c. Calculator : Computer
d. Documentary : Movie

5. Cub : Bear

a. Piano : Orchestra
b. Puppy : Dog
c. Cat : Kitten
d. Eagle : Predator

6. Medicine : Illness

a. Law : Anarchy
b. Hunger : Thirst
c. Etiquette : Discipline
d. Stimulant : Sensitivity

7. Gold : Metal

a. Carnivorous : Veterinarian
b. Surgeon : Doctor
c. Secretary : Lawyer
d. Potato : Farmer

8. Melt : Liquid :: Freeze : _____

a. Ice
b. Condense
c. Solid
d. Steam

9. Clock : Time :: Thermometer : _____

a. Heat
b. Radiation
c. Energy
d. Temperature

10. Car : Garage :: Plane : _____

a. Depot
b. Port
c. Hanger
d. Harbor

11. Select the synonym of peculiar.

   a. New
   b. Strange
   c. Imaginative
   d. Funny

12. Select the synonym of tippet.

   a. Necktie
   b. Shawl
   c. Sweater
   d. Blouse

13. Select the synonym of vivid.

   a. Glamorous
   b. Bountiful
   c. Varied
   d. Brilliant

14. Select the synonym of semblance.

   a. Personality
   b. Image
   c. Attitude
   d. ambition

15. Select the synonym of impregnable.

   a. Unconquerable
   b. Impossible
   c. Unlimited
   d. Imperfect

16. Choose the synonym pair.

   a. Jargon and Slang
   b. Slander and Plagiarism
   c. Devotion and Devout
   d. Current and Outdated

17. Choose the synonym pair.

   a. Render and Give
   b. Recognition and Cognizant
   c. Stem and Root
   d. Adjust and Redo

18. Choose the synonym pair.

   a. Private and Public
   b. Intrusive and Invasive
   c. Mysterious and Unknown
   d. Common and Unique

19. Choose the synonym pair.

   a. Renowned and Popular
   b. Guard and Safe
   c. Aggressive and Shy
   d. Curtail and Avoid

20. Choose the synonym pair.

   a. Brevity and Ambiguous
   b. Fury and Light-hearted
   c. Incoherent and Jumbled
   d. benign and malignant

21. Choose the synonym pair.

   a. Congenial and Pleasant
   b. Distort and Similar
   c. Valuable and Rich
   d. Asset and Liability

22. Choose the synonym pair.

a. Circumstance and Plan
b. Negotiate and Scheme
c. Ardent and Whimsical
d. Plight and Situation

23. Choose the synonym pair.

a. Berate and Criticize
b. Unspoken and Unknown
c. Tenet and Favor
d. Turf and Seashore

24. Choose the synonym pair.

a. Adequate and Inadequate
b. Sate and Satisfy
c. Sufficient and Lacking
d. Spectator and Teacher

25. Choose the synonym pair.

a. Pensive and Alibi
b. Terminate and End
c. Plot and Point
d. Jaded and Honest

26. Which does not belong?

a. abcabc
b. defdef
c. ghihij
d. mnomno

27. Which does not belong?

a. Anguish
b. Distress
c. Despair
d. Pain

28. Which does not belong?

a. DDDdddEEE
b. MMMnnnOOO
c. GGGhhhIII
d. JJJkkkLLL

29. Which does not belong?

a. cde
b. mno
c. stu
d. abc

30. Which does not belong?

a. 446688
b. 224466
c. 336699
d. 446688

31. Which does not belong?

a. Slant
b. Lean
c. Tilt
d. Incline

32. Which does not belong?

a. MnOp
b. AbCD
c. QrSt
d. WxYz

33. Which does not belong?

a. Look
b. See
c. Perceive
d. Surmise

34. Which does not belong?

a. Count
b. Number
c. Add up
d. List

35. Which does not belong?

a. Secure
b. Discard
c. Throw out
d. Abandon

36. Which does not belong?

a. Nop
b. Tuv
c. efg
d. Def

37. Which does not belong?

a. Dog
b. Wolf
c. Terrier
d. Cougar

38. Which does not belong?

a. Awkward
b. Graceless
c. Overweight
d. Inept

39. Which does not belong?

a. Smart
b. Great
c. Noteworthy
d. Supreme

40. Which does not belong?

a. Ask
b. Question
c. Query
d. Command

41. Which does not belong?

a. Assume
b. Certain
c. Sure
d. Positive

42. Choose the antonym pair.

a. Dissatisfied and Unsatisfied
b. Disentangle and Acknowledge
c. Discord and Harmony
d. Fruition and Fusion

43. Choose the antonym pair.

a. Late and Later
b. Latter and Former
c. Structure and Organization
d. Latter and Rushed

44. Choose the antonym pair.

a. Belittle and Bemuse
b. Shrunk and Minimal
c. Shrink and Expand
d. Smelly and Odor

45. Choose the antonym pair.

a. Repulsive and Repentant
b. Reluctant and Enthusiastic
c. Prepare and Ready
d. Release and Give

46. Choose the antonym pair.

   a. Sovereign and Autonomy
   b. Disdain and Contempt
   c. Disorder and Disarray
   d. Refute and Agree

47. Choose the antonym pair.

   a. Gentle and Soft
   b. Fragile and Breakable
   c. Vulnerable and Strong
   d. Vain and Tidy

48. Choose the antonym pair.

   a. Daring and Bold
   b. Colossal and Foreign
   c. Awesome and Amazing
   d. Intrepid and Timid

49. Choose the antonym pair.

   a. Liaise and Uncoordinated
   b. Coalesce and Coordinate
   c. Collaborate and Combine
   d. Encourage and Urge

50. Choose the antonym pair.

   a. Ridiculous and Funny
   b. Laughter and Bliss
   c. Famous and Popular
   d. Ridicule and Praise

51. Choose the antonym pair.

   a. Perception and Belief
   b. Fixed and Indefinite
   c. Signal and Symbol
   d. Appearance and Look

52. Select the antonym of flamboyant.

   a. Plain
   b. Colored
   c. Dark
   d. Light

53. Select the antonym of sporadic.

   a. Frequent
   b. Irregular
   c. Regular
   d. Movement

54. Whenever I swim in the ocean I get cold. I went swimming today. I will be getting cold very soon. If the first 2 statements are true, then the third statement is:

True False Uncertain

55. Fish can't breathe out of the water. Fish use their gills to breathe. Gills don't work out of water. If the first 2 statements are true, then the third statement is:

True False Uncertain

56. I eat steak when I am hungry. I ate steak last night. I was hungry last night. If the first 2 statements are true, then the third statement is:

True False Uncertain

57. I read a lot. My favorite author is Herman Melville. I have read all of Herman Melville's books. If the first 2 statements are true, then the third statement is:

True   False   Uncertain

58. All books are very informative. I am reading a book. I will learn something from this book. If the first 2 statements are true, then the third statement is:

True   False   Uncertain

59. Some cats have no tails. All cats are mammals. Some mammals have no tails. If the first 2 statements are true, then the third statement is:

True   False   Uncertain

60. All students carry backpacks. My grandfather carries a backpack. Therefore, my grandfather is a student. If the first 2 statements are true, then the third statement is:

True   False   Uncertain

Section II – Quantitative Skills

1. Consider the following series: 6, 11, 18, 27 ... What number should come next?

    a. 38
    b. 35
    c. 29
    d. 30

2. Consider Box A and the relationship to the numbers in Box B. What is the missing number in Box B?

Box A

6	3
9	5

Box B

36	?
81	25

    a. 49
    b. 51
    c. 9
    d. 12

3. Consider Box A and the relationship to the numbers in Box B. What is the missing number in Box B?

Box A

8	12
5	9

Box B

19	27
13	?

    a. 18
    b. 21
    c. 24
    d. 14

4. Consider the following series: 13, 26, 52, 104. What number should come next?

    a. 208

    b. 106

    c. 200

    d. 400

5. Consider the following series: 32, 26, 20, 14. What number should come next?

    a. 12

    b. 19

    c. 10

    d. 8

6. Consider the following series: 12, 4, 16, ..., 36. What is the missing number?

    a. 18

    b. 22

    c. 20

    d. 30

7. Consider the following series: 3, 9, 27, ..., 243. What is the missing number?

    a. 30

    b. 39

    c. 18

    d. 81

8. Consider the series in row A compared to row B. What is the missing number?

A	5	20	100	3	24
B	20	80	400	12	?

    a. 96

    b. 48

    c. 64

    d. 66

9. Consider the following series: 29, 39, 46, 56, ..., 25. What is the missing number?

    a. 40

    b. 20

    c. 15

    d. 39

10. Consider the following series: L, N, P, R. What letter should come next?

    a. S

    b. T

    c. U

    d. V

11. Consider the following series: M, P, S, ..., Y. What is the missing letter?

    a. V

    b. T

    c. U

    d. X

12. Consider the following series: 14, 21, 28, 35. What number should come next?

    a. 63

    b. 24

    c. 49

    d. 42

13. Consider the following series: 8, 11, 9, 12, 10, 13. What number should come next?

    a. 11

    b. 10

    c. 15

    d. 16

14. Consider the following series: 2, 1, 1/2, 1/4. What number should come next?

    a. 1/3

    b. 1/8

    c. 1/16

    d. 2/8

15. Consider the following series: 17, 23, 29, 35. What 3 numbers should come next?

    a. 41, 47, 54

    b. 42, 47, 53

    c. 40, 45, 50

    d. 41, 47, 53

16. Consider the following series: 11, 15, 20, 26. What 3 numbers should come next?

    a. 31, 37, 42

    b. 33, 41, 50,

    c. 32, 38, 46

    d. 36, 46, 56

17. Consider the following series: 17, 14, 8, -4. What 2 numbers should come next?

    a. -12, -36

    b. -28, -76

    c. -12, -24

    d. -28, -48

18. Consider the following series: -7, -3, 1, 5. What 2 numbers should come next?

    a. 9, 13

    b. 8, 11

    c. -9, 14

    d. 8, 12

19. Examine (A), (B) and (C) and find the best answer.

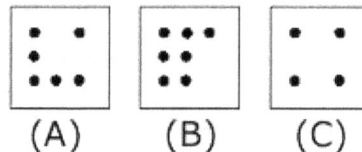

(A)   (B)   (C)

    a. (A) has more dots than (B)

    b. (A) has more than (C)

    c. (A) has more than (B) and (C)

    d. (A) (B) and (C) have an equal number of dots.

20. Examine (A), (B) and (C) and find the best answer.

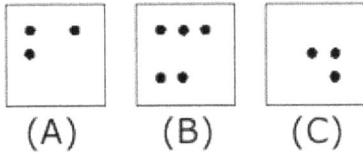

(A)   (B)   (C)

    a. (A) has more dots than (B)

    b. (B) has more than (A)

    c. (A) has more than (B) and (C)

    d. (A) (B) and (C) have an equal number of dots.

21. Examine (A) (B) and (C) and find the best answer.

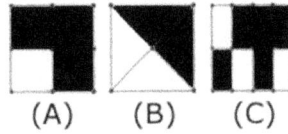

(A)   (B)   (C)

    a. The shaded area in (A) is equal to (B)

    b. The shaded area in (B) is greater than (A)

    c. The shaded area in (A) is less than (C)

    d. The shaded area in (B) is greater than (C)

22. Examine (A) (B) and (C) and find the best answer.

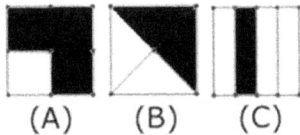

(A)   (B)   (C)

    a. The shaded area in (A) is equal to (C)

    b. The shaded area in (C) is greater than (B)

    c. The shaded area in (A) is greater than (C)

    d. The shaded area in (B) is equal to (C)

23. Examine (A) (B) and (C) and find the best answer.

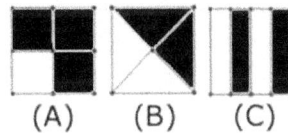

(A)   (B)   (C)

    a. The shaded area in (A) is equal to (C)

    b. The shaded area in (C) is greater than (B)

    c. The shaded area in (A) is greater than (C)

    d. The shaded area in (B) is greater than (C)

24. Examine (A) (B) and find the best answer.

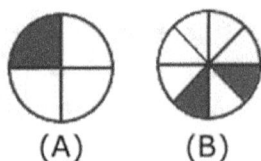

(A)   (B)

a. The shaded area in (A) is equal to (B)

b. The shaded area in (A) is greater than (B)

c. The shaded area in (B) is less than (A)

25. Examine (A) (B) and (C) and find the best answer.

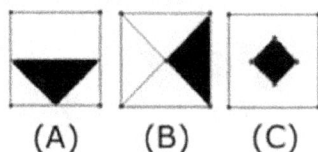

(A)   (B)   (C)

a. The shaded area in (A) is equal to (C)

b. The shaded area in (C) is greater than (B)

c. The shaded area in (A) is greater than (C)

d. The shaded area in (B) is equal to (C)

26. Examine (A) (B) and (C) and find the best answer.

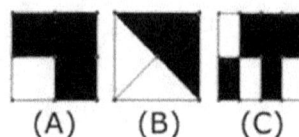

(A)   (B)   (C)

a. The shaded area in (A) is equal to (C)

b. The shaded area in (B) is greater than (C)

c. The shaded area in (A) is greater than (C)

d. The shaded area in (B) is equal to (C)

27. Examine (A) (B) and (C) and find the best answer.

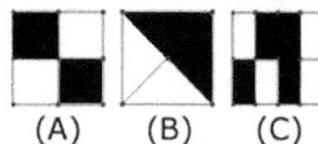

(A)   (B)   (C)

a. The shaded area in (A) is equal to (C)

b. The shaded area in (C) is greater than (B)

c. The shaded area in (A) is greater than (C)

d. The shaded area in (B) is less than (C)

28. Examine the following and find the best answer.

1. (4 X 7) - 12
2. (2 X 14) + 5
3. (3 X 10) – 8

    a. 1 < 2 < 3

    b. 1 < 2 > 3

    c. 2 > 3 < 1

    d. 3 > 2 < 1

29. Examine the following and find the best answer.

1. (8 X 2) X (2 X 3)
2. (4 X 8) + (2 X 6)
3. (3 X 4) X (9 - 2)
4. (3 X 7) - (2 X 6)

    a. 1 < 3 < 4

    b. 1 > 4 < 3

    c. 2 > 1 > 3

    d. 4 < 1 < 3

30. Examine the following and find the best answer.

1. 12 + (15 - 4)
2. 9 + (24 - 2)
3. 2 + (19 + 7)
4. 15 + (26 - 19)

    a. 1 < 3 < 4

    b. 1 < 4 < 3

    c. 2 > 1 < 3

    d. 4 > 1 < 3

31. Examine the following and find the best answer.

1. (23 - 7) * 2
2. (9 + 12) / 7
3. (13 - 7) X 2
4. (17 + 4) + 1

    a. 2 is the smallest

    b. 4 is the largest

    c. 1 is the smallest

    d. None of the Above

32. Examine the following and find the best answer.

1. 1 + (6 * 7)
2. 7 - 22
3. 9 + (13 X 2)
4. 6 * (5 + 2)

    a. 3 and 4 are greater than 1

    b. 3 and 2 are greater than 1

    c. 3 is less than 2

    d. None of the Above

33. Examine the following and find the best answer.

1. 19 + (4 X 5)
2. 13 - (4 + 6)
3. 7 + (3 X 7)

    a. 1 > 2 < 3

    b. 2 > 3 < 1

    c. 2 < 3 > 1

    d. 1 < 2 < 3

34. Examine the following and find the best answer.

1. 18 + 7
2. 4 X 8
3. 3 X 5
4. 2 X 10

    a. (#2 - #4) > #1
    b. (#4 - #3) > #2
    c. (#2 - #1) < #3
    d. (#1 + #2) > #4

35. Examine the following and find the best answer.

1. (6 X 3) X (3 X 4)
2. (4 X 5) + (3 X 6)
3. (3 X 4) X (5 - 2)

    a. 3 is the largest
    b. 1 is less than 2
    c. 3 is greater than 1
    d. None of the Above

36. What is the smallest value?

    a. 4 % of 4
    b. 5 % of 5
    c. 0.3% of 12
    d. 1/5 of 100

37. What is 8 more than 2/5 of 20?

    a. 10
    b. 12
    c. 16
    d. 8

38. What is 6 more than 50% of 50?

    a. 31
    b. 41
    c. 25
    d. 26

39. What number subtracted from 100 leaves 7 more than 3/4 of 40?

    a. 50
    b. 63
    c. 47
    d. 75

40. What number divided by 5 is 1/4 of 100?

    a. 125
    b. 150
    c. 75
    d. 225

41. 1/5 of what number is 5 times 10?

    a. 150
    b. 200
    c. 250
    d. 100

42. What number multiplied by 5 is 10 less than 52?

    a. 8.4
    b. 10.24
    c. 20
    d. 22.5

43. What number subtracted from 25 is 1/5 of 20?

    a. 125

    b. 150

    c. 50

    d. 21

44. What number is 15 less than 3/5 of 40?

    a. 42

    b. 17

    c. 9

    d. 18

45. What number is 10 times 1/2 of 60?

    a. 100

    b. 300

    c. 250

    d. 75

46. 1/4 of what number is 8 times 10?

    a. 150

    b. 200

    c. 320

    d.100

47. 1/2 of what number is 4 X 15

    a. 120

    b. 40

    c. 50

    d. 60

48. 5 X 60 = 1/3 of what number?

    a. 50

    b. 900

    c. 150

    d. 200

49. 1/4 of what number added to 20 is 4 times 8?

    a. 10

    b. 8

    c. 6

    d. 48

50. What number subtracted from 500 leaves 10 more than 3/4 of 100?

    a. 600

    b. 415

    c. 525

    d. 400

Section III - Reading

Questions 1 – 4 refer to the following passage.

Passage 1 - The Life of Helen Keller

Many people have heard of Helen Keller. She is famous because she was unable to see or hear, but learned to speak and read and went onto attend college and earn a degree. Her life is a very interesting story, one that she developed into an autobiography, which was then adapted into both a stage play and a movie. How did Helen Keller overcome her disabilities to become a famous woman? Read onto find out.

Helen Keller was not born blind and deaf. When she was a small baby, she had a very high fever for several days. As a result of her sudden illness, baby Helen lost her eyesight and her hearing. Because she was so young when she went deaf and blind, Helen Keller never had any recollection of being able to see or hear. Since she could not hear, she could not learn to talk. Since she could not see, it was difficult for her to move around. For the first six years of her life, her world was very still and dark.

Imagine what Helen's childhood was like. She could not hear her mother's voice. She could not see the beauty of her parent's farm. She could not recognize who was giving her a hug, or a bath or even where her bedroom was each night. More sad, she could not communicate with her parents in any way. She could not express her feelings or tell them the things she wanted. It must have been a very sad childhood.

When Helen was six years old, her parents hired her a teacher named Anne Sullivan. Anne was a young woman who was almost blind. However, she could hear and she could read Braille, so she was a perfect teacher for young Helen. At first, Anne had a very hard time teaching Helen anything. She described her first impression of Helen as a "wild thing, not a child." Helen did not like Anne at first either. She bit and hit Anne when Anne tried to teach her. However, the two of them eventually came to have a great deal of love and respect.

Anne taught Helen to hear by putting her hands on people's throats. She could feel the sounds that people made. In time, Helen learned to feel what people said. Next, Anne taught Helen to read Braille, which is a way that books are written for the blind. Finally, Anne taught Helen to talk. Although Helen did learn to talk, it was hard for anyone but Anne to understand her.

As Helen grew older, more and more people were amazed by her story. She went to college and wrote books about her life. She gave talks to the public, with Anne at her side, translating her words. Today, both Anne Sullivan and Helen Keller are famous women who are respected for their lives' work.

1. Helen Keller could not see and hear and so, what was her biggest problem in childhood?

    a. Inability to communicate

    b. Inability to walk

    c. Inability to play

    d. Inability to eat

2. Helen learned to hear by feeling the vibrations people made when they spoke. What were these vibrations were felt through?

    a. Mouth

    b. Throat

    c. Ears

    d. Lips

3. From the passage, we can infer that Anne Sullivan was a patient teacher. We can infer this because

    a. Helen hit and bit her and Anne still remained her teacher.

    b. Anne taught Helen to read only.

    c. Anne was hard of hearing too.

    d. Anne wanted to be a teacher.

4. Helen Keller learned to speak but Anne translated her words when she spoke in public. The reason Helen needed a translator was because

    a. Helen spoke another language.

    b. Helen's words were hard for people to understand.

    c. Helen spoke very quietly.

    d. Helen did not speak but only used sign language.

Questions 5 – 7 refer to the following passage.

Passage 2 - Ways Characters Communicate in Theater

Playwrights give their characters voices in a way that gives depth and added meaning to what happens on stage during their play. There are different types of speech in scripts that allow characters to talk with themselves, with other characters, and even with the audience.

It is very unique to theater that characters may talk "to themselves." When characters do this, the speech they give is called a soliloquy. Soliloquies are usually poetic, introspective, moving, and can tell audience members about the feelings, motivations, or suspicions of an individual character without that character having to reveal them to other characters on stage. "To be or not to be" is a famous soliloquy given by Hamlet as he considers difficult but important themes, such as life and death.

The most common type of communication in plays is when one character is speaking to another or a group of other characters. This is generally called dialogue, but can also be called monologue if one character speaks without being interrupted for a long time. It is not necessarily the most important type of communication, but it is the most common because the plot of the play cannot really progress without it.

Lastly, and most unique to theater (although it has been used somewhat in film) is when a character speaks directly to the audience. This is called an aside, and scripts usually specifically direct actors to do this. Asides are usually comical, an inside joke between the character and the audience, and very short. The actor will usually face the audience when delivering them, even if it's for a moment, so the audience can recognize this move as an aside.

All three of these types of communication are important to the art of theater, and have been perfected by famous playwrights like Shakespeare. Understanding these types of communication can help an audience member grasp what is artful about the script and action of a play.

5. According to the passage, characters in plays communicate to

    a. move the plot forward
    b. show the private thoughts and feelings of one character
    c. make the audience laugh
    d. add beauty and artistry to the play

6. When Hamlet delivers "To be or not to be," he can most likely be described as

    a. solitary
    b. thoughtful
    c. dramatic
    d. hopeless

7. The author uses parentheses to punctuate "although it has been used somewhat in film,"

    a. to show that films are less important
    b. instead of using commas so that the sentence is not interrupted
    c. because parenthesis help separate details that are not as important
    d. to show that films are not as artistic

Questions 8 – 10 refer to the following passage.

Passage 3 - Low Blood Sugar

As the name suggest, low blood sugar is low sugar levels in the bloodstream. This can occur when you have not eaten properly and undertake strenuous activity, or, when you are very hungry. When Low blood sugar occurs regularly and is ongoing, it is a medical condition called hypoglycemia. This condition can occur in diabetics and in healthy adults.

Causes of low blood sugar can include excessive alcohol consumption, metabolic problems, stomach surgery, pancreas, liver or kidneys problems, as well as a side-effect of some medications.

Symptoms

There are different symptoms depending on the severity of the case.

Mild hypoglycemia can lead to feelings of nausea and hunger. The patient may also feel nervous, jittery and have fast heart beats. Sweaty skin, clammy and cold skin are likely symptoms.
Moderate hypoglycemia can result in a short temper, confusion, nervousness, fear and blurring of vision. The patient may feel weak and unsteady.

Severe cases of hypoglycemia can lead to seizures, coma, fainting spells, nightmares, headaches, excessive sweats and severe tiredness.
Diagnosis of low blood sugar

A doctor can diagnosis this medical condition by asking the patient questions and testing blood and urine samples. Home testing kits are available for patients to monitor blood sugar levels. It is important to see a qualified doctor though. The doctor can administer tests to ensure that will safely rule out other medical conditions that could affect blood sugar levels.

Treatment

Quick treatments include drinking or eating foods and drinks with high sugar contents. Good examples include soda, fruit juice, hard candy and raisins. Glucose energy tablets can also help. Doctors may also recommend medications and well as changes in diet and exercise routine to treat chronic low blood sugar.

8. Based on the article, which of the following is true?

   a. Low blood sugar can happen to anyone.

   b. Low blood sugar only happens to diabetics.

   c. Low blood sugar can occur even.

   d. None of the statements are true.

9. Which of the following are the author's opinion?

a. Quick treatments include drinking or eating foods and drinks with high sugar contents.

b. None of the statements are opinions.

c. This condition can occur in diabetics and also in healthy adults.

d. There are different symptoms depending on the severity of the case

10. What is the author's purpose?

a. To inform

b. To persuade

c. To entertain

d. To analyze

11. Which of the following is not a detail?

a. A doctor can diagnosis this medical condition by asking the patient questions and testing.

b. A doctor will test blood and urine samples.

c. Glucose energy tablets can also help.

d. Home test kits monitor blood sugar levels.

d. None of the above.

Questions 12 – 15 refer to the following passage.

How To Get A Good Nights Sleep

Sleep is just as essential for healthy living as water, air and food. Sleep allows the body to rest and replenish depleted energy levels. Sometimes we may for various reasons experience difficulty sleeping which has a serious effect on our health. Those who have prolonged sleeping problems are facing a serious medical condition and should see a qualified doctor when possible for help. Here is simple guide that can help you sleep better at night.

Try to create a natural pattern of waking up and sleeping around the same time everyday. This means avoiding going to bed too early and oversleeping past your usual wake up time. Going to bed and getting up at radically different times everyday confuses your body clock. Try to establish a natural rhythm as much as you can.

Exercises and a bit of physical activity can help you sleep better at night. If you are having problem sleeping, try to be as active as you can during the day.

If you are tired from physical activity, falling asleep is a natural and easy process
for your body. If you remain inactive during the day, you will find it harder to
sleep properly at night. Try walking, jogging, swimming or simple stretches as
you get close to your bed time.

Afternoon naps are great to refresh you during the day, but they may also
keep you awake at night. If you feel sleepy during the day, get up, take a walk
and get busy to keep from sleeping. Stretching is a good way to increase blood
flow to the brain and keep you alert so that you don't sleep during the day.
This will help you sleep better night.

> A warm bath or a glass of milk in the evening
> can help your body relax and prepare for
> sleep. A cold bath will wake you up and keep
> you up for several hours. Also avoid eating too
> late before bed.

12. How would you describe this sentence?

a. A recommendation

b. An opinion

c. A fact

d. A diagnosis

13. Which of the following is an alternative title for this article?

a. Exercise and a good night's sleep

b. Benefits of a good night's sleep

c. Tips for a good night's sleep

d. Lack of sleep is a serious medical condition

14. Which of the following cannot be inferred from this article?

a. Biking is helpful for getting a good night's sleep

b. Mental activity is helpful for getting a good night's
sleep

c. Eating bedtime snacks is not recommended

d. Getting up at the same time is helpful for a good
night's sleep

15. What is a disadvantage of taking naps?

a. They may keep you awake.

b. There are no disadvantages

c. They may help you sleep better

d. They may affect your diet

Question 16 refers to the following Table of Contents.

Contents

Science Self-assessment 81
Answer Key 91
Science Tutorials 96
Scientific Method 96
Biology 99
Heredity: Genes and Mutation 104
Classification 108
Ecology 110
Chemistry 112
Energy: Kinetic and Mechanical 126
Energy: Work and Power 130
Force: Newton's Three Laws 132

16. Consider the table of contents above. What page would you find information about natural selection and adaptation?

a. 81

b. 90

c. 110

d. 132

Questions 17 – 19 refer to the following passage.

Passage 5 - Pearl Harbor

A Day That Will Live in Infamy! Attack on Pearl Harbor
In 1941, the world was at war. The United States was trying very hard to keep itself out of the conflict. In Europe, the countries of Germany and Italy had formed an alliance to expand their land and territory. Germany had already taken over Poland, Denmark, and parts of France. They were heading next toward England and due to all the fighting in Europe, there were battles taking place as far south as North Africa, where the German and Italian armies were fighting the British.

This got even worse when the Asian nation of Japan formed an alliance with

Germany and Italy. Together, the three countries called themselves, the AXIS. Now, the war was in the Pacific as well as in Europe and Northern Africa. A great deal of Americans felt that perhaps now was the time for the United States to join with its ally, Great Britain and stop the Axis from taking over more regions of the world.

In 1941, Franklin Roosevelt was President of the United States. His fear at the time was that Japan would try to take over many countries in Asia. He did not want to see that happen, so he moved some of the United States warships that had been stationed in San Diego, to the military base at Pearl Harbor, in Honolulu, Hawaii.

Japan quietly plotted their attack. They waited until the early hours of the morning on Sunday, December 7, 1941. Then, 350 Japanese war plans began to drop bombs on the U.S. ships at Pearl Harbor. The first bombs fell at 7:48 am and a mere 90 minutes later, the attack was over. Pearl Harbor was decimated. 8 battleships were damaged. Eleven ships were sunk and 300 U.S. planes were destroyed. Most devastating was the loss of life 2,400 U.S. military members was killed in the attack and 1, 282 were injured.

President Roosevelt addressed the country via the radio and said "Today is a day that will live in infamy." He asked Congress to declare war on Japan. War was declared on Japan on December 8th and on Germany and Italy on December 11th. The United States had entered World War Two.

17. After reading the passage, what can we infer infamy means?

    a. Famous

    b. Remembered in a good way

    c. Remembered in a bad way

    d. Easily forgotten

18. What three countries formed the Axis?

    a. Italy, England, Germany

    b. United States, England, Italy

    c. Germany, Japan, Italy

    d. Germany, Japan, United States

19. What do you think was President Roosevelt's reason for moving warships to Pearl Harbor?

    a. He feared Japan would bomb San Diego

    b. He knew Japan was going to attack Pearl Harbor

    c. He was planning to attack Japan

    d. He wanted to try and protect Asian countries from Japanese takeover

20. Why do you think Japan chose a Sunday morning at 7:48 am for their attack?

    a. They knew the military slept late

    b. There is a law against bombing countries on a Sunday

    c. They wanted the attack to catch people by surprise

    d. That was the only free time they had to attack.

Questions 21 - 24 refer to the following recipe.

If You Have Allergies, You're Not Alone

People who experience allergies might joke that their immune systems have let them down or are seriously lacking. Truthfully though, people who experience allergic reactions or allergy symptoms during certain times of the year have heightened immune systems that are, "better" than those of people who have perfectly healthy but less militant immune systems.

Still, when a person has an allergic reaction, they are having an adverse reaction to a substance that is considered normal to most people. Mild allergic reactions usually have symptoms like itching, runny nose, red eyes, or bumps or discoloration of the skin. More serious allergic reactions, such as those to animal and insect poisons or certain foods, may result in the closing of the throat, swelling of the eyes, low blood pressure, inability to breath, and can even be fatal.

Different treatments help different allergies, and which one a person uses depends on the nature and severity of the allergy. It is recommended to patients with severe allergies to take extra precautions, such as carrying an EpiPen, which treats anaphylactic shock and may prevent death, always in order for the remedy to be readily available and more effective. When an allergy is not so severe, treatments may be used just relieve a person of uncomfortable symptoms. Over the counter allergy medicines treat milder symptoms, and can be bought at any grocery store and used in moderation to help people with allergies live normally.

There are many tests available to assess whether a person has allergies or what they may be allergic to, and advances in these tests and the medicine used to treat patients continues to improve. Despite this fact, allergies still affect many people throughout the year or even every day. Medicines used to treat allergies have side effects of their own, and it is difficult to bring the body into balance with the use of medicine. Regardless, many of those who live with allergies are grateful for what is available and find it useful in maintaining their lifestyles.

21. According to this passage, it can be understood that the word "militant" belongs in a group with the words:

    a. sickly, ailing, faint

    b. strength, power, vigor

    c. active, fighting, warring

    d. worn, tired, breaking down

22. The author says that "medicines used to treat allergies have side-effects of their own" to

    a. point out that doctors aren't very good at diagnosing and treating allergies

    b. argue that because of the large number of people with allergies, a cure will never be found

    c. explain that allergy medicines aren't cures and some compromise must be made

    d. argue that more wholesome remedies should be researched and medicines banned

23. It can be inferred that _____ recommend that some people with allergies carry medicine with them.

    a. the author

    b. doctors

    c. the makers of EpiPen

    d. people with allergies

24. The author has written this passage to

    a. inform readers on symptoms of allergies so people with allergies can get help

    b. persuade readers to be proud of having allergies

    c. inform readers on different remedies so people with allergies receive the right help

    d. describe different types of allergies, their symptoms, and their remedies

Questions 25 – 26 refer to the following email.

SUBJECT: MEDICAL STAFF CHANGES

To all staff:

This email is to advise you of a paper on recommended medical staff changes has been posted to the Human Resources website.

The contents are of primary interest to medical staff, other staff may be interested in reading it, particularly those in medical support roles.

The paper deals with several major issues:

1. Improving our ability to attract top quality staff to the hospital, and retain our existing staff. These changes will make our position and departmental names internationally recognizable and comparable with North American and North Asian departments and positions.

2. Improving our ability to attract top quality staff by introducing greater flexibility in the departmental structure.

3. General comments on issues to be further discussed in relation to research staff.

The changes outlined in this paper are significant. I encourage you to read the document and send to me any comments you may have, so that it can be enhanced and improved.

Gordon Simms
Administrator,
Seven Oaks Regional Hospital

25. Are all hospital staff required to read the document posted to the Human Resources website?

   a. Yes all staff are required to read the document.
   b. No, reading the document is optional.
   c. Only medical staff are required to read the document.
   d. none of the above are correct.

26. Have the changes to medical staff been made?

   a. Yes, the changes have been made.
   b. No, the changes are only being discussed.
   c. Some of the changes have been made.
   d. None of the choices are correct.

Questions 27 – 30 refer to the following passage.

When a Poet Longs to Mourn, He Writes an Elegy

Poems are an expressive, especially emotional, form of writing. They have been present in literature virtually from the time civilizations invented the written word. Poets often portrayed as moody, secluded, and even troubled, but this is because poets are introspective and feel deeply about the current events and cultural norms they are surrounded with. Poets often produce the most telling literature, giving insight into the society and mind-set they come from. This can be done in many forms.

The oldest types of poems often include many stanzas, may or may not rhyme, and are more about telling a story than experimenting with language or words. The most common types of ancient poetry are epics, which are usually extremely long stories that follow a hero through his journey, or ellegies, which are often solemn in tone and used to mourn or lament something or someone. The Mesopotamians are often said to have invented the written word, and their literature is among the oldest in the world, including the epic poem titled "Epic of Gilgamesh." Similar in style and length to "Gilgamesh" is "Beowulf," an ellegy written in Old English and set in Scandinavia. These poems are often used by professors as the earliest examples of literature.

The importance of poetry was revived in the Renaissance. At this time, Europeans discovered the style and beauty of ancient Greek arts, and poetry was among those. Shakespeare is the most well-known poet of the time, and he used poetry not only to write poems but also to write plays for the theater. The most popular forms of poetry during the Renaissance included villanelles, (a nineteen-line poetic form) sonnets, as well as the epic. Poets during this time focused on style and form, and developed very specific rules and outlines for how an exceptional poem should be written.

As often happens in the arts, modern poets have rejected the constricting rules of Renaissance poets, and free form poems are much more popular. Some modern poems would read just like stories if they weren't arranged into lines and stanzas. It is difficult to tell which poems and poets will be the most important, because works of art often become more famous in hindsight, after the poet has died and society can look at itself without being in the moment. Modern poetry continues to develop, and will no doubt continue to change as values, thought, and writing continue to change.

Poems can be among the most enlightening and uplifting texts for a person to read if they are looking to connect with the past, connect with other people, or try to gain an understanding of what is happening in their time.

27. In summary, the author has written this passage

    a. as a foreword that will introduce a poem in a book or magazine

    b. because she loves poetry and wants more people to like it

    c. to give a brief history of poems

    d. to convince students to write poems

28. The author organizes the paragraphs mainly by

    a. moving chronologically, explaining which types of poetry were common in that time

    b. talking about new types of poems each paragraph and explaining them a little

    c. focusing on one poet or group of people and the poems they wrote

    d. explaining older types of poetry so she can talk about modern poetry

29. The author's claim that poetry has been around "virtually from the time civilizations invented the written word" is supported by the detail that

    a. Beowulf is written in Old English, which is not really in use any longer

    b. epic poems told stories about heroes

    c. the Renaissance poets tried to copy Greek poets

    d. the Mesopotamians are credited with both inventing the word and writing "Epic of Gilgamesh"

30. According to the passage, it can be understood that the word "telling" means

    a. speaking

    b. significant

    c. soothing

    d. wordy

Section III
Part II – Vocabulary

31. Choose a verb that means fearless or invulnerable to intimidation and fear.

    a. Feeble

    b. Strongest

    c. Dauntless

    d. Super

32. Choose a word that means the same as the underlined word.

I see the differences when they are placed side-by-side and <u>juxtaposed.</u>

    a. Compared

    b. Eliminated

    c. Overturned

    d. Exonerated

33. Choose the best definition of regicide.

    a. v. To endow or furnish with requisite ability, character, knowledge and skill

    b. n. killing of a king

    c. adj. Disposed to seize by violence or by unlawful or greedy methods

    d. v. To refresh after labor

34. Choose the best definition of pernicious.

    a. Deadly

    b. Infectious

    c. Common

    d. Rare

35. Fill in the blank.

After she received her influenza vaccination, Nan thought that she was _____ to the common cold.

    a. Immune

    b. Susceptible

    c. Vulnerable

    d. At risk

36. Choose a word that means the same as the underlined word.

She performed the gymnastics and stretches so well! I have never seen anyone so <u>nimble</u>.

    a. Awkward

    b. Agile

    c. Quick

    d. Taut

37. Choose a word that means the same as the underlined word.

Are there any more <u>queries</u>? We have already had so many questions today.

    a. Questions

    b. Commands

    c. Obfuscations

    d. Paradoxes

38. Choose a verb that means to remove a leader or high official from position.

    a. Sack

    b. Suspend

    c. Depose

    d. Dropped

39. Choose the best definition of pedestrian.

    a. Rare
    b. Often
    c. Walking or Running
    d. Commonplace

40. Choose the best definition of petulant.

    a. Patient
    b. Childish
    c. Impatient
    d. Mature

41. Fill in the blank.

Paul's rose bushes were being destroyed by Japanese beetles, so he invested in a good _____.

    a. Fungicide
    b. Fertilizer
    c. Sprinkler
    d. Pesticide

42. Choose the best definition of salient.

    a. v. To make light by fermentation, as dough
    b. adj. Not stringent or energetic
    c. adj. negligible
    d. adj. worthy of note or relevant

43. Choose the best definition of sedentary.

    a. n. A morbid condition, due to obstructed excretion of bile or characterized by yellowing of the skin
    b. adj. not moving or sitting in one place
    c. v. To wander from place to place
    d. n. Perplexity

44. Fill in the blank.

The last time that the crops failed, the entire nation experienced months of _____.

    a. Famine
    b. Harvest
    c. Plenitude
    d. Disease

45. Choose the best definition of stint.

    a. Thrifty
    b. Annoyed
    c. Dislike
    d. Insult

46. Choose the best definition of precipitate.

    a. To rain
    b. To throw down
    c. To throw up
    d. to snow

47. Choose the verb that means to build up or strengthen in relation to morals or religion.

   a. Sanctify

   b. Amplify

   c. Edify

   d. Wry

48. Choose the noun that means exit or way out.

   a. Door-jamb

   b. Egress

   c. Regress

   d. Furtherance

49. Choose the best definition of the underlined word.

The tide was in this morning but now it is starting to <u>recede</u>.

   a. Go out

   b. Flow

   c. Swell

   d. Come in

50. Choose the word that means private, personal.

   a. Confidential

   b. Hysteric

   c. Simplistic

   d. Promissory

Section IV – Math

1. A square lawn has an area of 62,500 square meters. What is the cost of building fence around it at a rate of $5.5 per meter?

   a. $4000

   b. $4500

   c. $5000

   d. $5500

2. The following numbers are the ages of people on a bus – 3, 6, 27, 13, 6, 8, 12, 20, 5, 10. Calculate their average of their ages.

   a. 11

   b. 6

   c. 9

   d. 110

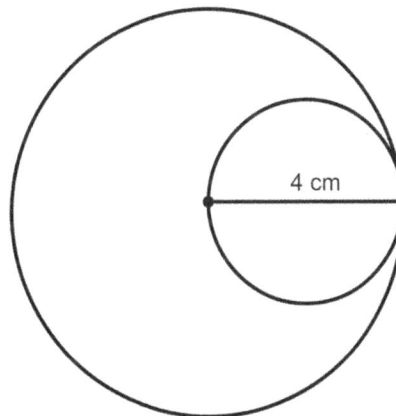

4 cm

Note: Figure not drawn to scale

3. What is (area of large circle) - (area of small circle) in the figure above? Assume the diameter of the small circle is the radius of the larger circle.

   a. 8π cm^2

   b. 10π cm^2

   c. 12π cm^2

   d. 16π cm^2

4. Estimate 4,210,987 – 210,078

    a. 4,000,000

    b. 40,000,000

    c. 400,000

    d. 40,000

5. A distributor purchased 550 kilograms of potatoes for $165. He distributed these at a rate of $6.4 per 20 kilograms to 15 shops, $3.4 per 10 kilograms to 12 shops and the remainder at $1.8 per 5 kilograms. If his total distribution cost is $10, what will his profit be?

    a. $10.4

    b. $13.6

    c. $14.9

    d. $23.4

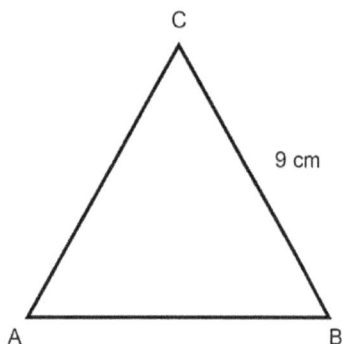

Note: figure not drawn to scale

6. What is the perimeter of the equilateral △ABC above?

    a. 18 cm

    b. 12 cm

    c. 27 cm

    d. 15 cm

7. How much pay does Mr. Johnson receive if he gives half of his pay to his family, $250 to his landlord, and has exactly 3/7 of his pay left after these expenses?

    a. $3600

    b. $3500

    c. $2800

    d. $1750

8. A boy has 4 red, 5 green and 2 yellow balls. He chooses two balls randomly. What is the probability that one is red and other is green?

    a. 2/11

    b. 19/22

    c. 20/121

    d. 9/11

9. Smith and Simon are playing a card game. Smith will win if a card drawn from a deck of 52 is either a 7 or a diamond, and Simon will win if the drawn card is an even number. Which statement is more likely to be correct?

    a. Simon will win more games.

    b. Smith will win more games.

    c. They have same winning probability.

    d. A decision cannot be made from the provided data.

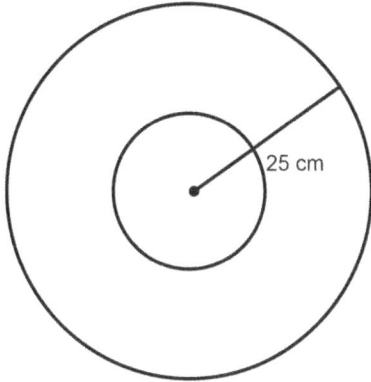

Note: Figure not drawn to scale

10. What is the distance travelled by the wheel above, when it makes 175 revolutions?

    a. 87.5 п m

    b. 875 п m

    c. 8.75 п m

    d. 8750 п m

11. How much water can be stored in a cylindrical container 5 meters in diameter and 12 meters high?

    a. 235.65 m³

    b. 223.65 m³

    c. 240.65 m³

    d. 252.65 m³

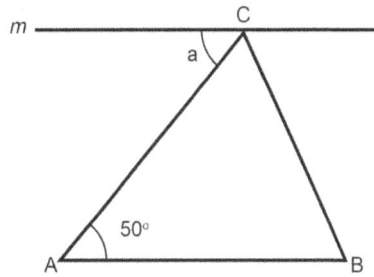

Note: Figure not drawn to scale

12. If the line m is parallel to the side AB of △ABC, what is angle a?

    a. 130°

    b. 25°

    c. 65°

    d. 50°

13. Estimate 215 x 65.

    a. 1,350

    b. 13,500

    c. 103,500

    d. 3,500

14. 4/5 – 2/3

    a. 2/2

    b. 2/13

    c. 1

    d. 2/15

15. If the speed of a train is 72 kilometers per hour, what distance will it cover in 12 seconds?

    a. 200 m

    b. 220 m

    c. 240 m

    d. 260 m

16. In a class of 83 students, 72 are present. What percent of the students are absent? Provide answer up to two significant digits.

    a. 12%

    b. 13%

    c. 14%

    d. 15%

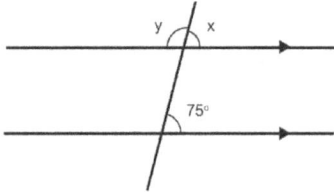

17. What is the value of the angle y?

    a. 25°

    b. 15°

    c. 30°

    d. 105°

18. A driver traveled from city A to city B in 1 hour and 13 minutes. On the way, he had to stop at 5 traffic signals, with an average time of 80 seconds. If the distance between the cities is 65 kilometers then what was the average driving speed?

    a. 56.42

    b. 58.77

    c. 60.34

    d. 63.25

19. A small business owner deposits $6000 in a savings account at a local bank. After 2 years, at 3% interest rate, what will be the interest earned?

    a. $6360

    b. $360

    c. $240

    d. $460

20. Richard gives 's' amount of salary to each of his 'n' employees weekly. If he has 'x' amount of money then how many days he can employ these 'n' employees.

    a. sx/7n

    b. 7x

    c. nx/7x

    d. 7x/ns

21. Mr. Micheal runs a factory. His total assets are $256,800 that consists of a building worth $80,500, machinery worth $125.000 and $51,300 cash. After one year what will be the value of his total assets if he has additional cash of $75,600 and the value of his building has increased by 10% per year, and his machinery depreciated by 20% per year?

    a. $243,450

    b. $252,450

    c. $264,150

    d. $272,350

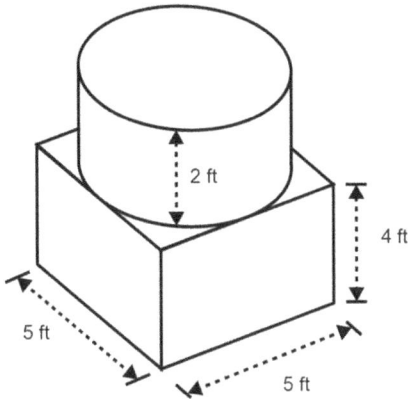

Note: Figure not drawn to scale

22. What is the approximate total volume of the above solid?

a. 120 ft³

b. 100 ft³

c. 140 ft³

d. 160 ft³

23. Martin earns $25,000 as basic pay, $500 rent and $860 for medical insurance. He spends 40% of his total earning on food and clothing, 10% on children's education and pays $800 for utility bills. What percent of his earning he is saving?

a. 54%

b. 50%

c. 47%

d. 44%

24. Below is the attendance for a class of 45.

Day   Absent Students
Monday   5
Tuesday   9
Wednesday 4
Thursday   10
Friday   6

What is the average attendance for the week?

a. 88%

b. 85%

c. 81%

d. 77%

25. Prize money of $1,050 is to be shared among top three contestants in ratio of 7:5:3 as 1st, 2nd and 3rd prizes respectively. How much more money will the 1st prize contestant receive than the 3rd prize contestant?

a. $210

b. $280

c. $350

d. $490

26. The manager of a weaving factory estimates that if 10 machines run on 100% efficiency for 8 hours, they will produce 1450 meters of cloth. Due to some technical problems, 4 machines run of 95% efficiency and the remaining 6 at 90% efficiency. How many meters of cloth can these machines will produce in 8 hours?

a. 1334 meters

b. 1310 meters

c. 1300 meters

d. 1285 meters

27. A driver at a speed of 's' miles per hour can reach his destination in 'h' hours. If his speed increased from 's' to 'x' then how much less time in hours will it take to reach his destination?

    a. h – xh/s

    b. h - sh/x

    c. s/x

    d. sh/x

28. A car covers a distance in 3.5 hours at an average speed of 60 km/hr. How much time in hours will a motorbike take to cover this distance at an average speed of 40km/hr?

    a. 4.5

    b. 4.75

    c. 5

    d. 5.25

29. A grandfather is 8 times older than his grandson is now. After 6 years, he will be 5 times older than his grandson will. How old is the grandfather now?

    a. 48

    b. 56

    c. 64

    d. 72

30. Solve for n. 5n + (19 – 2)) = 67.

    a. 21

    b. 10

    c. 15

    d. 7

31. A boy is given 2 apples while his sister is given 8 oranges. What is the ratio between the boy's apples and her oranges?

    a. 1:2

    b. 2:4

    c. 1:4

    d. 2:1

32. Solve for x. 5x + 21 = 66.

    a. 19

    b. 9

    c. 15

    d. 5

33. What is the least common multiple of 9 and 3?

    a. 27

    b. 9

    c. 3

    d. 18

34. A box contains 7 black pencils and 28 blue ones. What is the ratio between the black and blue pens?

    a. 1:4

    b. 2:7

    c. 1:8

    d. 1:9

35. If X + (32 + 356) = 920. What is x?

    a. 450

    b. 388

    c. 532

    d. 623

36. A boy buys 10 candies. The packet contains 3 green candies, 12 red and 9 blue candies. What is the ratio the green, red and blue sweets?

   a. 1:3:4

   b. 1:4:3

   c. 2:3:1

   d. 1:5:4

37. Solve for x. (12 x 12)/x = 12

   a. 12

   b. 13

   c. 8

   d. 14

38. Solve for A. A – (34 x 2) = 18.

   a. 86

   b. 78

   c. 50

   d. 73

39. Solve for X.   X% of 120 = 30.

   a. 15

   b. 12

   c. 4

   d. 25

40. Solve for X. X * 25% of 100 = 75.

   a. 5

   b. 3

   c. 21

   d. 13

41. There are 12 people sitting in a bus and 3 people standing. What is the ratio between the people sitting and standing?

   a. 4:2

   b. 3:1

   c. 1:4

   d. 4:1

42. Solve for X. X% of 250 = 50.

   a. 30

   b. 35

   c. 25

   d. 20

43. Write 41.061 to the nearest 10th.

   a. 41.1

   b. 41.06

   c. 41

   d. 41.6

44. What is the least common multiple of 4 and 3?

   a. 24

   b. 6

   c. 16

   d. 12

45. Write 51.738 to the nearest 100th.

   a. 51.735

   b. 51.7

   c. 51.73

   d. 51.74

46. What is the ratio between 2 gold coins, 6 silver coins and 12 bronze coins?

    a. 2:3:4

    b. 1:2:4

    c. 1:3:4

    d. 2:3:4

47. What is the least common multiple of 8 and 12?

    a. 24

    b. 36

    c. 12

    d. 8

48. Solve for x. -7 + 3x = 20.

    a. 7

    b. 5

    c. 4

    d. 9

49. What is the least common multiple of 2 and 3?

    a. 2

    b. 4

    c. 6

    d. 3

50. Solve for a, when 23 = 2a + 13.

    a. 6

    b. 12

    c. 5

    d. 8

51. Write 301.311 to the nearest 100th.

    a. 301.3

    b. 301.31

    c. 301

    d. 301.311

52. What is the least common multiple of 5 and 3?

    a. 35

    b. 25

    c. 15

    d. 12

53. Solve for c, when 124 = 12c - 20.

    a. 6

    b. 12

    c. 10

    d. 15

54. Write 765.3682 to the nearest 1000th.

    a. 765.368

    b. 765.361

    c. 765.369

    d. 765.378

55. Simplify 3 8/9 + 5 5/6.

    a. 8 13/15

    b. 8 3/9

    c. 9 13/18

    d. 8 12/18

56. Write 731.614 to the nearest 10th.

    a. 731.6

    b. 731.61

    c. 731.62

    d. 73

57. Simplify 7 4/5 + 2 2/5.

    a. 5 3/5

    b. 5 1/5

    c. 4 2/5

    d. 5 2/5

58. Write 765.3682 to the nearest 1000th.

    a. 765.368

    b. 765.361

    c. 765.369

    d. 765.378

59. Translate the following into an equation: three plus a number times 7 equals 42.

    a. $7(3 + X) = 42$

    b. $3(X + 7) = 42$

    c. $3X + 7 = 42$

    d. $(3 + 7)X = 42$

60. Estimate 5205 / 25

    a. 108

    b. 308

    c. 208

    d. 408

Section V – Language Arts

1. Choose the sentence below with the correct punctuation.

    a. Marcus who won the debate tournament, is the best speaker that I know.

    b. Marcus, who won the debate tournament, is the best speaker that I know.

    c. Marcus who won the debate tournament is the best speaker that I know.

    d. Marcus who won the debate tournament is the best speaker, that I know.

2. Choose the sentence below with the correct punctuation.

    a. To make chicken soup you must first buy a chicken.

    b. To make chicken soup you must first, buy a chicken.

    c. To make chicken soup, you must first buy a chicken.

    d. To make chicken soup; you must first buy a chicken.

3. Choose the sentence below with the correct punctuation.

    a. To travel around the globe you have to drive 25,000 miles.

    b. To travel around the globe, you have to drive 25000 miles.

    c. To travel around the globe, you have to drive, 25000 miles.

    d. To travel around the globe, you have to drive 25,000 miles.

4. Choose the sentence below with the correct punctuation.

    a. The dog loved chasing bones, but never ate them; it was running that he enjoyed.

    b. The dog loved chasing bones; but never ate them, it was running that he enjoyed.

    c. The dog loved chasing bones, but never ate them, it was running that he enjoyed.

    d. The dog loved chasing bones; but never ate them: it was running that he enjoyed.

5. Choose the sentence below with the correct punctuation.

    a. He had not paid the rent, therefore, the landlord changed the locks.

    b. He had not paid the rent; therefore, the landlord changed the locks.

    c. He had not paid the rent, therefore; the landlord changed the locks.

    d. He had not paid the rent therefore, the landlord changed the locks.

6. Choose the sentence below with the correct punctuation.

    a. Jessica's father was in the Navy, so she attended schools in Newark, New Jersey, Key   West, Florida, San Diego, California, and Fairbanks, Alaska.

    b. Jessica's father was in the Navy, so she attended schools in: Newark, New Jersey, Key West, Florida, San Diego, California, and Fairbanks, Alaska.

    c. Jessica's father was in the Navy, so she attended schools in Newark, New Jersey; Key West, Florida; San Diego, California; and Fairbanks, Alaska.

    d. Jessica's father was in the Navy, so she attended schools in Newark; New Jersey, Key West; Florida, San Diego, California, and Fairbanks, Alaska.

7. Choose the sentence below with the correct punctuation.

    a. George wrecked John's car that was the end of their friendship.

    b. George wrecked John's car. that was the end of their friendship.

    c. George wrecked John's car; that was the end of their friendship.

    d. None of the above

8. Choose the sentence below with the correct punctuation.

a. The dress was not Gina's favorite; however, she wore it to the dance.
b. The dress was not Gina's favorite, however, she wore it to the dance.
c. The dress was not Gina's favorite, however; she wore it to the dance.
d. The dress was not Gina's favorite however, she wore it to the dance.

9. Choose the sentence below with the correct punctuation.

a. Chris showed his dedication to golf in many ways, for example, he watched all of the tournaments on television.
b. Chris showed his dedication to golf in many ways; for example, he watched all of the   tournaments on television.
c. Chris showed his dedication to golf in many ways, for example; he watched all of the tournaments on television.
d. Chris showed his dedication to golf in many ways for example he watched all of the tournaments on television.

10. Choose the sentence with the correct capitalization.

a. I was able to speak with Susan Roberts, Mayor of Tampa.
b. I was able to speak with Susan Roberts, mayor of Tampa.
c. I was able to speak with Susan Roberts, Mayor of tampa.
d. None of the Above.

11. Choose the sentence with the correct capitalization.

a. I think thanksgiving is the best fall holiday.
b. I think Thanksgiving is the best Fall holiday.
c. I think Thanksgiving is the best fall holiday.
d. None of the above.

12. Choose the sentence with the correct capitalization.

a. I will be skipping the Fall 2012 Semester.
b. I will be skipping the fall 2012 semester.
c. I will be skipping the Fall 2012 semester.
d. None of the above.

13. Choose the sentence with the correct capitalization.

    a. They speak Spanish in Mexico.
    b. They speak spanish in Mexico.
    c. They speak spanish in mexico.
    d. None of the above.

14. Choose the sentence with the correct capitalization.

    a. My best friend said, "always count your change."
    b. My best friend said, "Always Count your Change."
    c. My best friend said, "Always count your change."
    d. None of the above.

15. Choose the sentence with the correct capitalization.

    a. The Victorian Era was in the nineteenth century.
    b. The victorian era was in the nineteenth century.
    c. The Victorian Era was in the Nineteenth century.
    d. The Victorian era was in the Nineteenth century.

16. Choose the sentence with the correct capitalization.

    a. I prefer Pepsi to coke.
    b. I prefer pepsi to Coke.
    c. I prefer Pepsi to Coke.
    d. None of the above.

17. Choose the sentence with the correct capitalization.

    a. I always have french fries with my coke.
    b. I always have french fries with my Coke.
    c. I always have French Fries with my Coke.
    d. None of the above.

18. Choose the sentence with the correct capitalization.

    a. The blue jays are my favorite team.
    b. the blue Jays are my favorite team.
    c. The Blue Jays are my favorite team.
    d. The blue Jays are my favorite team.

19. Choose the sentence with the correct capitalization.

    a. The Southwest is the best part of the country.

    b. The southwest is the best part of the country.

    c. The southwest is the best part of the Country.

    d. None of the above.

20. Choose the sentence with the correct capitalization.

    a. My favorite Dylan song is blowin' in the wind.

    b. My favorite dylan song is Blowin' in the Wind.

    c. My favorite Dylan song is Blowin' in the Wind.

    d. None of the above.

21. Choose the sentence with the correct capitalization.

    a. My latest novel, Danger on the Rhine will be published next year.

    b. My latest novel, danger on the Rhine will be published next year.

    c. My latest novel, danger on the rhine will be published next year.

    d. None of the above.

22. Choose the sentence with the correct usage.

    a. The Chinese live in one of the world's most populous nations, while a citizen of Bermuda lives in one of the least populous.

    b. The Chinese lives in one of the world's most populous nations, while a citizen of Bermuda live in one of the least populous.

    c. The Chinese live in one of the world's most populous nations, while a citizen of Bermuda live in one of the least populous.

    d. The Chinese lives in one of the world's most populous nations, while a citizen of Bermuda lives in one of the least populous.

23. Choose the sentence with the correct usage.

    a. Disease is highly prevalent in poorer nations; the most dominant disease is malaria.

    b. Disease are highly prevalent in poorer nations; the most dominant disease is malaria.

    c. Disease is highly prevalent in poorer nations; the most dominant disease are malaria.

    d. Disease are highly prevalent in poorer nations; the most dominant disease are malaria.

24. Choose the sentence with the correct usage.

a. Although I would prefer to have dog, I actually own a cat.
b. Although I would prefer to have a dog, I actually own cat.
c. Although I would prefer to have a dog, I actually own a cat.
d. Although I would prefer to have dog, I actually own cat.

25. Choose the sentence with the correct usage.

a. The principal of the school lived by one principle: always do your best.
b. The principle of the school lived by one principle: always do your best.
c. The principal of the school lived by one principal: always do your best.
d. The principle of the school lived by one principal: always do your best.

26. Choose the sentence with the correct usage.

a. Even with an speed limit sign clearly posted, an inattentive driver may drive too fast.
b. Even with a speed limit sign clearly posted, a inattentive driver may drive too fast.
c. Even with an speed limit sign clearly posted, a inattentive driver may drive too fast.
d. Even with a speed limit sign clearly posted, an inattentive driver may drive too fast.

27. Choose the sentence with the correct usage.

a. Except for the roses, she did not accept John's frequent gifts.
b. Accept for the roses, she did not except John's frequent gifts.
c. Accept for the roses, she did not accept John's frequent gifts.
d. Except for the roses, she did not except John's frequent gifts.

28. Choose the sentence with the correct usage.

a. Although he continued to advise me, I no longer took his advice.
b. Although he continued to advice me, I no longer took his advise.
c. Although he continued to advise me, I no longer took his advise.
d. Although he continued to advice me, I no longer took his advise.

29. Choose the sentence with the correct usage.

a. To adopt to the climate, we had to adopt a different style of clothing.

b. To adapt to the climate, we had to adapt a different style of clothing.

c. To adapt to the climate, we had to adopt a different style of clothing.

d. None of the above are correct.

30. Choose the sentence with the correct usage.

a. When he's between friends, Robert seems confident, but, between you and me, he is very shy.

b. When he's among friends, Robert seems confident, but, among you and me, he is very shy.

c. When he's between friends, Robert seems confident, but, among you and me, he is very shy.

d. When he's among friends, Robert seems confident, but, between you and me, he is very shy.

31. Choose the sentence with the correct usage.

a. I will be finished at ten in the morning, and will be arriving at home at about 6:30.

b. I will be finished at about ten in the morning, and will be arriving at home at 6:30.

c. I will be finished at about ten in the morning, and will be arriving at home at about 6:30.

d. I will be finished at ten in the morning, and will be arriving at home at 6:30.

32. Choose the sentence with the correct usage.

a. Beside the red curtains and pillows, there was a red rug beside the couch.

b. Besides the red curtains and pillows, there was a red rug beside the couch.

c. Besides the red curtains and pillows, there was a red rug besides the couch.

d. Beside the red curtains and pillows, there was a red rug besides the couch.

33. Choose the sentence with the correct usage.

a. Although John can swim very well, the lifeguard may not allow him to swim in the pool.

b. Although John may swim very well, the lifeguard may not allow him to swim in the pool.

c. Although John can swim very well, the lifeguard can not allow him to swim in the pool.

d. None of the choices are correct.

34. Choose the sentence with the correct usage.

a. Her continuous absences caused a continual disruption at the office.

b. Her continual absences caused a continuous disruption at the office.

c. Her continual absences caused a continual disruption at the office.

d. Her continuous absences caused a continuous disruption at the office.

35. Choose the sentence with the correct usage.

a. During the famine, the Irish people had to emigrate to other countries; many of them immigrated to the United States.

b. During the famine, the Irish people had to immigrate to other countries; many of them immigrated to the United States.

c. During the famine, the Irish people had to emigrate to other countries; many of them emigrated to the United States.

d. During the famine, the Irish people had to immigrate to other countries; many of them emigrated to the United States.

36. Choose the sentence with the correct usage.

a. His home was farther than we expected; farther, the roads were very bad.

b. His home was farther than we expected; further, the roads were very bad.

c. His home was further than we expected; further, the roads were very bad.

d. His home was further than we expected; farther, the roads were very bad.

37. Choose the sentence with the correct usage.

a. The volunteers brought groceries and toys to the homeless shelter; the latter were given to the staff, while the former were given directly to the children.

b. The volunteers brought groceries and toys to the homeless shelter; the former was given to the staff, while the latter was given directly to the children.

c. The volunteers brought groceries and toys to the homeless shelter; the groceries were given to the staff, while the former was given directly to the children.

d. The volunteers brought groceries and toys to the homeless shelter; the latter was given to the staff, while the groceries were given directly to the children.

38. Choose the sentence with the correct grammar.

a. His doctor suggested that he eat less snacks and do fewer lounging on the couch.

b. His doctor suggested that he eat fewer snacks and do less lounging on the couch.

c. His doctor suggested that he eat less snacks and do less lounging on the couch.

d. His doctor suggested that he eat fewer snacks and do fewer lounging on the couch.

39. Choose the sentence with the correct grammar.

a. However, I believe that he didn't really try that hard.
b. However I believe that he didn't really try that hard.
c. However; I believe that he didn't really try that hard.
d. However: I believe that he didn't really try that hard.

40. Choose the sentence with the correct grammar.

a. There was however, very little difference between the two.
b. There was, however very little difference between the two.
c. There was; however, very little difference between the two.
d. There was, however, very little difference between the two.

41. Choose the sentence with the correct grammar.

a. Don would never have thought of that book, but you could have reminded him.

b. Don would never of thought of that book, but you could have reminded him.

c. Don would never have thought of that book, but you could of have reminded him.

d. Don would never of thought of that book, but you could of reminded him.

42. Choose the sentence with the correct grammar.

a. The mother would not of punished her daughter if she could have avoided it.

b. The mother would not have punished her daughter if she could of avoided it.

c. The mother would not of punished her daughter if she could of avoided it.

d. The mother would not have punished her daughter if she could have avoided it.

43. Choose the sentence with the correct grammar.

a. There was scarcely no food in the pantry, because nobody ate at home.

b. There was scarcely any food in the pantry, because nobody ate at home.

c. There was scarcely any food in the pantry, because not nobody ate at home.

d. There was scarcely no food in the pantry, because not nobody ate at home.

44. Choose the sentence with the correct grammar.

a. Although you may not see nobody in the dark, it does not mean that nobody is there.

b. Although you may not see anyone in the dark, it does not mean that not nobody is there.

c. Although you may not see anyone in the dark, it does not mean that anyone is there.

d. Although you may not see nobody in the dark, it does not mean that not nobody is there.

45. Choose the sentence with the correct grammar.

a. Michael has lived in that house for forty years, while I has owned this one for only six weeks.

b. Michael have lived in that house for forty years, while I have owned this one for only six weeks.

c. Michael have lived in that house for forty years, while I has owned this one for only six weeks.

d. Michael has lived in that house for forty years, while I have owned this one for only six weeks.

46. Choose the sentence with the correct grammar.

a. The older children have already eat their dinner, but the baby has not yet eaten anything.

b. The older children have already eaten their dinner, but the baby has not yet ate anything.

c. The older children have already eaten their dinner, but the baby has not yet eaten anything.

d. The older children have already eat their dinner, but the baby has not yet ate anything.

47. Choose the sentence with the correct grammar.

a. If they had gone to the party, he would have gone too.

b. If they had went to the party, he would have gone too.

c. If they had gone to the party, he would have went too.

d. If they had went to the party, he would have went too.

48. Choose the sentence with the correct grammar.

a. He should have went to the appointment; instead, he went to the beach.

b. He should have gone to the appointment; instead, he went to the beach.

c. He should have went to the appointment; instead, he gone to the beach.

d. He should have gone to the appointment; instead, he gone to the beach.

49. Choose the correct spelling.

a. humoros
b. humouros
c. humorous
d. humorus

50. Choose the correct spelling.

a. knowlege
b. knowledge
c. knowlegde
d. knowlledge

51. Choose the correct spelling.

a. camaraderie
b. camaredere
c. camaradere
d. cameraderie

52. Choose the correct spelling.

a. mathematics
b. mathmatics
c. matematics
d. mathamatics

53. Choose the correct spelling.

a. conscentious
b. conscientios
c. conscientious
d. consceintious

54. Choose the correct spelling.

a. leisuire
b. lesure
c. lesure
d. leisure

55. Choose the correct spelling.

a. pigeone
b. pigoen
c. pigeon
d. pidgeon

56. Choose the correct spelling.

a. odyessy
b. odeyssey
c. odysey
d. odyssey

57. Choose the correct spelling.

a. sacreligious
b. sacriligious
c. sacrilegious
d. sacrilegous

58. Choose the correct spelling.

a. accommodate
b. accomodate
c. acommodate
d. accommodaite

59. Choose the correct spelling.

a. consenssus
b. conssensus
c. consensus
d. consemsus

60. Choose the correct spelling.

a. exhilirate
b. exhalirate
c. exhilerate
d. exhilarate

Answer Key

Section 1 – Verbal Skills

1. C
This is a functional relationship. A lawyer defends a client in a trial in the same way a doctor performs an operation on a patient.

2. B
This is a cause and effect relationship. You must eat to become fat, in the same way you must breathe to live.

3. D
This is a definition relationship. A dog is a canine in the same way a porpoise is a mammal.

4. A
This is a time relationship. A turntable is an early type of stereo, MP3 player is a modern stereo. In the same way, a horse drawn carriage is an earlier type of car.

5. B
This is a type relationship. A cub is a young bear, in the same way a puppy is a young dog.

6. A
Law cures anarchy in the same way medicine cures illness.

7. B
This is a type relationship. Gold is a type of metal in the same way a surgeon is a type of doctor.

8. C
This is a process relationship. The first word is the process which creates the second. For example, ice melts to liquid in the same way water freezes to create a solid.

9. D
This is a measurement relationship. Clocks measure time in the same way thermometers measure temperature.

10. C
A car is kept in a garage the same way a plane is kept in a hangar.

11. B
Peculiar and strange are synonyms.

12. B
Tippet and shawl are synonyms.

13. D
Vivid and brilliant are synonyms.

14. B
Semblance and image are synonyms.

15. A
Impregnable and unconquerable are synonyms.

16. A
Jargon and slang are synonyms.

17. A
Render and give are synonyms.

18. B
Intrusive and invasive are synonyms.

19. A
Renowned and popular are synonyms.

20. C
Incoherent and jumbled are synonyms.

21. A
Congenial and pleasant are synonyms.

22. D
Plight and situation are synonyms.

23. A
Berate and criticize are synonyms.

24. B
Sate and satisfy are synonyms.

25. B
Terminate and end are synonyms.

26. C
This is a repetition pattern. All the choices repeat a 3 number sequence.

27. D
This is a word meaning relationship. Pain is not a synonym for any of the choices.

28. D
This is a repetition vowel pattern. All the choices have 3 vowels except D.

29. D
This is a vowel and consonant relationship. All the choices have a vowel at the end, except abc.

30. C
This is a repetition pattern. All the choices repeat a 2-letter sequence obtained by adding 2 to the previous number.

31. B
This is a word meaning relationship. Lean is not a synonym for any of the choices.

32. B
This is a capital small letter relationship. All choices have alternate letters capitalized.

33. D
This is a relationship of words question. All the choices are synonyms of look and see, except surmise.

34. D
This is a word meaning relationship. List is not a synonym for any of the choices.

35. A
This is a word meaning relationship. List is not a synonym for any of the choices.

36. C
This is a capital letter small letter relationship. All the choices begin with a capital letter, as well as beginning with a consonant.

37. D
This is a relationship of words question. All the choices are dog or canine family except cougar.

38. C
This is a word meaning relationship. Overweight is not a synonym for any of the choices.

39. A
This is a relationship of words question. All the choices are synonyms of great, except smart.

40. D
This is a word meaning relationship. Command is not a synonym for any of the choices.

41. A
This is a word meaning relationship. Assume is not a synonym for any of the choices.

42. C
Discord and harmony are antonyms.

43. B
Latter and former are antonyms.

44. C
Shrink and expand are antonyms.

45. B
Reluctant and enthusiastic are antonyms.

46. D
Refute and agree are antonyms.

47. C
Vulnerable and strong are antonyms.

48. D
Intrepid and timid are antonyms.

49. A
Liaise and uncoordinated are antonyms.

50. D
Ridicule and praise are antonyms.

51. B
Fixed and indefinite are antonyms.

52. A
The antonym of flamboyant is plain.

53. C
The antonym of sporadic is regular.

54. Uncertain.
It does not say where they went swimming.

55. True
It must be true that if fish use their gills to breathe, and fish can't breathe out of water, then gills don't work out of water.

56. Uncertain.
It does not say that they eat steak every time they are hungry.

57. Uncertain.
It does not say where they went swimming. There could be Herman Melville books they can't find or haven't read.

58. True
The answer because the first statement says 'all.' Therefore the conclusion is also true. If the first sentence did NOT say 'all,' the conclusion would not be true.

59. True
The conclusion must be true, since all cats are mammals. The conclusion would be false if the first statement was 'all,' and the second statement was 'some.'

60. False
Although all students carry a backpack, not everyone who carries a backpack is a student. I.e. there are some people who carry a backpack who are not students.

Section II – Quantitative Skills

1. A
The interval begins with 5, increases by 2 and is added each time.

2. C
The numbers in Box B are squares of the numbers in Box A, so the missing number in Box B is 9.

3. B
The numbers in Box B are result of (number in Box A * 2) + 3. Therefore, the missing number is 21.

4. A
The number doubles each time.

5. D
The numbers decrease by 6 each time.

6. C
Each number is the sum of the previous two numbers.

7. D
The number triples each time.

8. A
The number in row B is 4 times the number in row A.

9. C
Each number is ten less than the next number. E.g. 29 is 10 less than 39.

10. B
One letter is missing after each letter.

11. A
Two letters are missing after each letter.

12. D
Each number is 7 greater than the previous.

13. A
The sequence increases initially and then decreases in the next term. The relationship between each increase is +3 and the relationship with the alternate decrease is -3. So the answer is -2 from the last given term. 13 – 2 = 11.

14. B
The sequence is decreasing by half. So half of 1/4 = 1/8

15. D
This sequence is increasing by adding 6.

16. B
The sequence is increasing by adding an increasing amount to the previous number e.g. 4, 5, 6, 7, 8, 9....etc. The next term is of the sequence is 26 + 7 =33 and then 33 + 8 = 41

17. B
The second term decreased by 3, and the subsequent terms decreased at twice the last rate of decrease. The next term of the sequence is thus -4 – 24= -28. The 6th term is -28 – 48 = -76.

18. A
The sequence is increasing by 4.
19. B
20. B
21. D
22. B
23. C
24. A
25. C
26. C
27. A

28. B
#1 = 16
#2 = 33
#3 = 22
1 < 2 > 3

29. B
1. 96
2. 44
3. 84
4. 9
1 > 4 < 3

30. C
#1 = 23
#2 = 31
#3 = 28
#4 = 22
2 > 1 < 3

31. A
#1 = 32
#2 = 3
#3 = 12
#4 = 22
2 is the smallest.

32. D
#1 = 43
#2 = 15
#3 = 35
#4 = 42
None of the Above.

33. A
#1 = 39
#2 = 3
#3 = 28
1 > 2 < 3

34. D
1. 25
2. 32
3. 15
4. 20
(#1 + #2) = 57 > 20

35. D
#1 = 216
#2 = 38
#3 = 36
None of the Above.

36. C
a. 4% of 4 = .16
b. 5% of 5 = 0.25
c. 0.3% of 12 = 0.036
d. 1/5 of 100 = 20
C is the smallest.

37. C
2/5 of 20 = 8 + 8 = 16

38. A
50% of 50 = 25 + 6 = 31

39. B
3/4 of 40 = 30 + 7 = 37
100 − X = 37
X = 63

40. A
x/5 = 1/4 * 100
x/5 = 25
x = 125

41. C
1/5X = 5 * 10
1/5X = 50
x = 250

42. A
5z = 52 − 10
Z = 10.4 − 2
Z = 8.4

43. D
25 - Z = 1/5 X 20
25 - Z = 4
Z = 21

44. C
Z = (3/5 * 40) - 15
Z = 24 - 15
Z = 9

45. B
Z = 10 X (1/2 X 60)
Z = 10 X 30
Z = 300

46. C
8 X 10 = 80
1/4Z = 80
Z = 4 X 80
Z = 320

47. A
4 X 15 = 60
1/2 x = 60
X = 120

48. B
5 X 60 = 300
300 = 1/3X
x = 900

49. D
4 X 8 = 32
1/4 X + 20 = 32
1/4 X = 12
x = 48

50. B
3/4 or 100 = 75
500 - x = 75 + 10
500 - x = 85
x = 500 - 85
x = 415

Section III – Reading

1. B

The correct answer because that fact is stated directly in the passage. The passage explains that Anne taught Helen to hear by allowing her to feel the vibrations in her throat.

2. A

We can infer that Anne is a patient teacher because she did not leave or lose her temper when Helen bit or hit her; she just kept trying to teach Helen. Choice B is incorrect because Anne taught Helen to read and talk. Choice C is incorrect because Anne could hear. She was partially blind, not deaf. Choice D is incorrect because it does not have to do with patience.

3. B

The passage states that it was hard for anyone but Anne to understand Helen when she spoke. Choice A is incorrect because the passage does not mention Helen spoke a foreign language. Choice C is incorrect because there is no mention of how quiet or loud Helen's voice was. Choice D is incorrect because we know from reading the passage that Helen did learn to speak.

4. D

This question tests the reader's summarization skills. The other choices A, B, and C focus on portions of the second paragraph that are too narrow and do not relate to the specific portion of text in question. The complexity of the sentence may mislead students into selecting one of these answers, but rearranging or restating the sentence will lead the reader to the correct answer. In addition, choice A makes an assumption that may or may not be true about the intentions of the company, choice B focuses on one product rather than the idea of the products, and choice C makes an assumption about women that may or may not be true and is not supported by the text.

5. D

This question tests the reader's summarization skills. The question is asking very generally about the message of the passage, and the title, "Ways Characters Communicate in Theater," is one indication of that. The other choices A, B, and C are all directly from the text, and therefore readers may be inclined to select one of them, but are too specific to encapsulate the entirety of the passage and its message.

6. B

The paragraph on soliloquies mentions "To be or not to be," and it is from the context of that paragraph that readers may understand that because "To be or not to be" is a soliloquy, Hamlet will be introspective, or thoughtful, while delivering it. It is true that actors deliver soliloquies alone, and may be "solitary" (choice A), but "thoughtful" (choice B) is more true to the overall idea of the paragraph. Readers may choose C because drama and theater can be used interchangeably and the passage mentions that soliloquies are unique to theater (and therefore drama), but this answer is not specific enough to the paragraph in question. Readers may pick up on the theme of life and death and Hamlet's true intentions and select that he is "hopeless" (choice D), but those themes are not discussed either by this paragraph or passage, as a close textual reading and analysis confirms.

7. C
This question tests the reader's grammatical skills. Choice B seems logical, but parenthesis are actually considered to be a stronger break in a sentence than commas are, and along this line of thinking, actually disrupt the sentence more.

Choices A and D make comparisons between theater and film that are simply not made in the passage, and may or may not be true. This detail does clarify the statement that asides are most unique to theater by adding that it is not completely unique to theater, which may have been why the author didn't chose not to delete it and instead used parentheses to designate the detail's importance (choice C).

8. A
Low blood sugar occurs both in diabetics and healthy adults.

9. B
None of the statements are the author's opinion.

10. A
The author's purpose is the inform.

11. A
The only statement that is not a detail is, "A doctor can diagnosis this medical condition by asking the patient questions and testing."

12. A
This sentence is a recommendation.

13. C
Tips for a good night's sleep is the best alternative title for this article.

14. B
Mental activity is helpful for a good night's sleep is cannot be inferred from this article.

15. A
From the passage, one disadvantage of taking naps is they may keep you awake at night.

16. A
Based on the partial table of contents, this book is most likely about how to answer multiple choice.

17. C
To be infamous means to be remembered for an evil or terrible action. Therefore, the word infamy means to remember a bad or terrible thing. Choice A is incorrect because being famous is not the same as being infamous. Choice B is incorrect because the attack on Pearl Harbor was not good. Choice D is incorrect because Pearl Harbor was not forgotten.

18. C
Each answer choice except choice C contains the name of at least one country that was not part of the AXIS powers.

19. D
It is stated in the passage. Choice A is not correct because there was no indication that Japan would attack San Diego. Choice B is incorrect because the attack on Pearl Harbor was a surprise. Choice C is incorrect because Roosevelt was not planning to attack Japan.

20. C
The passage clearly states that Japan planned a surprise attack. They chose that early time to catch the U.S. military off guard. Choice A is incorrect because the military does not sleep late. Choice B is incorrect because there is no law against bombing countries. Choice D is incorrect because it makes no sense.

21. C

This question tests the reader's vocabulary skills. The uses of the negatives "but" and "less," especially right next to each other, may confuse readers into answering with choices A or D, which list words that are antonyms to "militant." Readers may also be confused by the comparison of healthy people with what is being described as an overly healthy person--both people are good, but the reader may look for which one is "worse" in the comparison, and therefore stray toward the antonym words. One key to understanding the meaning of "militant" if the reader is unfamiliar with it is to look at the root of the word; readers can then easily associate it with "military" and gain a sense of what the word signifies: defense (especially considered that the immune system defends the body). Choice C is correct over choice B because "militant" is an adjective, just as the words in choice C are, whereas the words in choice B are nouns.

22. C

This question tests the reader's understanding of function within writing. The other choices are details included surrounding the quoted text, and may therefore confuse the reader. A somewhat contradicts what is said earlier in the paragraph, which is that tests and treatments are improving, and probably doctors are along with them, but the paragraph doesn't actually mention doctors, and the subject of the question is the medicine. Choice B may seem correct to readers who aren't careful to understand that, while the author does mention the large number of people affected, the author is touching on the realities of living with allergies rather about the likelihood of curing all allergies. Similarly, while the author does mention the "balance" of the body, which

is easily associated with "wholesome," the author is not really making an argument and especially is not making an extreme statement that allergy medicines should be outlawed. Again, because the article's tone is on living with allergies, choice C is an appropriate choice that fits with the title and content of the text.

23. B

This question tests the reader's inference skills. The text does not state who is doing the recommending, but the use of the "patients," as well as the general context of the passage, lends itself to the logical partner, "doctors," choice B. The author does mention the recommendation but doesn't present it as her own (i.e. "I recommend that"), so choice A may be eliminated. It may seem plausible that people with allergies (choice D) may recommend medicines or products to other people with allergies, but the text does not necessarily support this interaction taking place. Choice C may be selected because the EpiPen is specifically mentioned, but the use of the phrase "such as" when it is introduced is not limiting enough to assume the recommendation is coming from its creators.

24. D

This question tests the reader's global understanding of the text. Choice D includes the main topics of the three body paragraphs, and isn't too focused on a specific aspect or quote from the text, as the other questions are, giving a skewed summary of what the author intended. The reader may be drawn to choice B because of the title of the passage and the use of words like "better," but the message of the passage is larger and more general than this.

25. B
Reading the document posted to the Human Resources website is optional.

26. B
The document is recommended changes and have not be implemented yet.

27. C
This question tests the reader's summarization skills. The use of the word "actually" in describing what kind of people poets are, as well as other moments like this, may lead readers to selecting choices B or D, but the author is more information than trying to persuade readers. The author gives no indication that she loves poetry (choice B) or that people, students specifically (D), should write poems. Choice A is incorrect because the style and content of this paragraph do not match those of a foreword; forewords usually focus on the history or ideas of a specific poem to introduce it more fully and help it stand out against other poems. The author here focuses on several poems and gives broad statements. Instead, she tells a kind of story about poems, giving three very broad time periods in which to discuss them, thereby giving a brief history of poetry, as choice C states.

28. A
This question tests the reader's summarization skills. Key words in the topic sentences of each of the paragraphs ("oldest," "Renaissance," "modern") should give the reader an idea that the author is moving chronologically. The opening and closing sentence-paragraphs are broad and talk generally. B seems reasonable, but epic poems are mentioned in two paragraphs, eliminating the idea that only new types of poems are used in each paragraph. Choice C is also easily eliminated because the author clearly mentions several different poets, groups of people, and poems. Choice D also seems reasonable, considering that the author does move from older forms of poetry to newer forms, but use of "so (that)" makes this statement false, for the author gives no indication that she is rushing (the paragraphs are about the same size) or that she prefers modern poetry.

29. D
This question tests the reader's attention to detail. The key word is "invented"--it ties together the Mesopotamians, who invented the written word, and the fact that they, as the inventors, also invented and used poetry. The other selections focus on other details mentioned in the passage, such as that the Renaissance's admiration of the Greeks (choice C) and that Beowulf is in Old English (choice A). Choice B may seem like an attractive answer because it is unlike the others and because the idea of heroes seems rooted in ancient and early civilizations.

30. B
This question tests the reader's vocabulary and contextualization skills. "Telling" is not an unusual word, but it may be used here in a way that is not familiar to readers, as an adjective rather than a verb in gerund form. A may seem like the obvious answer to a reader looking for a verb to match the use they are familiar with. If the reader understands that the word is being used as an adjective and that choice A is a ploy, they may opt to select choice D, "wordy," but it does not make sense in context. Choice C can be easily eliminated, and doesn't have any connection to the paragraph or passage. "Significant" (choice B) makes sense con-

textually, especially relative to the phrase "give insight" used later in the sentence.

31. C
Dauntless: adj. Invulnerable to fear or intimidation.

32. A
Juxtaposed: adj. Placed side by side often for comparison or contrast.

33. B
Regicide: v. killing of a king.

34. A
Pernicious: adj. Causing much harm in a subtle way.

35. A
Immune: adj. Resistant to a particular infection or toxin owing to the presence of specific antibodies.

36. B
Nimble: adj. Quick and light in movement or action.

37. A
Queries: n. Questions or inquiries.

38. C
Depose: To remove (a leader) from (high) office, without killing the incumbent.

39. D
Pedestrian: Ordinary, dull; everyday; unexceptional.

40. B
Petulant: adj. Childishly irritable.

41. D
Pesticide: n. A substance used for destroying insects or other organisms harmful to cultivated plants or to animals.

42. D
Salient: adj. worthy or note or relevant.

43. B
Sedentary: adj. not moving or sitting in one place.

44. A
Famine: n. extreme scarcity of food.

45. A
Stint: n. To be sparing, thrifty.

46. A
Precipitate: v. to rain.

47. C
Edify: v. To instruct or improve morally or intellectually.

48. B
Egress: n. An exit or way out.

49. A
Recede: v. To move back, to move away.

50. A
Confidential: adj. kept secret within a certain circle of persons; not intended to be known publicly.

Section IV – Mathematics

1. D
As the lawn is square, the length of one side will be the square root of the area. $\sqrt{62,500} = 250$ meters. So, the perimeter is 4 times the length of one side:

250 * 4 = 1000 meters.

Since each meter costs $5.5, the total cost of the fence will be 1000 * 5.5 = $5,500.

2. A
First add all the numbers 3 + 6 + 27 + 13 + 6 + 8 + 12 + 20 + 5 + 10 = 110. Then divide by 10 (the number of data provided) = 110/10 = 11

3. C
In the figure, we are given a large circle and a small circle inside it; with the diameter equal to the radius of the large one. The diameter of the small circle is 4 cm. This means that its radius is 2 cm. Since the diameter of the small circle is the radius of the large circle, the radius of the large circle is 4 cm. The area of a circle is calculated by: πr^2 where r is the radius.

Area of the small circle: $\pi(2)^2 = 4\pi$

Area of the large circle: $\pi(4)^2 = 16\pi$

The difference area is found by:

Area of the large circle - Area of the small circle = $16\pi - 4\pi = 12\pi$

4. A
4,210,987 – 210,078 is about 4,000,000.

5. B
The distribution is at three different rates and amounts:

$6.4 per 20 kilograms to 15 shops ... 20 * 15 = 300 kilograms distributed

$3.4 per 10 kilograms to 12 shops ... 10 * 12 = 120 kilograms distributed

550 - (300 + 120) = 550 - 420 = 130 kilograms left. This amount is distributed by 5 kilogram portions. So, this means that there are 130/5 =

26 shops.

$1.8 per 130 kilograms.

We need to find the amount he earned overall these distributions.

$6.4 per 20 kilograms : 6.4 * 15 = $96 for 300 kilograms

$3.4 per 10 kilograms : 3.4 * 12 = $40.8 for 120 kilograms

$1.8 per 5 kilograms : 1.8 * 26 = $46.8 for 130 kilograms

So, he earned 96 + 40.8 + 46.8 = $ 183.6

The total distribution cost is given as $10

The profit is found by: Money earned - money spent ... It is important to remember that he bought 550 kilograms of potatoes for $165 at the beginning:

Profit = 183.6 - 10 - 165 = $8.6

6. C
Equilateral triangle with 9 cm sides
Perimeter = 9+9+9
= 27 cm.

7. B
We check the fractions taking place in the question. We see that there is a "half" (that is 1/2) and 3/7. So, we multiply the denominators of these fractions to decide how to name the total money. We say that Mr. Johnson has 14x at the beginning; he gives half of this, meaning 7x, to his family. $250 to his landlord. He has 3/7 of his money left. 3/7 of 14x is equal to:

14x * (3/7) = 6x

So,

Spent money is: 7x + 250

Unspent money is: 6x

Total money is: 14x

We write an equation: total money = spent money + unspent money

14x = 7x + 250 + 6x

14x - 7x - 6x = 250

x = 250

We are asked to find the total money that is 14x:

14x = 14 * 250 = $3500

8. A
The probability that the 1st ball drawn is red = 4/11. The probability that the 2nd ball drawn is green = 5/10. The combined probability will then be 4/11 X 5/10 = 20/110 = 2/11.

9. B
There are 52 cards. Smith has 16 cards in which he can win. Therefore, his winning probability in a single game will be 16/52. Simon has 20 cards in which he can win, so his probability of winning in a single draw is 20/52.

10. A
The wheel travels $2\pi r$ distance when it makes one revolution. Here, r stands for the radius. The radius is given as 25 cm in the figure. So,

$2\pi r = 2\pi * 25 = 50\pi$ cm is the distance travelled in one revolution.

In 175 revolutions: $175 * 50\pi = 8750\pi$ cm is travelled.

We are asked to find the distance in meter.

1 m = 100 cm So;

8750π cm = 8750π / 100 = 87.5π m

11. B
The formula of the volume of cylinder is the base area multiplied by the height. As the formula:

Volume of a cylinder = $\pi r^2 h$. Where π is 3.142, r is radius of the cross sectional area, and h is the height.

We know that the diameter is 5 meters, so the radius is 5/2 = 2.5 meters.

The volume is: V = 3.142 * 2.52 * 12 = 235.65 m³.

12. D
Two parallel lines (m & side AB) intersected by side AC. This means that 50° and a angles are interior angles. So:
a = 50° (interior angles).

13. B
215 X 65 = 13975, or about 13,500.

14. D
A common denominator is needed, 12-10/15 = 2/15

15. C
1 hour is equal to 3600 seconds and 1 kilometer is equal to 1000 meters. Therefore, a train covers 72000 meters in 36000 seconds.

Distance covered in 12 seconds = 12 × 72000/3600 = 240 meters.

16. B
Number of absent students = 83 – 72 = 11

Percentage of absent students is found by proportioning the number of absent students to total number of students in the class = (11 * 100)/83 = 13.25

Checking the answers, we round 13.25 to the nearest whole number: 13%

17. D
As shown in the figure, two parallel lines intersecting with a third line with angle of 75°.

x = 75° (corresponding angles)

x + y = 180° (supplementary angles) ... inserting the value of x here:

y = 180° - 75°
y = 105°

18. B
Time taken to travel from A to B in seconds = 3600 + (13 X 60) = 3600 + 780 = 4380 seconds.
Total time spent at traffic signals = 80 X 5 = 400 seconds.
The remaining driving time = 4380 – 400 = 3980 seconds = 3980/3600 = 1.106 hours
The speed will be 65/1.106 = 58.77 km/hr

19. B
I = ?, r = 3%, t = 2 years, P = 6000.
Convert the rate to decimal. 3% = 0.03. Then plug in variables into the simple interest formula. I = P x r x t, I = 6000 x 0.03 x 2, I = $360

20. D
We understand that each of the n employees earn s amount of salary weekly. This means that one employee earns s salary weekly. So; Richard has ns amount of money to employ n employees for a week.

We are asked to find the number of days n employees can be employed with x amount of money. We can do simple direct proportion:

If Richard can employ n employees for 7 days with ns amount of money,

Richard can employ n employees for y days with x amount of money ... y is the number of days we need to find.

We can do cross multiplication:

y = (x * 7)/(ns)

y = 7x/ns

21. C
Cash assets = 75600
Building assets after one year = 80500 X 1.1 = $88550
Machinery assets after one year = 125000 X 0.8 = 100,000
Total value of assets = 264150

22. C
Volume of a cylinder is π x r^2 x h
Diameter = 5 ft. so radius is 2.5 ft.
Volume of the cylinder = π x 2.5^2 x 2
= π x 6.25 x 2 = 12.5 π
Approximate π to 3.142
Volume of the cylinder = 39.25

Volume of a rectangle = height X width X length.
= 5 X 5 X 4 = 100

Total volume = Volume of rectangular solid + volume of cylinder
Total volume = 100 + 39.25
Total volume = 139.25 ft^3 or approximately 140 ft^3

23. C
Total earnings = 25000 + 500 + 860 = $26360
Food and Clothing expenses = 0.4 X 26360 = 10544
Children's education expense = 26360 X 0.1 = $2636
Utility Bills = $800
Savings = 26360 – 10544 – 2636 – 800 = $12380
Percent savings = 100 X 12380/26360 = 47%

24. B
Percentage attendance will be 85%

25. B
1st prize winner receives, 7 X
1050/15 = $490
3rd price winner receives, 3 X
1050/15 = $210
Difference = 490 – 210 = $280

26. A
At 100% efficiency 1 machine
produces 1450/10 = 145 m of cloth.

At 95% efficiency, 4 machines
produce (4 * 145 * 95)/100 = 551 m
of cloth.

At 90% efficiency, 6 machines
produce (6 * 145 * 90)/100 = 783 m
of cloth.

Total cloth produced by all 10
machines = 551 + 783 = 1334 m

Since the information provided and
the question are based on 8 hours,
we did not need to use time to reach
the answer.

27. B
If the driver increases their speed
from 's' to 'x' miles per hour, the
equation will be h - sh/x.

28. D
Distance covered by the car = 60 X
3.5 = 210 km.
Time required by the motorbike =
210/40 = 5.25 hr.

29. C
Let the grandson's age be X and the
grandfather's age be Y. According we
have,
y = 8x
and
y + 6 = 5(x + 6)
Solving we get y = 64

30. B
5n + (19 – 2)) = 67, 5n + 17 = 67, 5n =
67 -17, 5n = 50, n = 50/5 = 10

31. C
The ratio between apples and oranges
is 2 to 8 or 2:8. Bring to the lowest
terms by dividing both sides by 2
gives 1:4.

32. B
5x + 21 = 66, 5x = 66 – 21 = 45, 5x =
45, x = 45/5 = 9

33. B
Multiples of 3 are 3, 6, 9 and Multiples of 9 are 9, 18, therefore the least
common multiple is 9.

34. A
The ratio between black and blue
pens is 7 to 28 or 7:28. Bring to the
lowest terms by dividing both sides by
7 gives 1:4.

35. C
32 + 356 = 388. Therefore X + 388 =
920, X = 920 – 388 = 532

36. B
The ratio between green, red and blue
candies is 3:12:9. Bring to the lowest
terms by dividing the sides by 3 gives
1:4:3.

37. A
12 x 12 = 144, so 144/x = 12
144 = 12X
X = 12

38. A
34 x 2 = 68, so A – 68 = 18, A = 68 +
18 = 86

39. D
X% of 120 = 30, so X = 30/120 x
100/1 = 300/12 = 25

40. B
X * (25% of 100) = 75,
25X = 75, X = 75/25 = 3

41. D
The ratio between people sitting and

standing is 12 to 3 or 12:3. Bring to the lowest terms by dividing both sides by 3 gives 4:1.

42. D
X% of 250 = 50, so X = 50/250 x 100/1= 100/5 = 20

43. B
The number is 41.061. The last digit 1 is less than 5, and so it's discarded. The next digit, 6, is greater than 5 and so is removed and 1 is added to the next digit to the left. Answer = 41.1

44. D
Multiples of 3 are 3, 6, 9, 12 and Multiples of 4 are 4, 8, 12, Therefore the least common multiple is 12.

45. D
The number is 51.738. The last digit is greater than 5, so it is removed and 1 is added to the next number to the left. Answer = 51.74.

46. C
The ratio between gold, silver and bronze coins is 2:6:8. Bring to the lowest terms by dividing each side by 2 gives 1:3:4.

47. A
Multiples of 8 are 8, 16, 24 and multiples of 12 are 12, 24, 36, so the least common multiple is 24.

48. D
3x = 20 + 7 = 27, x = 27/3, x = 9.

49. C
Multiples of 2 are 2, 4, 6 and Multiples of 3 are 3, 6, so the least common is 6.

50. C
23 = 2a + 13, 23 – 13 = 2a, 10 = 2a, a = 10/2 = 5.
51. B

301.311, since the last digit is less than 5 it is removed. Answer = 301.31.

52. C
Multiples of 5 are 5, 10, 15, 20 and multiples of 3 are 3, 6, 9, 12, 15... so the answer is 15.

53. B
124 = 12c - 20, 124 + 20 = 12c, 144 = 12c, c = 144/12 = 12.

54. A
The number is 765.3682. The last digit, 2, is less than 5, so it is discarded. Answer = 765.368.

55. C
Add the whole numbers and then add the fractions, therefore 3 + 5 {8/9 + 5/6}, then find a common denominator for the fractions 8 {16/18 + 15/18} = 8 31/18, then simplify to 9 13/18

56. A
The number is 731.614. The last digit is less than 5 so it is removed. Answer = 731.6

57. D
Subtract the whole numbers and then subtract the fractions, therefore 7 - 2 {4/5 - 2/5}, the fractions has a common denominator, so 5 (4-2/5) = 5 2/5.

58. A
The number is 51.738. The last digit, 2, is less than 5, so it is discarded. Answer = 765.368.

59. C
Three plus a number times 7 equals 42. Let X be the number.
(3 + X) times 7 = 42
7(3 + X) = 42

60. C
5205 / 25 = 208.20 or, about 208.

Section V – Language Arts

1. B
Comma separate phrases.

2. C
The comma separates phrases.

3. D
To travel around the globe, you have to drive 25,000 miles.

4. A
The dog loved chasing bones, but never ate them; it was running that he enjoyed.

5. B
The semicolon links independent clauses with a conjunction (therefore).

6. C
Use a semicolon in a list where the list items have internal punctuation, such as "Key West, Florida."

7. C
The semicolon links independent clauses. An independent clause can form a complete sentence by itself.

8. A
The semicolon links independent clauses with a conjunction (However).

9. B
The semicolon links independent clauses. An independent clause can form a complete sentence by itself.

10. B
Titles preceding names are capitalized, but not titles that follow names.

11. C
Holidays are capitalized; the names of seasons are not.

12. C
The names of seasons are not capitalized because they are generic nouns. If a season is used in a title, such as the "Fall 2012 semester," Fall 2012 is a title and capitalized.

13. A
The names of languages and countries are capitalized.

14. C
Quoted speech is not capitalized.

15. A
Periods and events are capitalized but not century numbers.

16. C
Brand names are capitalized.

17. B
Brand names are capitalized but generic terms such as 'french fries' are not.

18. C
The names of sports teams, as proper nouns, are capitalized.

19. A
North, south, east, and west when used as sections of the country, are capitalized, but not as compass directions

20. C
The major words in the titles of books, articles, and songs are capitalized. (but not short prepositions or the articles "the," "a," or "an," if they are not the first word of the title)

21. A
Titles of publications are capitalized.

22. A
Singular subjects. "The Chinese" is plural, and "a citizen of Bermuda" is singular.

23. A
Disease is singular.

24. C
Articles of speech. Both dog and cat in this sentence are singular and require the article 'a.'

25. A
Principle vs. Principal. A principal is the First, highest, or foremost in importance, or rank. A principle is a fundamental truth.

26. D
A vs. An. The article 'a' come before a consonant and 'an' comes before a vowel.

27. A
Accept vs. Except. To accept is to receive or to say yes. Except is a preposition that means excluding.

28. A
Advise vs. Advice. To advise is to give advice. Advice is an opinion that someone offers.

29. C
Adapt vs. Adopt.
Adapt means "to change." Usually we adapt to someone or something. Adopt means "to take as one's own."

30. D
Among vs. Between. Among is for more than 2 items, and between is only for 2 items.

When he's among friends (many or more than 2), Robert seems confident, but, between you and I (two), he is very shy.

31. D
At vs. About. 'At' refers to a specific time and 'about' refers to a more general time. A common usage is 'at about 10,' but it isn't proper grammar.

32. B
Beside vs. Besides. 'Beside' means next to, and 'besides' means in addition to.

33. A
Can vs. May. 'Can' refers to ability and 'may' refers to permission.

Although John can swim (is able to. very well, he may not (permission. be allowed to swim in the pool.

34. B
Continual vs. Continuous. 'Continuous' means a time with no interruption and 'continual' means a time with interruption.

Her continual absences (with interruption – not always absent. caused a continuous disruption (the disruption was ongoing without interruption at the office.

35. A
Emigrate vs. Immigrate. 'To emigrate' means to leave one's country and to 'immigrate' means to come to a country.

36. B
Further vs. Farther. 'Farther' is used for physical distance, and 'further' is used for figurative distance.

37. B
Former vs. Latter. 'Former' refers to the first of two things, 'latter' to the second.

38. B
Fewer vs. Less. 'Fewer' is used with countables and 'less' is used with uncountables.

39. A
'However' usage. 'However' usually has a comma before and after.

40. D
'However' Usage. 'However' usually has a comma before and after.

41. A
The third conditional is used for talking about an unreal situation (that did not happen) in the past. For example, "If I had studied harder, [if clause] I would have passed the exam [main clause]. Which is the same as, "I failed the exam, because I didn't study hard enough."

42. D
The third conditional is used for talking about an unreal situation (that did not happen) in the past. For example, "If I had studied harder, [if clause] I would have passed the exam [main clause]. Which is the same as, "I failed the exam, because I didn't study hard enough."

43. B
Double negative sentence. In double negative sentences, one negative is replaced with 'any.'

44. C
Double negative sentence. In double negative sentences, one negative is replaced with 'any.'

45. D
Present perfect. You cannot use the present perfect with specific time expressions such as, yesterday, one year ago, last week, when I was a child, at that moment, that day, one day, etc. The Present Perfect is used with unspecific expressions such as, ever, never, once, many times, several times, before, so far, already, yet, etc.

46. C
Present perfect. You cannot use the Present Perfect with specific time expressions such as, yesterday, one year ago, last week, when I was a child, at that moment, that day, one day, etc. The Present Perfect is used with unspecific expressions such as, ever, never, once, many times, several times, before, so far, already, yet, etc.

47. A
Went vs. Gone. Went is the simple past tense. Gone is used in the past perfect.

48. B
Went vs. Gone. 'Went' is the simple past tense. 'Gone' is used in the past perfect.

49. C
50. B
51. A
52. A
53. C
54. D
55. C
56. D
57. C
58. A
59. C
60. D

Practice Test Questions Set 2

The questions below are not the same as you will find on the HSPT® - that would be too easy! And nobody knows what the questions will be and they change all the time. Below are general questions that cover the same subject areas as the HSPT®. So the format and exact wording of the questions may differ slightly, and change from year to year, if you can answer the questions below, you will have no problem with the HSPT®.

For the best results, take these Practice Test Questions as if it were the real exam. Set aside time when you will not be disturbed, and a location that is quiet and free of distractions. Read the instructions carefully, read each question carefully, and answer to the best of your ability.
Use the bubble answer sheets provided. When you have completed the Practice Questions, check your answer against the Answer Key and read the explanation provided.

Do not attempt more than one set of practice test questions in one day. After completing the first practice test, wait two or three days before attempting the second set of questions.

Section I – Verbal Skills

Questions: 50
Time: 16 Minutes

Section II – Quantitative Skills

Questions: 50
Time: 30 Minutes

Section III – Reading & Vocabulary

Questions: 60
Time: 25 Minutes

Section IV – Math

Questions: 60
Time: 45 Minutes

Section V – Language

Questions: 60
Time: 25 Minutes

Verbal Skills

1. Ⓐ Ⓑ Ⓒ Ⓓ
2. Ⓐ Ⓑ Ⓒ Ⓓ
3. Ⓐ Ⓑ Ⓒ Ⓓ
4. Ⓐ Ⓑ Ⓒ Ⓓ
5. Ⓐ Ⓑ Ⓒ Ⓓ
6. Ⓐ Ⓑ Ⓒ Ⓓ
7. Ⓐ Ⓑ Ⓒ Ⓓ
8. Ⓐ Ⓑ Ⓒ Ⓓ
9. Ⓐ Ⓑ Ⓒ Ⓓ
10. Ⓐ Ⓑ Ⓒ Ⓓ
11. Ⓐ Ⓑ Ⓒ Ⓓ
12. Ⓐ Ⓑ Ⓒ Ⓓ
13. Ⓐ Ⓑ Ⓒ Ⓓ
14. Ⓐ Ⓑ Ⓒ Ⓓ
15. Ⓐ Ⓑ Ⓒ Ⓓ
16. Ⓐ Ⓑ Ⓒ Ⓓ
17. Ⓐ Ⓑ Ⓒ Ⓓ

18. Ⓐ Ⓑ Ⓒ Ⓓ
19. Ⓐ Ⓑ Ⓒ Ⓓ
20. Ⓐ Ⓑ Ⓒ Ⓓ
21. Ⓐ Ⓑ Ⓒ Ⓓ
22. Ⓐ Ⓑ Ⓒ Ⓓ
23. Ⓐ Ⓑ Ⓒ Ⓓ
24. Ⓐ Ⓑ Ⓒ Ⓓ
25. Ⓐ Ⓑ Ⓒ Ⓓ
26. Ⓐ Ⓑ Ⓒ Ⓓ
27. Ⓐ Ⓑ Ⓒ Ⓓ
28. Ⓐ Ⓑ Ⓒ Ⓓ
29. Ⓐ Ⓑ Ⓒ Ⓓ
30. Ⓐ Ⓑ Ⓒ Ⓓ
31. Ⓐ Ⓑ Ⓒ Ⓓ
32. Ⓐ Ⓑ Ⓒ Ⓓ
33. Ⓐ Ⓑ Ⓒ Ⓓ
34. Ⓐ Ⓑ Ⓒ Ⓓ

35. Ⓐ Ⓑ Ⓒ Ⓓ
36. Ⓐ Ⓑ Ⓒ Ⓓ
37. Ⓐ Ⓑ Ⓒ Ⓓ
38. Ⓐ Ⓑ Ⓒ Ⓓ
39. Ⓐ Ⓑ Ⓒ Ⓓ
40. Ⓐ Ⓑ Ⓒ Ⓓ
41. Ⓐ Ⓑ Ⓒ Ⓓ
42. Ⓐ Ⓑ Ⓒ Ⓓ
43. Ⓐ Ⓑ Ⓒ Ⓓ
44. Ⓐ Ⓑ Ⓒ Ⓓ
45. Ⓐ Ⓑ Ⓒ Ⓓ
46. Ⓐ Ⓑ Ⓒ Ⓓ
47. Ⓐ Ⓑ Ⓒ Ⓓ
48. Ⓐ Ⓑ Ⓒ Ⓓ
49. Ⓐ Ⓑ Ⓒ Ⓓ
50. Ⓐ Ⓑ Ⓒ Ⓓ

Quantitative Skills

1. A B C D
2. A B C D
3. A B C D
4. A B C D
5. A B C D
6. A B C D
7. A B C D
8. A B C D
9. A B C D
10. A B C D
11. A B C D
12. A B C D
13. A B C D
14. A B C D
15. A B C D
16. A B C D
17. A B C D

18. A B C D
19. A B C D
20. A B C D
21. A B C D
22. A B C D
23. A B C D
24. A B C D
25. A B C D
26. A B C D
27. A B C D
28. A B C D
29. A B C D
30. A B C D
31. A B C D
32. A B C D
33. A B C D
34. A B C D

35. A B C D
36. A B C D
37. A B C D
38. A B C D
39. A B C D
40. A B C D
41. A B C D
42. A B C D
43. A B C D
44. A B C D
45. A B C D
46. A B C D
47. A B C D
48. A B C D
49. A B C D
50. A B C D

Reading Comprehension and Vocabulary

1. (A) (B) (C) (D)
2. (A) (B) (C) (D)
3. (A) (B) (C) (D)
4. (A) (B) (C) (D)
5. (A) (B) (C) (D)
6. (A) (B) (C) (D)
7. (A) (B) (C) (D)
8. (A) (B) (C) (D)
9. (A) (B) (C) (D)
10. (A) (B) (C) (D)
11. (A) (B) (C) (D)
12. (A) (B) (C) (D)
13. (A) (B) (C) (D)
14. (A) (B) (C) (D)
15. (A) (B) (C) (D)
16. (A) (B) (C) (D)
17. (A) (B) (C) (D)

18. (A) (B) (C) (D)
19. (A) (B) (C) (D)
20. (A) (B) (C) (D)
21. (A) (B) (C) (D)
22. (A) (B) (C) (D)
23. (A) (B) (C) (D)
24. (A) (B) (C) (D)
25. (A) (B) (C) (D)
26. (A) (B) (C) (D)
27. (A) (B) (C) (D)
28. (A) (B) (C) (D)
29. (A) (B) (C) (D)
30. (A) (B) (C) (D)
31. (A) (B) (C) (D)
32. (A) (B) (C) (D)
33. (A) (B) (C) (D)
34. (A) (B) (C) (D)

35. (A) (B) (C) (D)
36. (A) (B) (C) (D)
37. (A) (B) (C) (D)
38. (A) (B) (C) (D)
39. (A) (B) (C) (D)
40. (A) (B) (C) (D)
41. (A) (B) (C) (D)
42. (A) (B) (C) (D)
43. (A) (B) (C) (D)
44. (A) (B) (C) (D)
45. (A) (B) (C) (D)
46. (A) (B) (C) (D)
47. (A) (B) (C) (D)
48. (A) (B) (C) (D)
49. (A) (B) (C) (D)
50. (A) (B) (C) (D)

Mathematics

1. (A) (B) (C) (D)	21. (A) (B) (C) (D)	41. (A) (B) (C) (D)
2. (A) (B) (C) (D)	22. (A) (B) (C) (D)	42. (A) (B) (C) (D)
3. (A) (B) (C) (D)	23. (A) (B) (C) (D)	43. (A) (B) (C) (D)
4. (A) (B) (C) (D)	24. (A) (B) (C) (D)	44. (A) (B) (C) (D)
5. (A) (B) (C) (D)	25. (A) (B) (C) (D)	45. (A) (B) (C) (D)
6. (A) (B) (C) (D)	26. (A) (B) (C) (D)	46. (A) (B) (C) (D)
7. (A) (B) (C) (D)	27. (A) (B) (C) (D)	47. (A) (B) (C) (D)
8. (A) (B) (C) (D)	28. (A) (B) (C) (D)	48. (A) (B) (C) (D)
9. (A) (B) (C) (D)	29. (A) (B) (C) (D)	49. (A) (B) (C) (D)
10. (A) (B) (C) (D)	30. (A) (B) (C) (D)	50. (A) (B) (C) (D)
11. (A) (B) (C) (D)	31. (A) (B) (C) (D)	51. (A) (B) (C) (D)
12. (A) (B) (C) (D)	32. (A) (B) (C) (D)	52. (A) (B) (C) (D)
13. (A) (B) (C) (D)	33. (A) (B) (C) (D)	53. (A) (B) (C) (D)
14. (A) (B) (C) (D)	34. (A) (B) (C) (D)	54. (A) (B) (C) (D)
15. (A) (B) (C) (D)	35. (A) (B) (C) (D)	55. (A) (B) (C) (D)
16. (A) (B) (C) (D)	36. (A) (B) (C) (D)	56. (A) (B) (C) (D)
17. (A) (B) (C) (D)	37. (A) (B) (C) (D)	57. (A) (B) (C) (D)
18. (A) (B) (C) (D)	38. (A) (B) (C) (D)	58. (A) (B) (C) (D)
19. (A) (B) (C) (D)	39. (A) (B) (C) (D)	59. (A) (B) (C) (D)
20. (A) (B) (C) (D)	40. (A) (B) (C) (D)	60. (A) (B) (C) (D)

Language Arts

1. (A) (B) (C) (D)   21. (A) (B) (C) (D)   41. (A) (B) (C) (D)

2. (A) (B) (C) (D)   22. (A) (B) (C) (D)   42. (A) (B) (C) (D)

3. (A) (B) (C) (D)   23. (A) (B) (C) (D)   43. (A) (B) (C) (D)

4. (A) (B) (C) (D)   24. (A) (B) (C) (D)   44. (A) (B) (C) (D)

5. (A) (B) (C) (D)   25. (A) (B) (C) (D)   45. (A) (B) (C) (D)

6. (A) (B) (C) (D)   26. (A) (B) (C) (D)   46. (A) (B) (C) (D)

7. (A) (B) (C) (D)   27. (A) (B) (C) (D)   47. (A) (B) (C) (D)

8. (A) (B) (C) (D)   28. (A) (B) (C) (D)   48. (A) (B) (C) (D)

9. (A) (B) (C) (D)   29. (A) (B) (C) (D)   49. (A) (B) (C) (D)

10. (A) (B) (C) (D)   30. (A) (B) (C) (D)   50. (A) (B) (C) (D)

11. (A) (B) (C) (D)   31. (A) (B) (C) (D)   51. (A) (B) (C) (D)

12. (A) (B) (C) (D)   32. (A) (B) (C) (D)   52. (A) (B) (C) (D)

13. (A) (B) (C) (D)   33. (A) (B) (C) (D)   53. (A) (B) (C) (D)

14. (A) (B) (C) (D)   34. (A) (B) (C) (D)   54. (A) (B) (C) (D)

15. (A) (B) (C) (D)   35. (A) (B) (C) (D)   55. (A) (B) (C) (D)

16. (A) (B) (C) (D)   36. (A) (B) (C) (D)   56. (A) (B) (C) (D)

17. (A) (B) (C) (D)   37. (A) (B) (C) (D)   57. (A) (B) (C) (D)

18. (A) (B) (C) (D)   38. (A) (B) (C) (D)   58. (A) (B) (C) (D)

19. (A) (B) (C) (D)   39. (A) (B) (C) (D)   59. (A) (B) (C) (D)

20. (A) (B) (C) (D)   40. (A) (B) (C) (D)   60. (A) (B) (C) (D)

Section I – Verbal Skills

Choose the word with the same relationship as the given pair.

1. Acting : Theater :: Gambling : _____

    a. Gym
    b. Bar
    c. Club
    d. Casino

2. Pork : Pig :: Beef : _____

    a. Herd
    b. Farmer
    c. Cow
    d. Lamb

3. Fruit : Banana :: Mammal : _____

    a. Rabbit
    b. Snake
    c. Fish
    d. Sparrow

4. Slumber : Sleep :: Bog : _____

    a. Dream
    b. Foray
    c. Swamp
    d. Night

5. Petal: Flower :: Fur : _____

    a. Coat
    b. Warm
    c. Woman
    d. Rabbit

6. Present : Birthday :: Reward : _____

    a. Accomplishment
    b. Medal
    c. Acceptance
    d. Cash

7. Shovel : Dig :: Scissors : _____

    a. Scoop
    b. Carry
    c. Snip
    d. Rip

8. Finger : Hand :: Leg : _____

    a. Body
    b. Foot
    c. Toe
    d. Hip

Choose the pair with the same relationship

9. Zoology : Animals

    a. Ecology : Pollution
    b. Botany : Plants
    c. Chemistry : Atoms
    d. History : People

10. Child : Human

    a. Dog : Pet
    b. Kitten : Cat
    c. Cow : Milk
    d. Bird : Robin

11. **Wax : Candle**

    a. Ink : Pen
    b. Clay : Bowl
    c. String : Kite
    d. Liquid : Cup

12. **Choose the synonym pair.**

    a. Pensive and Alibi
    b. Able and Competent
    c. Allow and Forbid
    d. Capable and Honest

13. **Choose the synonym pair.**

    a. Antidote and Cure
    b. Potion and Lure
    c. Craft and Magic
    d. Affiliation and Member

14. **Choose the synonym pair.**

    a. Quality and Measure
    b. Compensation and Wage
    c. Consensus and Agreement
    d. Command and Obey

15. **Choose the synonym pair.**

    a. Magnify and Amplify
    b. Emphasize and Trace
    c. Blot and Shade
    d. Stamina and Agility

16. **Choose the synonym pair.**

    a. Haphazard and Order
    b. Immaculate and Perfect
    c. Clean and Fresh
    d. Debt and Payment

17. **Choose the synonym pair.**

    a. Haste and Deadline
    b. Manuscript and Bible
    c. Feasible and Viable
    d. Priest and Priestess

18. **Choose the synonym pair.**

    a. Deduct and Induct
    b. Reason and Rationale
    c. Genuine and Congenial
    d. Fraudulent and Errant

19. **Choose the synonym pair.**

    a. Tinge and Touch
    b. Spot and Dirt
    c. Slur and Narration
    d. Rant and Ask

20. **Choose the synonym pair.**

    a. Context and Content
    b. Flourish and Colorful
    c. Gist and Summary
    d. Speculate and Witness

21. **Choose the synonym pair.**

    a. Problem and Solution
    b. Solute and Solvent
    c. Initiate and Instigate
    d. Lament and Joyful

22. **Choose the synonym pair.**

    a. Expertise and Specialty
    b. Professionalism and Diploma
    c. Accentuate and Articulate
    d. Brazen and Bashful

Choose the synonym of the underlined word.

23. Her <u>amazing</u> talent wowed the audience during the contest.

    a. Ugly

    b. Extraordinary

    c. Plain

    d. Ordinary

24. Jean was <u>furious</u> when her little brother destroyed her favorite doll.

    a. Happy

    b. Lonely

    c. Angry

    d. Surprised

25. We will <u>inquire</u> about our scores on the pop quiz.

    a. Ask

    b. Complain

    c. Suggest

    d. Command

26. The car accident was an <u>awful</u> experience the victims want to forget.

    a. Terrible

    b. Pleasant

    c. Wonderful

    d. Unforgettable

27. Cinderella's <u>wicked</u> stepmother failed in the end.

    a. Understanding

    b. Happy

    c. Evil

    d. Supportive

28.

All colonels are officers.
All officers are soldiers.
No colonels are soldiers.

If the first 2 statements are true, then the third statement is:

True   False   Uncertain

29.

No houses on Appleby Street or Francisco streets cost more than $500,000. My house is not on Appleby or Francisco Street.
My house does not cost more than $500,000.

If the first 2 statements are true, then the third statement is:

True   False   Uncertain

30.

Some tropical fish are very sensitive.
I have many types of tropical fish.
Some of my fish are very sensitive.

If the first 2 statements are true, then the third statement is:

True   False   Uncertain

31.

Most people in oil producing countries are rich.
I live in an oil producing country.
I am rich.

If the first 2 statements are true, then the third statement is:

True   False   Uncertain

32.

Science can explain all events. Making a decision is an event. Science cannot explain how I make a decision.

If the first 2 statements are true, then the third statement is:

True False Uncertain

33.

Doctors can sometimes predict epidemics.
Bird Flu is becoming an epidemic. Doctors know where bird flu will spread.

If the first 2 statements are true, then the third statement is:

True False Uncertain

34.

That store sells new and used books.
My textbook is used.
My textbook came from that store.

If the first 2 statements are true, then the third statement is:

True False Uncertain

35. Which does not belong?

   a. Plate
   b. Spoon
   c. Dish
   d. Dinner

36. Which does not belong?

   a. Moon
   b. Venus
   c. Neptune
   d. Saturn

37. Which does not belong?

   a. Cat
   b. Lion
   c. Tiger
   d. Fox

38. Which does not belong?

   a. Tree
   b. Garden
   c. Bush
   d. Shrub

39. Which does not belong?

   a. Grass
   b. Flowers
   c. Lawn
   d. Weeds

Choose the word that completes the relationship.

**40. Beautiful : Attractive
Powerful : _____**

   a. Influential
   b. Poor
   c. Deprived
   d. Gorgeous

41. Chaos : Order ::
Reckless : _____

    a. Bitter

    b. Grief

    c. Joy

    d. Careful

42. Servant : Master ::
Predator : _____

    a. Nurse

    b. Pupil

    c. Prey

    d. Utensil

43. Winner : Champion ::
Sheen : _____

    a. Shimmer

    b. Dark

    c. Sweet

    d. Garbage

44. Pal : Friend ::
Enemy : _____

    a. Relative

    b. Business

    c. Foe

    d. Career

45. Strange : Odd ::
Offbeat : _____

    a. Melody

    b. Guitar

    c. Drums

    d. Unconventional

46. Frog : Amphibian ::
Snake : _____

    a. Reptile

    b. Protozoan

    c. Mammals

    d. Bacteria

47. Color : Red :: Shape : _____

    a. Yellow

    b. Black

    c. Triangle

    d. Hard

48. Clothes : Skirt ::
Planets : _____

    a. Comets

    b. Galaxy

    c. Mars

    d. Clouds

49. Fat : Obese :: Brilliant : _____

    a. Glowing

    b. Robust

    c. Intelligent

    d. Poor

50. Bland : Plain :: Broken : _____

    a. Fixed

    b. Busted

    c. Creative

    d. Glass

51. Two : Binary :: Work : _____

a. Occupation
b. Vocation
c. Street
d. Challenge

52. Botanist : Plants :: Zoologist : _____

a. Rocks
b. Planets
c. Animals
d. Shells

53. Choose the antonym pair.

a. Perception and Belief
b. Fixed and Indefinite
c. Signal and Symbol
d. Appearance and Look

54. Choose the antonym pair.

a. Stratify and Categorize
b. Plan and Scheme
c. Strategic and Unplanned
d. Confused and Mistaken

55. Select the antonym of authentic.

a. Real
b. Imitation
c. Apparition
d. Dream

56. Select the antonym of villain.

a. Actor
b. Actress
c. Antagonist
d. Hero

57. Select the antonym of vanish.

a. Appear
b. Lose
c. Reflection
d. Empty

58. Select the antonym of literal.

a. Manuscript
b. Writing
c. Figurative
d. Untrue

59. Select the antonym of harsh.

a. Mild
b. Light
c. Bulky
d. Bothersome

60. Select the antonym of splurge.

a. Spend
b. Count
c. Use
d. Save

Section II – Quantitative Skills

1. Consider the following series: 10, 20, 40, 80. What number should come next?

a. 150
b. 120
c. 90
d. 160

2. Consider the following series: 18395, 18295, 18195, 18095. What number should come next?

    a. 18000

    b. 18950

    c. 17995

    d. 17905

3. Consider the following series: -45, -39, -33, -27. What number should come next?

    a. 21

    b. -21

    c. -25

    d. 25

4. Consider the following series: -100, 100, -200, 0, -300. What number should come next?

    a. 0

    b. -200

    c. -100

    d. 100

5. Consider the following series: 2.3, 2.3, 4.6, 12.18. What number should come next?

    a. 24.36

    b. 48.72

    c. 48

    d. 12.19

6. Consider the following series: 3, 9, 11, 33, 36. What number should come next?

    a. 106

    b. 39

    c. 33

    d. 108

7. Consider the following series: 345, 347, 344, 346. What number should come next?

    a. 345

    b. 343

    c. 348

    d. 349

8. Consider the following series: 21, 21, 31, 31, 41, 41. What number should come next?

    a. 51

    b. 50

    c. 61

    d. 31

9. Consider the following series: 14, 17, 22, 29. What number should come next?

    a. 38

    b. -36

    c. -39

    d. 34

10. Consider the following series: 39, 28, 19, 12, 7. What number should come next?

    a. 1

    b. 4

    c. 0

    d. 2

11. Consider the following series: 3, 5, 10, 12, 24. What 2 numbers should come next?

    a. 48, 58

    b. 26, 28

    c. 48, 50

    d. 26, 52

12. Consider the following series: 1000, 992, 984, 976. What 2 numbers should come next?

    a. 968, 961
    b. 967, 960
    c. 968, 960
    d. 970, 964

13. Consider the following series: 0.1, 0.3, 0.9, 2.7. What 2 numbers should come next?

    a. -8.1, -24.3
    b. 8.1, 24.3
    c. 5.4, 10.8
    d. -5.4, -10.8

14. Consider the following series: 32, 16, 8, 4. What 3 numbers should come next?

    a. 2, 1, 0.5
    b. 2, 0,-2
    c. 0,-4,-8
    d. 2, 1, 0

15. Consider the following series: 3, ..., 17, 24, 31. What is the missing number?

    a. 8
    b. 12
    c. 10
    d. 5

16. Consider the following series: 3, ..., 9, 12, 15. What is the missing number?

    a. 4
    b. 7
    c. 6
    d. 5

17. Consider the following series: 95, 90, ..., 80, 75. What is the missing number?

    a. 87
    b. 85
    c. 86
    d. 80

18. Consider the following series: ..., 75, 65, 60, 50, 45, 35, ... What 2 numbers are missing?

    a. 70, 35
    b. 65, 35
    c. 80, 30
    d. 65, 30

19. Examine (A) and (B) and find the best answer.

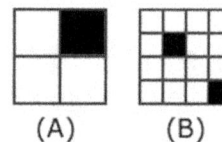

(A)   (B)

a. The shaded area in (A) is greater than (B)

b. The shaded area in (B) is greater than (A)

c. The shaded area in (A) is equal to (B)

20. Examine (A) and (B) and find the best answer.

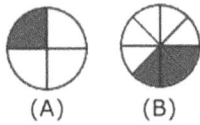

(A)   (B)

a. The shaded area in (A) is greater than (B)

b. The shaded area in (B) is greater than (A)

c. The shaded area in (A) is equal to (B)

21. Examine (A) and (B) and find the best answer.

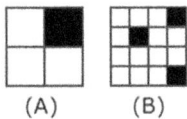

(A)   (B)

a. The shaded area in (A) is greater than (B)

b. The shaded area in (B) is greater than (A)

c. The shaded area in (A) is equal to (B)

22. Examine (A) (B) and (C) and find the best answer.

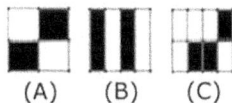

(A)   (B)   (C)

a. The shaded area in (A) is equal to (B) and (C).

b. The shaded area in (C) is less than (A) and (B).

c. The shaded area in (A) is greater than (B) and (C).

d. The shaded area in (B) is equal to (A) and (C).

23. Examine (A) (B) and (C) and find the best answer.

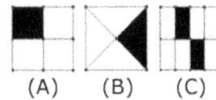

(A)   (B)   (C)

a. (A) (B) and (C) are equal.

b. The shaded area in (C) is greater than (A) and (B).

c. The shaded area in (A) is greater than (B) and (C).

d. The shaded area in (B) is greater than (A) and (C).

24. Examine (A) (B) and (C) and find the best answer.

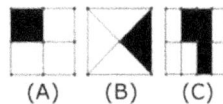

(A)   (B)   (C)

a. (A) (B) and (C) are equal.

b. The shaded area in (C) is greater than (A) and (B).

c. The shaded area in (A) is greater than (B) and (C).

d. The shaded area in (B) is greater than (A) and (C).

25. Examine (A) (B) and (C) and find the best answer.

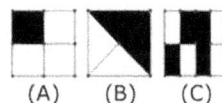

(A)   (B)   (C)

a. (A) (B) and (C) are equal.

b. The shaded area in (C) is greater than (A) and (B).

c. The shaded area in (A) is less than (B) and (C).

d. The shaded area in (B) is greater than (A) and (C).

26. Examine (A) (B) and (C) and find the best answer.

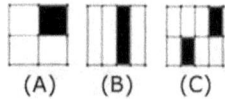
(A)   (B)   (C)

a. (A) (B) and (C) are equal.

b. The shaded area in (C) is greater than (A) and (B).

c. The shaded area in (A) is greater than (B) and (C).

d. The shaded area in (B) is greater than (A) and (C).

27. Examine (A) (B) and (C) and find the best answer.

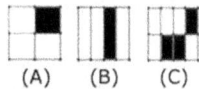
(A)   (B)   (C)

a. (A) (B) and (C) are equal.

b. The shaded area in (C) is greater than (A) and (B).

c. The shaded area in (A) is greater than (B) and (C).

d. The shaded area in (B) is greater than (A) and (C).

28. Examine the following and find the best answer.

1. (6 X 1) X (2 X 4)
2. (4 X 7) + (5 X 6)
3. (3 X 4) X (9 - 2)

a. 2 is the largest

b. 3 is greater than 1

c. 1 is greater than 2

d. None of the Above.

29. Examine the following and find the best answer.

1. 6 X (4 + 3)
2. 4 X (5 X 3)
3. 7 + (3 X 6)

a. 1 < 2 < 3

b. 1 < 2 > 3

c. 2 > 3 > 1

d. 2 < 3 > 1

30. Examine the following and find the best answer.

1. 50 - (5 X 4)
2. 100 - (6 X 6)
3. 45 - (4 X 2)

a. 1 < 3 < 2

b. 1 > 3 > 2

c. 2 > 1 > 3

d. 2 < 1 > 3

31. Examine the following and find the best answer.

1. 35 - (6 X 3)
2. 100 - (6 X 10)
3. 75 - (4 X 7)

a. 1 < 3 < 2

b. 1 > 3 > 2

c. 2 > 1 > 3

d. 2 < 1 > 3

32. Examine the following and find the best answer.

1. 4 X (2 + 3)
2. 5 X (7 X 3)
3. 9 + (3 X 7)

    a. 3 < 2 > 1

    b. 1 > 2 < 3

    c. 2 > 3 < 1

    d. 2 < 3 < 1

33. Examine the following and find the best answer.

(4 X 3) X (3 X 7)
(7 X 5) + (2 X 5)
(4 X 3) X (7 - 2)

    a. 1 > 2 > 3

    b. 2 > 1 > 3

    c. 3 < 2 < 1

    d. 2 < 1 < 3

34. Examine the following and find the best answer.

1. 12 + (5 X 3)
2. 15 - (9 + 4)
3. 4 + (2 X 9)

    a. 1 > 2 > 3

    b. 2 < 1 > 3

    c. 3 < 2 < 1

    d. 2 < 1 < 3

35. Examine the following and find the best answer.

1. 15 X 6
2. 37 X 5
3. 24 X 2

    a. 1 = 3

    b. 1 = 2

    c. 1 > 2 > 3

    d. 3 < 1 < 2

36. Examine the following and find the best answer.

1. (6 X 4) - 5
2. (2 X 8) - 3
3. (3 X 5) – 8

    a. 1 and 3 are equal

    b. 1 and 3 are not equal

    c. 1 and 2 are equal

    d. 2 and 3 are equal

37. 2/3 of what number added to 10 is 3 times 15?

    a. 50

    b. 52.5

    c. 65

    d. 72.8

38. What number is 25 more than 1/3 of 27?

    a. 34

    b. -16

    c. 20

    d. 18

39. What number is 10 less than 5 squared?

    a. 25
    b. 10
    c. 15
    d. 40

40. What is 12 more than 3/4 of 40?

    a. 42
    b. 35
    c. 52
    d. 18

41. What is 25 more than 30% of 120?

    a. 75
    b. 50
    c. 65
    d. 35

42. What number subtracted from 75 leaves 15 more than 3/5 of 75?

    a. 25
    b. 15
    c. 30
    d. 12

43. What number divided by 5 is 2/3 of 100?

    a. 333.33
    b. 444.44
    c. 250
    d. 100

44. 1/2 of what number is 9 times 5?

    a. 60
    b. 120
    c. 90
    d. 45

45. What number multiplied by 8 is 10 less than 58?

    a. 5
    b. 6
    c. 7
    d. 8

46. What number subtracted from 25 is 1/5 of 40?

    a. 22
    b. 17
    c. 34
    d. 12

47. What number is 1 less than 1/4 of 16?

    a. 1
    b. 2
    c. 3
    d. 4

48. 1/2 of what number is 8 times 7?

    a. 60
    b. 120
    c. 112
    d. 45

49. What number multiplied by 10 is 15 less than 65?

     a. 5
     b. 6
     c. 7
     d. 8

50. What number subtracted from 25 is 1/5 of 60?

     a. 22
     b. 13
     c. 34
     d. 12

Section III - Reading

Questions 1 - 4 refer to the following passage.

Passage 1 - The Crusades

In 1095 Pope Urban II proclaimed the First Crusade with the intent and stated goal to restore Christian access to holy places in and around Jerusalem. Over the next 200 years there were 6 major crusades and numerous minor crusades in the fight for control of the "Holy Land." Historians are divided on the real purpose of the Crusades, some believing that it was part of a purely defensive war against Islamic conquest; some see them as part of a long-running conflict at the frontiers of Europe; and others see them as confident, aggressive, papal-led expansion attempts by Western Christendom. The impact of the crusades was profound, and judgment of the Crusaders ranges from laudatory to highly critical. However, all agree that the Crusades and wars waged during those crusades were brutal and often bloody. Several hundred thousand Roman Catholic Christians joined the Crusades, they were Christians from all over Europe.

Europe at the time was under the Feudal System, so while the Crusaders made vows to the Church they also were beholden to their Feudal Lords. This led to the Crusaders not only fighting the Saracen, the commonly used word for Muslim at the time, but also each other for power and economic gain in the Holy Land. This infighting between the Crusaders is why many historians hold the view that the Crusades were simply a front for Europe to invade the Holy Land for economic gain in the name of the Church. Another factor contributing to this theory is that while the army of crusaders marched towards Jerusalem they pillaged the land as they went. The church and feudal Lords vowing to return the land to its original beauty, and inhabitants, this rarely happened though as the Lords often kept the land for themselves. A full 800 years after the Crusades, Pope John Paul II expressed his sorrow for the massacre of innocent people and the lasting damage the Medieval church caused in that area of the World.

1. What is the tone of this article?

    a. Subjective

    b. Objective

    c. Persuasive

    d. None of the Above

2. What can all historians agree on concerning the Crusades?

    a. It achieved great things

    b. It stabilized the Holy Land

    c. It was bloody and brutal

    d. It helped defend Europe from the Byzantine Empire

3. What impact did the feudal system have on the Crusades?

a. It unified the Crusaders

b. It helped gather volunteers

c. It had no effect on the Crusades

d. It led to infighting, causing more damage than good

4. What does Saracen mean?

a. Muslim

b. Christian

c. Knight

d. Holy Land

Questions 5 - 8 refer to the following passage.

ABC Electric Warranty

ABC Electric Company warrants that its products are free from defects in material and workmanship. Subject to the conditions and limitations set forth below, ABC Electric will, at its option, either repair or replace any part of its products that prove defective due to improper workmanship or materials.

This limited warranty does not cover any damage to the product from improper installation, accident, abuse, misuse, natural disaster, insufficient or excessive electrical supply, abnormal mechanical or environmental conditions, or any unauthorized disassembly, repair, or modification.

This limited warranty also does not apply to any product on which the original identification information has been altered, or removed, has not been handled or packaged correctly, or has been sold as second-hand.

This limited warranty covers only repair, replacement, refund or credit for defective ABC Electric products, as provided above.

5. I tried to repair my ABC Electric blender, but could not, so can I get it repaired under this warranty?

a.   Yes, the warranty still covers the blender

b.   No, the warranty does not cover the blender

c.   Uncertain. ABC Electric may or may not cover repairs under this warranty

6. My ABC Electric fan is not working. Will ABC Electric provide a new one or repair this one?

    a. ABC Electric will repair my fan

    b. ABC Electric will replace my fan

    c. ABC Electric could either replace or repair my fan can request either a replacement or a repair.

7. My stove was damaged in a flood. Does this warranty cover my stove?

    a. Yes, it is covered.

    b. No, it is not covered.

    c. It may or may not be covered.

    d. ABC Electric will decide if it is covered

8. Which of the following is an example of improper workmanship?

    a. Missing parts

    b. Defective parts

    c. Scratches on the front

    d. None of the above

Questions 9 – 12 refer to the following passage.

Passage 2 - Women and Advertising

Only in the last few generations have media messages been so widespread and so readily seen, heard, and read by so many people. Advertising is an important part of both selling and buying anything from soap to cereal to jeans. For whatever reason, more consumers are women than are men. Media message are subtle but powerful, and more attention has been paid lately to how these message affect women.

Of all the products that women buy, makeup, clothes, and other stylistic or cosmetic products are among the most popular. This means that companies focus their advertising on women, promising them that their product will make her feel, look, or smell better than the next company's product will. This competition has resulted in advertising that is more and more ideal and less and less possible for everyday women. However, because women do look to these ideals and the products they represent as how they can potentially become, many women have developed unhealthy attitudes about themselves when they have failed to become those ideals.

In recent years, more companies have tried to change advertisements to be healthier for women. This includes featuring models of more sizes and addressing a huge outcry against unfair tools such as airbrushing and photo editing. There is debate about what the right balance between real and ideal is, because fashion is also considered art and some changes are made to purposefully elevate fashionable products and signify that they are creative, innovative, and the work of individual people. Artists want their freedom protected as much as women do, and advertising agencies are often caught in the middle.

Some claim that the companies who make these changes are not doing enough. Many people worry that there are still not enough models of different sizes and different ethnicities. Some people claim that companies use this healthier type of advertisement not for the good of women, but because they would like to sell products to the women who are looking for these kinds of messages. This is also a hard balance to find: companies do need to make money, and women do need to feel respected.

While the focus of this change has been on women, advertising can also affect men, and this change will hopefully be a lesson on media for all consumers.

9. The second paragraph states that advertising focuses on women

    a. to shape what the ideal should be

    b. because women buy makeup

    c. because women are easily persuaded

    d. because of the types of products that women buy

10. According to the passage, fashion artists and female consumers are at odds because

    a. there is a debate going on and disagreement drives people apart

    b. both of them are trying to protect their freedom to do something

    c. artists want to elevate their products above the reach of women

    d. women are creative, innovative, individual people

11. The author uses the phrase "for whatever reason" in this passage to

    a. keep the focus of the paragraph on media messages and not on the differences between men and women

    b. show that the reason for this is unimportant

    c. argue that it is stupid that more women are consumers than men

    d. show that he or she is tired of talking about why media messages are important

12. This passage suggests that

    a. advertising companies are still working on making their messages better

    b. all advertising companies seek to be more approachable for women

    c. women are only buying from companies that respect them

    d. artists could stop producing fashionable products if they feel bullied

Questions 13 - 16 refer to the following passage.

FDR, the Treaty of Versailles, and the Fourteen Points

At the conclusion of World War I, those who had won the war and those who were forced to admit defeat welcomed the end of the war and expected that a peace treaty would be signed. The American president, Franklin D. Roosevelt, played an important part in proposing what the agreements should be and did so through his Fourteen Points.
World War I had begun in 1914 when an Austrian archduke was assassinated, leading to a domino effect that pulled the world's most powerful countries into war on a large scale. The war catalyzed the creation and use of deadly weapons that had not previously existed, resulting in a great loss of soldiers on both sides of the fighting. More than 9 million soldiers were killed.

The United States agreed to enter the war right before it ended, and many believed that its decision to become finally involved brought on the end of the war. FDR made it very clear that the U.S. was entering the war for moral reasons and had an agenda focused on world peace. The Fourteen Points were individual goals and ideas (focused on peace, free trade, open communication, and self reliance) that FDR wanted the power nations to strive for now that the war had concluded. He was optimistic and had many ideas about what could be accomplished through and during the post-war peace. However, FDR's fourteen points were poorly received when he presented them to the leaders of other world powers, many of whom wanted only to help their own countries and to punish the Germans for fueling the war, and they fell by the wayside. World War II was imminent, for Germany lost everything.

Some historians believe that the other leaders who participated in the Treaty of Versailles weren't receptive to the Fourteen Points because World War I was fought almost entirely on European soil, and the United States lost much less than did the other powers. FDR was in a unique position to determine the fate of the war, but doing it on his own terms did not help accomplish his goals. This is only one historical example of how the United State has tried to use its power as an important country, but found itself limited because of geological or ideological factors.

13. The main idea of this passage is that

a. World War I was unfair because no fighting took place in America

b. World War II happened because of the Treaty of Versailles

c. the power the United States has to help other countries also prevents it from helping other countries

d. Franklin D. Roosevelt was one of the United States' smartest presidents

14. According to the second paragraph, World War I started because

a. an archduke was assassinated

b. weapons that were more deadly had been developed

c. a domino effect of allies agreeing to help each other

d. the world's most powerful countries were large

15. The author includes the detail that 9 million soldiers were killed

a. to demonstrate why European leaders were hesitant to accept peace

b. to show the reader the dangers of deadly weapons

c. to make the reader think about which countries lost the most soldiers

d. to demonstrate why World War II was imminent

16. According to this passage, it can be understood that the word catalyzed means

a. analyzed

b. sped up

c. invented

d. funded

Questions 17 - 20 refer to the following passage.

Chocolate Chip Cookies

3/4 cup sugar
3/4 cup packed brown sugar
1 cup butter, softened
2 large eggs, beaten
1 teaspoon vanilla extract
2 1/4 cups all-purpose flour
1 teaspoon baking soda
3/4 teaspoon salt
2 cups semisweet chocolate chips
If desired, 1 cup chopped pecans, or chopped walnuts.
Preheat oven to 375 degrees.

Mix sugar, brown sugar, butter, vanilla and eggs in a large bowl. Stir in flour, baking soda, and salt. The dough will be very stiff.

Stir in chocolate chips by hand with a sturdy wooden spoon. Add the pecans, or other nuts, if desired. Stir until the chocolate chips and nuts are evenly dispersed.

Drop dough by rounded tablespoonfuls 2 inches apart onto a cookie sheet.

Bake 8 to 10 minutes or until light brown. Cookies may look underdone, but they will finish cooking after you take them out of the oven.

17. What is the correct order for adding these ingredients?

    a. Brown sugar, baking soda, chocolate chips
    b. Baking soda, brown sugar, chocolate chips
    c. Chocolate chips, baking soda, brown sugar
    d. Baking soda, chocolate chips, brown sugar

18. What does sturdy mean?

    a. Long
    b. Strong
    c. Short
    d. Wide

19. What does disperse mean?

a. Scatter

b. To form a ball

c. To stir

d. To beat

20. When can you stop stirring the nuts?

a. When the cookies are cooked.

b. When the nuts are evenly distributed.

c. When the nuts are added.

d. After the chocolate chips are added.

Questions 21 - 24 refer to the following passage.

Passage 5 - Frankenstein

Great God! What a scene has just taken place! I am yet dizzy with the remembrance of it. I hardly know whether I shall have the power to detail it; yet the tale which I have recorded would be incomplete without this final and wonderful catastrophe. I entered the cabin where lay the remains of my ill-fated and admirable friend. Over him hung a form which I cannot find words to describe—gigantic in stature, yet uncouth and distorted in its proportions. As he hung over the coffin, his face was concealed by long locks of ragged hair; but one vast hand was extended, in color and apparent texture like that of a mummy. When he heard the sound of my approach, he ceased to utter exclamations of grief and horror and sprung towards the window. Never did I behold a vision so horrible as his face, of such loathsome yet appalling hideousness. I shut my eyes involuntarily and endeavored to recollect what were my duties with regard to this destroyer. I called on him to stay.

He paused, looking on me with wonder, and again turning towards the lifeless form of his creator, he seemed to forget my presence, and every feature and gesture seemed instigated by the wildest rage of some uncontrollable passion.

"That is also my victim!" he exclaimed. "In his murder my crimes are consummated; the miserable series of my being is wound to its close! Oh, Frankenstein! Generous and self-devoted being! What does it avail that I now ask thee to pardon me? I, who irretrievably destroyed thee by destroying all thou lovedst. Alas! He is cold, he cannot answer me."

His voice seemed suffocated, and my first impulses, which had suggested to me the duty of obeying the dying request of my friend in destroying his enemy, were now suspended by a mixture of curiosity and compassion. I approached this tremendous being; I dared not again raise my eyes to his face, there was something so scaring and unearthly in his ugliness. I attempted to speak, but the words died away on my lips. The monster continued to utter wild and incoherent self-reproaches. At length I gathered resolution to address him in a pause of the tempest of his passion.

"Your repentance," I said, "is now superfluous. If you had listened to the voice of conscience and heeded the stings of remorse before you had urged your diabolical vengeance to this extremity, Frankenstein would yet have lived." [7]

21. Who is the "ill-fated and admirable friend" who is lying in the coffin?

    a. Frankenstein's monster

    b. Frankenstein

    c. Mary Shelley

    d. Unknown

22. Why is the speaker 'suspended" from following through on his duty to destroy the monster?

    a. The way the monster looks

    b. The monster's remorse

    c. Curiosity and compassion

    d. Fear the monster might kill him too

23. How does Frankenstein's monster destroy Frankenstein?

    a. By killing Frankenstein

    b. By letting himself be the monster everyone sees him as

    c. By destroying everything Frankenstein loved

    d. All of the above

24. When the Speaker says the monster's repentance is "superfluous, what does he mean?

    a. That it is unnecessary and unused because Frankenstein is already dead and cannot hear him

    b. That he accepts the repentance on behalf of Frankenstein

    c. That the monster does not actually feel remorseful

    d. That his repentance is unneeded because he did not do anything wrong

Questions 25 - 28 refer to the following passage.

Lowest Price Guarantee

Get it for less. Guaranteed!

ABC Electric will beat any advertised price by 10% of the difference.

1) If you find a lower advertised price, we will beat it by 10% of the difference.

2) If you find a lower advertised price within 30 days* of your purchase we will beat it by 10% of the difference.

3) If our own price is reduced within 30 days* of your purchase, bring in your receipt and we will refund the difference.

*14 days for computers, monitors, printers, laptops, tablets, cellular & wireless devices, home security products, projectors, camcorders, digital cameras, radar detectors, portable DVD players, DJ and pro-audio equipment, and air conditioners.

25. I bought a radar detector 15 days ago and saw an ad for the same model only cheaper. Can I get 10% of the difference refunded?

a. Yes. Since it is less than 30 days, you can get 10% of the difference refunded.

b. No. Since it is more than 14 days, you cannot get 10% of the difference re-funded.

c. It depends on the cashier.

d. Yes. You can get the difference refunded.

26. I bought a flat-screen TV for $500 10 days ago and found an advertisement for the same TV, at another store, on sale for $400. How much will ABC refund under this guarantee?

a. $100

b. $110

c. $10

d. $400

27. What is the purpose of this passage?

a. To inform

b. To educate

c. To persuade

d. To entertain

Questions 28 - 30 refer to the following passage.

Passage 6 - What Is Mardi Gras?

Mardi Gras is fast becoming one of the South's most famous and most celebrated holidays. The word Mardi Gras comes from the French and the literal
translation is "Fat Tuesday." The holiday has also been called Shrove Tuesday, due to its associations with Lent. The purpose of Mardi Gras is to celebrate and enjoy before the Lenten season of fasting and repentance begins.

What originated by the French Explorers in New Orleans, Louisiana in the
17th century is now celebrated all over the world. Panama, Italy, Belgium
and Brazil all host large scale Mardi Gras celebrations, and many smaller cities and towns celebrate this fun loving Tuesday as well. Usually held in Feb-
ruary or early March, Mardi Gras is a day of extravagance, a day for people to
eat, drink and be merry, to wear costumes, masks and to dance to jazz music.
The French explorers on the Mississippi River would be in shock today if they
saw the opulence of the parades and floats that grace the New Orleans streets
during Mardi Gras these days. Parades in New Orleans are divided by organi-
zations. These are more commonly known as Krewes.

Being a member of a Krewe is quite a task because Krewes are responsible for
overseeing the parades. Each Krewe's parade is ruled by a Mardi Gras "King
and Queen." The role of the King and Queen is to "bestow" gifts on their ador-
ing fans as the floats ride along the street. They throw doubloons, which is
fake money and usually colored green, purple and gold, which are the colors
of Mardi Gras. Beads in those color shades are also thrown and cups are
thrown as well. Beads are by far the most popular souvenir of any Mardi Gras
parade, with each spectator attempting to gather as many as possible.

28. The purpose of Mardi Gras is to

    a. Repent for a month.

    b. Celebrate in extravagant ways.

    c. Be a member of a Krewe.

    d. Explore the Mississippi.

29. From reading the passage we can infer that "Kings and Queens,"

    a. Have to be members of a Krewe.

    b. Have to be French.

    c. Have to know how to speak French.

    d. Have to give away their own money.

30. Which group of people first began to hold Mardi Gras celebrations?

    a. Settlers from Italy

    b. Members of Krewes

    c. French explorers

    d. Belgium explorers

31. In the context of the passage, what does spectator mean?

    a. Someone who participates actively

    b. Someone who watches the parade's action

    c. Someone on one of the parade floats

    d. Someone who does not celebrate Mardi Gras

Questions 32 - 33 refer to the following passage.

Passage 7 - Peter Pan

All children, except one, grow up. They soon know that they will grow up, and the way Wendy knew was this. One day when she was two years old she was playing in a garden, and she plucked another flower and ran with it to her mother. I suppose she must have looked rather delightful, for Mrs. Darling put her hand to her heart and cried, "Oh, why can't you remain like this for ever!" This was all that passed between them on the subject, but henceforth Wendy knew that she must grow up. You always know after you are two. Two is the beginning of the end.

Of course they lived at 14 [their house number on their street], and until Wendy came her mother was the chief one. She was a lovely lady, with a romantic mind and such a sweet mocking mouth. Her romantic mind was like the tiny boxes, one within the other, that come from the puzzling East, however many you discover there is always one more; and her sweet mocking mouth had one kiss on it that Wendy could never get, though there it was, perfectly conspicuous in the right-hand corner.

The way Mr. Darling won her was this: the many gentlemen who had been boys when she was a girl discovered simultaneously that they loved her, and they all ran to her house to propose to her except Mr. Darling, who took a cab and nipped in first, and so he got her. He got all of her, except the innermost box and the kiss. He never knew about the box, and in time he gave up trying for the kiss. Wendy thought Napoleon could have got it, but I can picture him trying, and then going off in a passion, slamming the door.

32. The author's description of Mrs. Darling's "sweet mocking mouth" implies:

a. While pretty, Mrs. Darling frequently chides others.

b. Although subject to slight disfigurement, Mrs. Darling's mouth is still pleasant in appearance.

c. Mrs. Darling uses her words to get her way.

d. Mrs. Darling is a loving woman, yet she does not wholly give her love away.

33. Overall, from this passage you can infer that Mrs. Darling:

a. Is a dominant, complex woman.

b. Accidentally denies those around her.

c. Is artistic and absent-minded.

d. Has a troubled marriage.

Section III - Part II - Vocabulary

34. Choose the best definition of anecdote.

a. A short account of an incident

b. Something that comes before

c. The use of humour, irony, exaggeration, or ridicule

d. Constant fluctuations

35. Choose the adjective that means shocking, terrible or wicked.

a. Pleasantries

b. Heinous

c. Shrewd

d. Provencal

36. Choose the noun that means a person or thing that tells or announces the coming of someone or something.

a. Harbinger

b. Evasion

c. Bleak

d. Craven

37. Choose a word that means the same as the underlined word.

He wasn't especially generous. All the servings were very <u>judicious</u>.

    a. Abundant

    b. Careful

    c. Extravagant

    d. Careless

38. Fill in the blank.

Because of the growing use of _____ as a fuel, corn production has greatly increased.

    a. Alcohol

    b. Ethanol

    c. Natural gas

    d. Oil

39. Fill in the blank.

In heavily industrialized areas, the pollution of the air causes many to develop _____ diseases.

    a. Respiratory

    b. Cardiac

    c. Alimentary

    d. Circulatory

40. Choose the best definition of inherent.

    a. To receive money in a will

    b. An essential part of

    c. To receive money from a will

    d. None of the above

41. Choose the best definition of vapid.

    a. adj. tasteless or bland

    b. v. To inflict, as a revenge or punishment

    c. v. to convert into gas

    d. v. to go up in smoke

42. Choose the best definition of waif.

    a. n. a sick and hungry child

    b. n. an orphan staying in a foster home

    c. n. homeless child or stray

    d. n. a type of French bread eaten with cheese

43. Choose the adjective that means similar or identical.

    a. Soluble

    b. Assembly

    c. Conclave

    d. Homologous

44. Choose a word with the same meaning as the underlined word.

We used that operating system 20 years ago, now it is <u>obsolete</u>.

    a. Functional

    b. Disused

    c. Obese

    d. None of the Above

45. Choose the word with the same meaning as the underlined word

His bad manners really <u>rankle</u> me.

    a. Annoy

    b. Obsolete

    c. Enliven

    d. None of the above

46. Fill in the blank.

Because hydroelectric power is a _____ source of energy, its use is excellent for the environment.

    a. Significant

    b. Disposable

    c. Renewable

    d. Reusable

47. Choose the best definition of torpid.

    a. Fast

    b. Rapid

    c. Sluggish

    d. Violent

48. Choose the best definition of gregarious.

    a. Sociable

    b. Introverted

    c. Large

    d. Solitary

49. Choose the best definition of mutation.

    a. v. To utter with a loud and vehement voice

    b. n. change or alteration

    c. n. An act or exercise of will

    d. v. To cause to be one

50. Choose the best definition of lithe.

    a. adj. small in size

    b. adj. Artificial

    c. adj. flexible or plaint

    d. adj. fake

Section IV – Math

1. The sum of the digits of a 2-digit number is 12. If we switch the digits, the number we get will be greater than the initial one by 36. Find the initial number.

    a. 39

    b. 48

    c. 57

    d. 75

5 cm

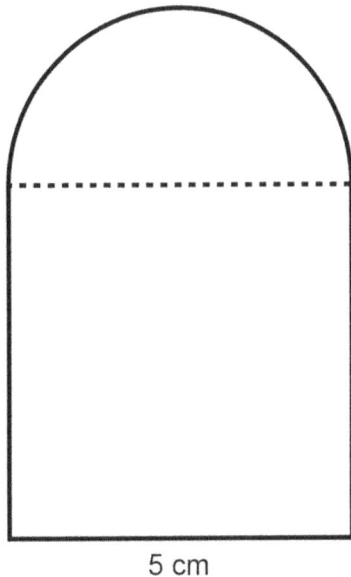

Note: Figure not drawn to scale

2. What is the perimeter of the above shape?

    a. 17.5 π cm

    b. 20 π cm

    c. 15 π cm

    d. 25 π cm

3. Kate's father is 32 years older than Kate is. In 5 years, he will be five times older. How old is Kate?

    a. 2

    b. 3

    c. 5

    d. 6

4. If Lynn can type a page in p minutes, what portion of the page can she do in 5 minutes?

    a. 5/p

    b. p - 5

    c. p + 5

    d. p/5

5. If Sally can paint a house in 4 hours, and John can paint the same house in 6 hours, how long will it take for both of them to paint the house together?

    a. 2 hours and 24 minutes

    b. 3 hours and 12 minutes

    c. 3 hours and 44 minutes

    d. 4 hours and 10 minutes

6. The following are the number of people that attended a particular church, every Friday for 7 weeks – 62, 18, 39, 13, 16, 37, 25. Find the average.

    a. 25

    b. 210

    c. 62

    d. 30

7. Sales of a local football team's season tickets have gone up 10% in the current season to 880 tickets. Last year, they sold X season tickets. X equals:

    a. 700

    b. 800

    c. 880

    d. 928

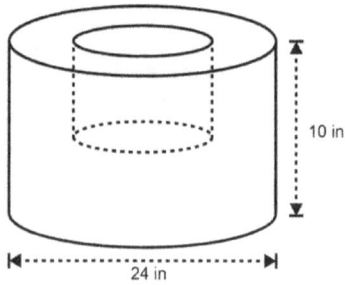

Note: Figure not drawn to scale

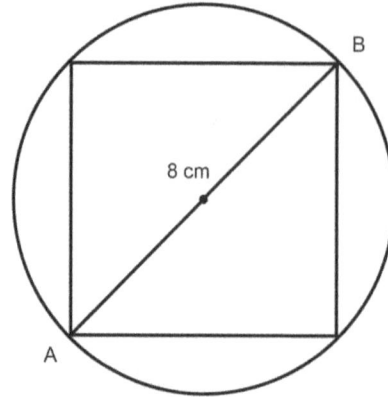

Note: Figure not drawn to scale

8. What is the volume of the above solid made by a hollow cylinder that is half the size (in all dimensions) of the larger cylinder?

    a. 1440 π in³
    b. 1260 π in³
    c. 1040 π in³
    d. 960 π in³

9. Two trains start at the same time in different directions. One travels at an average speed of 72 km/hr., and the other at 52 km/hr. After 20 minutes how far apart are they?

    a. 6.67 km
    b. 17.33 km
    c. 24.3 km
    d. 41.33 km

10. There were some oranges in a basket, by adding 8/5 of these, the total became 130. How many oranges were in the basket before?

    a. 60
    b. 50
    c. 40
    d. 35

11. What is area of the circle?

    a. 4 π cm²
    b. 12 π cm²
    c. 10 π cm²
    d. 16 π cm²

12. John jogs around a 75-meter diameter track 7 times. How much linear distance did he cover?

    a. 1250 meters
    b. 1450 meters
    c. 1650 meters
    d. 1725 meters

13. In an office, 12 employees can finish a task in 7 hours. If two of them are absent, how much more time will they have to work to complete the task?

    a. 10 minutes
    b. 12 minutes
    c. 15 minutes
    d. 20 minutes

14. A bullet train traveling at 300km/hr passes station A at 8:56 pm. What time will the train reach station B, which is 45km away?

    a. 9:03 pm

    b. 9:05 pm

    c. 9:07 pm

    d. 9:10 pm

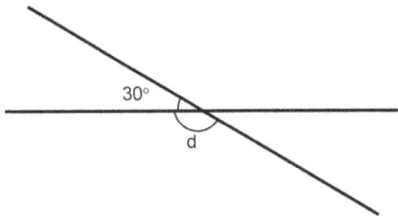

15. What is the indicated angle above?

    a. 150°

    b. 330°

    c. 60°

    d. 120°

16. In an 80 km marathon race, George runs 2 km/hr. faster than Marsha does. George reaches the finish line in 3.2 hrs. At that time, how far is Marsh from finish line?

    a. 6.4 km

    b. 5.6 km

    c. 5.2 km

    d. 4.8 km

17. On a circular jogging track with a circumference of 1.2 km, John, Tony and David walk at the rate of 120, 100 and 75 meters per minute respectively. If they all start walking in the same direction, how long will it take until they are together again?

    a. 200 minutes

    b. 220 minutes

    c. 240 minutes

    d. 260 minutes

18. On a scaled map, city A is 12.4 cm away from city B. If the scale is 1 cm = 5 km then what is the actual distance between these two cities?

    a. 12.4 km

    b. 48.4 km

    c. 58 km

    d. 62 km

19. In a 30-minute test, there are 40 problems. A student solved 28 problems in first 25 minutes. How many seconds should she give to each of the remaining problems?

    a. 20 seconds

    b. 23 seconds

    c. 25 seconds

    d. 27 seconds

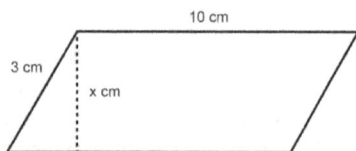

Note: Figure not drawn to scale

20. What is the perimeter of the parallelogram above?

    a. 12 cm

    b. 26 cm

    c. 13 cm

    d. (13+x) cm

21. Estimate 2009 x 108.

    a. 110,000

    b. 2,0000

    c. 21,000

    d. 210,000

22. Richard sold 12 shirts for total revenue of $336 at 8% profit. What is the purchase price of each shirt?

    a. $25.76

    b. $24.50

    c. $23.75

    d. $22.50

23. If we know it takes 12 men to operate four machines, how many are required to operate 20 machines?

    a. 6

    b. 20

    c. 60

    d. 9

24. The playing times for three songs on a compact disc are: 4 minutes 56 seconds for song A, 2 minutes 30 seconds for song B, 10 minutes 16 seconds for song C. What's the average playing time for the three songs?

    a. 17 minutes 42 seconds

    b. 6 minutes 7 seconds

    c. 6 minutes

    d. 5 minutes 54 seconds

25. John is a barber and receives 40% of the amount paid by his customers, and all the tips. If a customer pays $8.50 for a haircut and leaves a tip of $1.30, how much money does John receive?

    a. $3.92

    b. $4.70

    c. $5.30

    d. $6.40

26. A company paid a total of $2850 to book 6 single rooms and 4 double rooms in a hotel for one night. Another company paid $3185 to book for 13 single rooms for one night in the same hotel. What is the cost for single and double rooms in that hotel?

    a. Single $250, double $345

    b. Single $254, double $350

    c. single $245, double $305

    d. single $245, double $345

27. The length of a rectangle is 5 in. more than its width. The perimeter of the rectangle is 26 in. What is the width and length of the rectangle?

a. Width 6 in., Length 9 in.
b. Width 4 in., Length 9 in.
c. Width 4 in., Length 5 in.
d. Width 6 in., Length 11 in.

28. A basket contains 125 oranges, mangos and apples. If 3/5 of the fruits in the basket are mangos, and only 2/5 of the mangos are ripe, how many ripe mangos are there in the basket?

a. 30
b. 68
c. 55
d. 47

29. Calculate (3a + 4b) * d when A = 2, b = 4 and d = 8

a. 40
b. 150
c. 112
d. 176

30. c = 4, n = 5 and x = 3. Calculate 2cnx/2n

a. 12
b. 50
c. 8
d. 21

31. Simplify 3 1/2 / 2 4/5

a. 1 1/4
b. 2 1/4
c. 1 1/3
d. 2 1/3

32. Solve 2b/3 + 3a/5 – 2, where b = 9 and a = 10

a. 5
b. 10
c. 20
d. 9

33. Simplify (1/3 + 2/6) - (3/4 - 1/3)

a. 1/4
b. 5/11
c. 3/7
d. 2/9

34. Simplify (4/5 - 3/10) + (2/3 – 3/9) =

a. 4/11
b. 5/6
c. 7/15
d. 9/11

35. Translate the following into an equation: 2 + a number divided by 7.

a. (2 + X)/7
b. (7 + X)/2
c. (2 + 7)/X
d. 2/(7 + X)

36. If a = 12 and b = 8, solve 6b - a + 2a

a. 12/9
b. 18
c. 16
d. 12

37. Simplify 3 2/3 - 1 2/8

    a. 3/5
    b. 3/5
    c. 2 5/12
    d. 5/12

38. Simplify 7 2/5 – 4 3/10

    a. 3 1/10
    b. 3 2/5
    c. 4 1/5
    d. 3 7/10

39. Solve for x. -5 – 5x = 8x + 8

    a. 6
    b. 3
    c. 1
    d. 2

40. Solve 2 1/3 x 1 3/7 x 3/4

    a. 2 1/2
    b. 9
    c. 3 2/3
    d. 2 2/5

41. Simplify 7 4/5 – 4 2/3

    a. 4 2/5
    b. 3 2/15
    c. 3 7/15
    d. 4 3/5

42. Solve for x. 12x - 8 = 3x + 10

    a. 6
    b. 4
    c. 2
    d. 3

43. Simplify (3/5 - 2/5) + (3/4 – 2/8)

    a. 18/45
    b. 7/11
    c. 14/20
    d. 12/19

44. Solve for a. 6a + 4 = 28 + 2a

    a. 4
    b. 8
    c. 2
    d. 6

45. Simplify (3/4 - 1/4) - (3/5 – 2/5)

    a. 9/20
    b. 4/15
    c. 7/15
    d. 11/20

46. Solve for x. 6 + 9x = 12 + 7x

    a. 5
    b. 2
    c. 4
    d. 3

47. Simplify 6 2/5 / 2 2/7

    a. 2 1/4
    b. 1 1/5
    c. 2 4/5
    d. 2 2/3

48. Solve for a. -6 + 7a = 9 + 4a

    a. 3
    b. 5
    c. 2
    d. 6

49. Simplify 2 1/3 / 1 2/5

   a. 1 2/5
   b. 1 2/3
   c. 1 1/7
   d. 2 2/5

50. 2/3 x 1 4/7 x 5 1/4

   a. 3 1/4
   b. 5 1/2
   c. 6 2/3
   d. 4 2/5

51. Simplify 4 1/5 / 2 1/3

   a. 1 4/5
   b. 2 1/4
   c. 1 3/7
   d. 2 1/4

52. 10/3 x 2 1/4 x 3 1/5

   a. 1 3/4
   b. 24
   c. 7 2/7
   d. 5 1/5

53. Simplify 3 1/9 / 2 2/3

   a. 2 1/5
   b. 2 3/4
   c. 1 1/6
   d. 1 1/4

54. What is -9 + (+6) – (-2)

   a. -3
   b. 1
   c. -1
   d. -5

55. Simplify 5 1/2 – 5 3/7

   a. 1/10
   b. 1/14
   c. 1/7
   d. 2/7

56. What is -3 - (-7) - (+5)?

   a. -6
   b. 6
   c. 3
   d. -1

57. Solve 3 3/4 x 4/5 x 1 3/4

   a. 1 4/5
   b. 4 1/3
   c. 6
   d. 5 1/4

58. Simplify 6 3/5 – 4 4/5

   a. 2 4/5
   b. 2 3/5
   c. 2 9/5
   d. 1 1/5

59. Estimate 46,227 + 101,032.

   a. 14,700
   b. 147,000
   c. 14,700,000
   d. 104,700

60. Solve √121

   a. 11
   b. 12
   c. 21
   d. None of the above

Section V – Language Arts

1. Choose the sentence below with the correct punctuation.

a. There are many species of owls, the Great-Horned Owl, the Snowy Owl, and the Western Screech Owl, and the Barn Owl.

b. There are many species of owls, the Great-Horned Owl: the Snowy Owl: and the Western Screech Owl, and the Barn Owl.

c. There are many species of owls: the Great-Horned Owl, the Snowy Owl, and the Western Screech Owl, and the Barn Owl.

d. There are many species of owls: the Great-Horned Owl, the Snowy Owl, and the Western Screech Owl, and the Barn Owl.

2. Choose the sentence below with the correct punctuation.

a. In his most famous speech, Reverend King proclaimed: "I have a dream!"

b. In his most famous speech, Reverend King proclaimed; "I have a dream!"

c. In his most famous speech, Reverend King proclaimed. "I have a dream!"

d. In his most famous speech: Reverend King proclaimed, "I have a dream!"

3. Choose the sentence below with the correct punctuation.

a. Puzzled — Joe said, "You aren't going to pay me until ?"

b. Puzzled, Joe said, "You aren't going to pay me until ?"

c. Puzzled, Joe said, "You aren't going to pay me until —?"

d. Puzzled, Joe said, "You aren't going to pay me until, ?"

4. Choose the sentence below with the correct punctuation.

a. The years of his employment were not consecutive, being from 1999 to 2001 and 2002 – 2004.

b. The years of his employment were not consecutive, being from 1999 – 2001 and 2002 – 2004.

c. The years of his employment were not consecutive, being from 1999 _ 2001   and 2002_ 2004.

d. The years of his employment were not consecutive, being from 1999, 2001 and 2002, 2004.

5. Which sentence uses the period correctly?

    a. Henry VIII

    b. Henry VIII

    c. Pope John XXIII

    d. Vol. IV

6. Choose the correct answer.

    a. Ph.D.

    b. BSN.

    c. N.A.S.A.

    d. F.B.I.

7. Sit up straight _____

    a. ;

    b. ?

    c. .

    d. :

8. Choose the sentence with the correct capitalization.

    a. The Pharmalife Drugstore is on the north corner.

    b. The Pharmalife Drugstore is on the North corner.

    c. The pharmalife drugstore is on the north corner.

    d. None of the above.

9. Choose the sentence with the correct capitalization.

    a. The motto of The New York times is "All The News That's Fit to Print."

    b. The Motto of The New York Times is "All The News That's Fit to Print."

    c. The motto of The New York Times is "All The News That's Fit to Print."

    d. The motto of The New York Times is "All the News That's Fit to Print."

10. Choose the sentence with the correct capitalization.

    a. During the years he was President, the country fought two wars.

    b. During the years he was president, the country fought two wars.

    c. During the years he was president, the Country fought two wars.

    d. During the years he was President, the Country fought two wars.

11. Choose the sentence with the correct capitalization.

a. Shakespeare wrote more than 37 Plays, including Much Ado about Nothing.

b. Shakespeare wrote more than 37 plays, including Much ado about nothing.

c. Shakespeare wrote more than 37 plays, including Much Ado about Nothing.

d. None of the above.

12. Choose the sentence with the correct capitalization.

a. George forgot to call his Grandmother and Aunt Sue during the holidays.

b. George forgot to call his Grandmother and Aunt Sue during the Holidays.

c. George forgot to call his grandmother and Aunt Sue during the holidays.

d. George forgot to call his grandmother and aunt Sue during the holidays.

13. Choose the sentence with the correct capitalization.

a. The Sahara Desert is found in the northern part of Africa.

b. The Sahara Desert is found in the Northern part of Africa.

c. The Sahara desert is found in the northern part of Africa.

d. The Sahara desert is found in the Northern part of Africa.

14. Choose the sentence with the correct capitalization.

a. The State of Georgia is located south of North Carolina.

b. The state of Georgia is located South of North Carolina.

c. The state of Georgia is located south of north Carolina.

d. The state of Georgia is located south of North Carolina.

15. Choose the sentence with the correct capitalization.

a. The best known rivers in China are the Yangtze river, the Yellow river, and the Pearl river.

b. The best known Rivers in China are the Yangtze River, the Yellow River, and the Pearl River.

c. The best known rivers in China are the Yangtze River, the Yellow River, and the Pearl River.

d. The best known Rivers in China are the Yangtze river, the Yellow river, and the Pearl river.

16. Choose the sentence with the correct capitalization.

a. The abbreviation of the American medical association is the AMA.

b. The abbreviation of the american medical association is the AMA.

c. The abbreviation of the American Medical Association is the AMA.

d. The abbreviation of the American medical Association is the AMA.

17. Choose the sentence with the correct capitalization.

a. Mrs. Jones is my English teacher, but I have Mr. Brown for Science and mathematics.

b. Mrs. Jones is my English teacher, but I have Mr. Brown for Science and Mathematics.

c. Mrs. Jones is my english teacher, but I have Mr. Brown for science and mathematics.

d. Mrs. Jones is my English teacher, but I have Mr. Brown for science and mathematics.

18. Choose the sentence with the correct capitalization.

a. That country was ruled by a Dictator for decades, but recently, its people elected their first president.

b. That country was ruled by a dictator for decades, but recently, its people elected their first President.

c. That country was ruled by a dictator for decades, but recently, its people elected their first president.

d. That country was ruled by a Dictator for decades, but recently, its people elected their first President.

19. Choose the sentence with the correct usage.

a. Vegetables are a healthy food; eating them can make you more healthful.

b. Vegetables are a healthful food; eating them can make you more healthful.

c. Vegetables are a healthy food; eating them can make you more healthy.

d. Vegetables are a healthful food; eating them can make you more healthy.

20. Choose the sentence with the correct usage.

a. When James went into his room, he found that his clothes had been put in the closet.

b. When James went in his room, he found that his clothes had been put in the closet.

c. When James went into his room, he found that his clothes had been put into the closet.

d. When James went in his room, he found that his clothes had been put into the closet.

21. Choose the sentence with the correct usage.

a. After you lay the books on the counter, you may lay down for a nap.

b. After you lie the books on the counter, you may lay down for a nap.

c. After you lay the books on the counter, you may lie down for a nap.

d. After you lay the books on the counter, you may lay down for a nap.

22. Choose the sentence with the correct usage.

a. Once the chickens had layed their eggs, they lay on their nests to hatch them.

b. Once the chickens had lay their eggs, they lay on their nests to hatch them.

c. Once the chickens had laid their eggs, they lay on their nests to hatch them.

d. Once the chickens had laid their eggs, they laid on their nests to hatch them.

23. Choose the sentence with the correct usage.

a. Mrs. Foster taught me many things, but I learned the most from Mr. Wallace.

b. Mrs. Foster learned me many things, but I was taught the most by Mr. Wallace.

c. Mrs. Foster learned me many things, but I learned the most from Mr. Wallace.

d. Mrs. Foster taught me many things, but I taught the most from Mr. Wallace.

24. Choose the sentence with the correct usage.

a. He did not have to loose the race; if only his shoes weren't so lose!

b. He did not have to lose the race; if only his shoes weren't so loose!

c. He did not have to loose the race; if only his shoes weren't so lose!

d. He did not have to lose the race; if only his shoes weren't so lose!

25. Choose the sentence with the correct usage.

a. The attorney did not want to prosecute the defendant; his goal was to prosecute the guilty party.

b. The attorney did not want to persecute the defendant; his goal was to persecute the guilty party.

c. The attorney did not want to prosecute the defendant; his goal was to persecute the guilty party.

d. The attorney did not want to persecute the defendant; his goal was to prosecute the guilty party.

26. Choose the sentence with the correct usage.

a. The speeches must precede the election; the election cannot proceed without hearing from the candidates.

b. The speeches must precede the election; the election cannot precede without hearing from the candidates.

c. The speeches must proceed the election; the election cannot precede without hearing from the candidates.

d. The speeches must proceed the election; the election cannot proceed without hearing from the candidates.

27. Choose the sentence with the correct usage.

a. Before a lawyer can rise an objection, he must first rise to his feet.

b. Before a lawyer can raise an objection, he must first raise to his feet.

c. Before a lawyer can raise an objection, he must first rise to his feet.

d. Before a lawyer can rise an objection, he must first raise to his feet.

28. Choose the sentence with the correct usage.

a. You shouldn't sit in that chair wearing black pants; I set the white cat there just a moment ago.

b. You shouldn't set in that chair wearing black pants; I sit the white cat there just a moment ago.

c. You shouldn't set in that chair wearing black pants; I set the white cat there just a moment ago.

d. You shouldn't sit in that chair wearing black pants; I sit the white cat there just a moment ago.

For each of the sentences below choose the correct word to replace the underlined word or phrase.

29. Sarah bought some stationeries.

a. stationary
b. stationarys
c. stationaryes
d. None of the Above

30. He is a man of his words.

a. wordy
b. word
c. wordes
d. None of the Above

31. I have two son in laws.

a. sons in laws.
b. sons on law.
c. sons in law.
d. None of the Above.

32. We'll go to the beach in our vacation.

a. on
b. at
c. from
d. None of the Above.

33. We'll go to the beach during the summer vocations.

a. summer vacation
b. summer's vacation
c. summer vocation
d. summers vacation

34. Richard is the tallest of the two boys.

a. tall
b. taller
c. taller than
d. None of the Above.

35. Choose the correct spelling.

a. lighting
b. lightning
c. lightining
d. lightming

36. Choose the correct spelling.

a. occasionaly
b. occassionally
c. occasionally
d. ocasionally

37. Choose the correct spelling.

a. pronounciation
b. pronuonciation
c. pronounciation
d. pronunciation

38. Choose the correct spelling.

a. questionnaire
b. questionnare
c. questionaire
d. questionare

39. Choose the correct spelling.

a. sergeant
b. sergent
c. sergant
d. sergernt

40. Choose the correct spelling.

    a. immeadiately

    b. imeddiately

    c. immediately

    d. immedaitely

41. Choose the correct spelling.

    a. vacume

    b. vaccum

    c. vacum

    d. vacuum

42. Choose the correct spelling.

    a. theshold

    b. treshold

    c. threshold

    d. threeshold

43. Choose the correct spelling.

    a. segie

    b. sigie

    c. seige

    d. siege

44. Choose the correct spelling.

    a. supersede

    b. supercede

    c. superseed

    d. supercede

45. Choose the correct spelling.

    a. rhytm

    b. rythym

    c. rhythm

    d. ryhtym

46. Choose the correct spelling.

    a. thourough

    b. thoruogh

    c. thourogh

    d. thorough

47. Choose the correct spelling.

    a. fictitiuos

    b. fictitious

    c. fictictious

    d. fictititous

48. Choose the correct spelling.

    a. partiscular

    b. particuler

    c. partticular

    d. particular

49. Choose the correct spelling.

    a. experinment

    b. experiment

    c. expirement

    d. ecperiment

50. Choose the correct spelling.

    a. disappereance

    b. disapperance

    c. disappearance

    d. disapearance

Revise these sentences to have better form and grammar.

51. When I was a child, my mother taught me to say thank you, holding the door open for other, and cover my mouth when yawning or coughing.

a. When I was a child, my mother teaching me to say thank you, to hold the door open for others, and cover my mouth when yawning or coughing.

b. When I was a child, my mother taught me say thank you, to hold the door open for others, and to covering my mouth when yawning or coughing.

c. When I was a child, my mother taught me saying thank you, holding the door open for others, and to cover my mouth when yawning or coughing.

d. When I was a child, my mother taught me to say thank you, hold the door open for others, and cover my mouth when yawning or coughing.

52. Mother is talking to a man that wants to hire her to be a receptionist.

a. Mother is talking to a man who wants to hire her to be a receptionist.

b. Mother is talked to a man who wants to hire her to be a receptionist.

c. Mother is talking to a man who wants to her. To be a receptionist.

d. Mother is talking to a man hiring her who to be a receptionist.

53. Those comic books, which was for sale at the magazine shop, are now quite valuable.

a. Those comics books which were for sale, at the magazine shop are now quite valuable.

b. Those comic books, which were for sale at the magazine, shop, are now quite valuable.

c. Those comic books, which were for sale at the magazine shop, are now, quite valuable

d. Those comic books, which were for sale at the magazine shop, are now quite valuable.

54. If you want to sell your car, it's important being honest with the buyer.

a. If you want to sell your car, being honest with the buyer is important.

b. If you want to sell your car, its important to be honest with the buyer.

c. If you wanting to sell your car, being honest with the buyer are important.

d. If you want to selling your car, to be honest with the buyer is important.

55. Although today the boy was nice to my brother, they usually was quite mean to him.

    a. Although today the boy was nice to my brother, they were usually quite mean to him.

    b. Although today the boy was nice to my brother, he was usually quite mean to him.

    c. Although today the boy was nice to my brother, he is usually quite mean to him.

    d. Although today the boy was nice to my brother, he were usually quite mean to him.

Combine the separate sentences into one simpler sentence with the same meaning.

56. The customers were impatient for the store to open. The customers rushed inside as soon as the doors were open.

    a. Although the customers were impatient for the store to open, the doors were opened as soon as the customers rushed inside.

    b. Although the doors were opened before customers rushed inside, the customers were impatient for the store to open.

    c. The customers, who were impatient for the store to open, rushed inside as soon as the doors were open.

    d. Although the doors were opened by impatient customers, they rushed inside before the store was open.

57. I should enter my dog in a dog pageant. Everyone says that my dog, whose name is Skipper, is the most beautiful one they've ever seen."

    a. Because my dog's name is Skipper, my dog was entered in the pageant and everyone said he was the mot beautiful dog that they've ever seen.

    b. I should enter my dog in a dog pageant, since everyone says that Skipper is the most beautiful dog they've ever seen.

    c. Before I entered my dog in the dog pageant, Skipper said that he was the most beautiful dog that he'd ever seen.

    d. Skipper entered my dog in the dog pageant because he was the most beautiful one that anyone had ever seen.

58. The doctor was not looking forward to meeting Mrs. Lucas. The doctor would have to tell Mrs. Lucas that she has cancer. The doctor hates giving bad news to patients.

a. The doctor hates giving bad news, and so he was not looking forward to meeting Mrs. Lucas because he would have to tell her that she has cancer.

b. The doctor has cancer and was not looking forward to meeting Mrs. Lucas and telling her this bad news.

c. Before the doctor met Mrs. Lucas, he had to give his the patients the bad news that Mrs. Lucas has cancer.

d. The doctor was not looking forward to giving the bad news to his patients that he had to tell Mrs. Lucas that his patients have cancer.

59. Mom hates shopping. We were out of bread, milk and eggs. Mom went to the supermarket.

a. Because we were out of bread, milk and eggs, Mom hated shopping at the supermarket.

b. Although she hates shopping, Mom went to the supermarket since we were out of bread, milk and eggs.

c. Although we were out of bread, milk and eggs, Mom still hated shopping at the supermarket and went there anyway.

d. Because Mom hated shopping at the supermarket, she went to there to buy her bread, milk and eggs.

60. I hate needles. I want to give blood. I can't give blood.

a. Although I hate needles, I couldn't give blood even if I wanted to.

b. Because I hate needles, I can't give blood, although I want to give blood.

c. Whenever I hate needles, I give blood although I can't give blood.

d. Whenever I can't give blood, I give blood anyway, although I hate needles.

Answer Key

Section I - Verbal Skills

1. D
This is a place relationship. Acting is done in a theater in the same way gambling is done in a casino.

2. C
Pork is the meat of a pig in the same way beef is the meat of a cow.

3. A
This is a classification relationship. The first is the class which the second belongs.

4. C
Slumber is a synonym for sleep and bog is a synonym for swamp.

5. D
This is a part-to-whole relationship. A petal is to a flower as fur is to a rabbit.

6. A
A present celebrates a birthday and a reward celebrates an accomplishment.

7. C
This is a functional relationship. A shovel is used to dig and scissors are used to snip.

8. A
This is a parts-to-whole relationship. The finger is part of the hand in the same way, a leg is part of a body.

9. B
The first is the study of the second. Zoology is the study of animals in the same way botany is the study of plants.

10. B
This is a type relationship. A child is a young human just as a kitten is a young cat.

11. B
This is a composition relationship. A candle is made of wax and a bowl is made of clay.

12. B
Able and competent are synonyms.

13. A
Antidote and cure are synonyms.

14. C
Consensus and agreement are synonyms.

15. A
Magnify and amplify are synonyms.

16. B
Immaculate and perfect are synonyms.

17. C
Feasible and viable are synonyms.

18. B
Reason and rationale are synonyms.

19. A
Tinge and touch are synonyms.

20. C
Gist and summary are synonyms.

21. C
Initiate and instigate are synonyms.

22. A
Expertise and specialty are synonyms.

23. B
Amazing and extraordinary are synonyms.

24. C
Furious and angry are synonyms.

25. A
Inquire and ask are synonyms.

26. A
Awful and terrible are synonyms.

27. C
Wicked and evil are synonyms.

28. False
You cannot real a negative conclusion from 2 positive statements.

29. Uncertain
No information is given about houses NOT on Appleby or Francisco streets.

30. Uncertain
It is possible that some of my tropical fish are very sensitive, but it is also possible that they are all insensitive varieties.

31. Uncertain
I may be rich or I may not be.

32. False
IF Science can explain all events, AND making a decision is an event, THEN science CAN explain how I make a decision.

33. False.
There are 2 problems. Doctors can sometimes predict epidemics. Bird Flu is becoming an epidemic.

Bird flu is not an epidemic yet, and doctors can only predict epidemics sometimes.

34. Uncertain.
My textbook MAY have come from that store or it may have come from another store.

35. D
This is a relationship of words question. All the choices are dinnerware except dinner.

36. A
This is a relationship of words question. All the choices are major planets except the moon.

37. D
This is a relationship of words question. All the choices are cat or feline family except fox.

38. B
This is a relationship of words question. All the choices are plants, except garden.

39. B
This is a relationship of words question. All the choices are related to lawn, except flowers.

40. A
This is a synonym relationship. Influential has the same meaning as powerful.

41. D
This is an antonym relationship. Careful is the opposite meaning of reckless.

42. C
This is an opposite relationship. Prey is the opposite meaning of predator.

43. A
This is a synonym relationship. Shimmer has the same meaning as sheen.

44. C
This is a synonym relationship. Foe has the same meaning as enemy.

45. D
This is a synonym relationship. Unconventional has the same meaning as offbeat.

46. A
This is a classification relationship. Frogs are amphibians, and snakes are reptiles.

47. C
Red is a color and triangle is a shape.

48. C
Skirt is a type of clothing as Mars is a planet.

49. C
Intelligent has the same relation to brilliant as fat to obese.

50. B
Busted has the same relation to broken as bland to plain.

51. A
Occupation has the same relation to work as two to binary.

52. C
A zoologist studies animals, and a botanist studies plants.

53. B
Fixed and indefinite are antonyms.

54. C
Strategic and unplanned are antonyms.

55. B
Authentic and imitation are antonyms.

56. D
Villian and hero are antonyms.

57. A
Vanish and appear are antonyms.

58. C
Literal and figurative are antonyms.

59. A
Harsh and mild are antonyms.

60. D
Splurge and save are antonyms.

Section II – Quantitative Skills

1. D
The sequence is increasing. Each new term is obtained by multiplying the last term by 2. Therefore, 80 x 2 = 160

2. C
Each new term is calculated by subtracting 100 from the last term. So, 18095 – 100 = 17995

3. B
Each new term is calculated by adding 6 to the last term, therefore, -27 + 6 = -21

4. C
The sequence increases initially and then decreases in the next term. The relationship between each increase is +200 and the relationship with the alternate decrease is -300. So the answer is -300 + 200 = -100

5. B
The sequence is increasing. Each new term is derived by multiplying the last term with an increasing number. The first term is multiplied by 1 to get the next term. That is multiplied by 2 to get the 3rd term, which is multiplied by 3 to get the 4th term. So the answer is 12.18 x 4 = 48.72

6. D
This sequence is increasing. The

sequence increases by multiplying by 3 and adding 3. The first term the sequence is increasing by multiplying and adding 3 alternatively. The first term was multiplied by 3 to get the second term, and that was added to 3. The answer = 36 x 3 = 108

7. B
The sequence increases and decreases alternatively. The rate of increase is +2 and decrease is -3, so the answer = 346 – 3 = 343

8. A
The sequence is increasing after repeating the last term. The answer = 41 + 10 = 51

9. A
The first two terms increased by +3. The difference between each subsequent term is the rate of last increase + 2. So answer is 29 + 7 + 2 = 38

10. B
First two terms decreased by 11 and the subsequent terms decreased by subtracting 2 from the last rate of decrease. Answer is 7 – (5-2) = 7-3 =4.

11. D
The sequence is increasing by adding 2 and multiplying 2 alternatively. The next 2 terms are 24 + 2= 26 and 26 x 2 = 52.

12. C
The sequence is decreasing by 8.

13. B
The sequence is increasing by multiplying the last term by 3. 2.7 x 3= 8.1 and 8.1 x 3 = 24.3

14. A
The sequence is decreasing by dividing the last term by 2.

15. C
The sequence is increasing by 7.

16. C
The sequence is increasing by 3.

17. B
The sequence is decreasing by 5.

18. C
The sequence is decreasing by -5 and -10 alternatively the first term is 75 – 5 = 70 and the last term is 35 – 5 = 30.

19. C
20. B
21. A
22. B
23. A
24. B
25. C
26. A
27. B

28. B
#1 = 48
#2 = 58
#3 = 84
3 is greater than 1

29. B
#1 = 42
#2 = 60
#3 = 25
1 < 2 > 3

30. A
#1 = 30
#2 = 64
#3 = 37
1 < 3 < 2

31. B
#1 = 17
#2 = 40
#3 = 47
1 < 3 > 2

32. A
#1 = 20
#2 = 105
#3 = 30
3 < 2 > 1

33. B
#1 = 252
#2 = 350
#3 = 60
2 > 1 > 3

34. B
#1 = 27
#2 = 2
#3 = 22
2 < 1 > 3

35. D
#1 = 90
#2 = 185
#3 = 48
3 < 1 < 2

36. B
#1 = 19
#2 = 13
#3 = 7
1 and 3 are not equal

37. B
$(2/3)Z + 10 = 3 \times 15$
$2/3 \ Z = 45 – 10$
$Z = 35 \times 3/2$
$Z = 52.5$

38. A
$X = 25 + (1/3 * 27)$
$X = 25 + 9$
$X = 34$

39. C
$Z = (5 \times 5) – 10$
$Z = 15$

40. A
$3/4 \times 40 = 30 + 12 = 42$

41. C
30% of 120 = 40 + 25 = 65

42. B
$75 - x = 15 + (3/5 * 75)$
$75 - x = 45 + 15$
$75 - x = 60$
$x = 75 – 60 = 15$

43. A
2/3 of 100 = 66.66 X 5 = 333.33

44. C
9 X 5 = 45 X 2 = 90

45. B
58 - 10 = 48 ÷ 8 = 6

46. B
1/5 of 40 = 8
25 – X = 8
X = 17

47. C
1/4 of 16 = 4
4 – 1 = 3

48. C
8 X 7 = 56 X 2 = 112

49. A
65 - 15 = 50 ÷ 10 = 5

50. B
1/5 of 60 = 12
25 – X = 12
X = 13

Section III – Reading

1. A
Choice B is incorrect; the author did not express their opinion on the subject matter. Choice C is incorrect, the author was not trying to prove a point, nor is the author trying to persuade.

2. C
Choice C is correct; historians believe it was brutal and bloody. Choice A is incorrect; there is no consensus that the Crusades achieved great things. Choice B is incorrect; it did not stabilize the Holy Lands. Choice D is incorrect, some historians do believe this was the purpose but not all historians.

3. D
The feudal system led to infighting. Choice A is incorrect, it had the opposite effect. Choice B is incorrect, though this is a good answer, it is not the best answer. The Church asked for volunteers not the Feudal Lords. Choice C is incorrect, it did have an effect on the Crusades.

4. A
Saracen was a generic term for Muslims widely used in Europe during the later medieval era.

5. B
This warranty does not cover a product that you have tried to fix yourself. From paragraph two, "This limited warranty does not cover ... any unauthorized disassembly, repair, or modification. "

6. C
ABC Electric could either replace or repair the fan, provided the other conditions are met. ABC Electric has the option to repair or replace.

7. B
The warranty does not cover a stove damaged in a flood. From the passage, "This limited warranty does not cover any damage to the product from improper installation, accident, abuse, misuse, natural disaster, insufficient or excessive electrical supply, abnormal mechanical or environmental conditions."

A flood is an "abnormal environmental condition," and a natural disaster, so it is not covered.

8. A
A missing part is an example of defective workmanship. This is an error made in the manufacturing process. A defective part is not considered workmanship.

9. D
This question tests the reader's summarization skills. The other choices A, B, and C focus on portions of the second paragraph that are too narrow and do not relate to the specific portion of text in question. The complexity of the sentence may mislead students into selecting one of these answers, but rearranging or restating the sentence will lead the reader to the correct answer. In addition, choice A makes an assumption that may or may not be true about the intentions of the company, choice B focuses on one product rather than the idea of the products, and choice C makes an assumption about women that may or may not be true and is not supported by the text.

10. B
This question tests reader's attention to detail. If a reader selects A, he or she may have picked up on the use of the word "debate" and assumed, very logically, that the two are at odds because they are fighting; however, this is simply not supported in the text. Choice C also uses very specific quotes from the text, but it rearranges and gives them false meaning. The artists want to elevate their creations above the creations of other artists, thereby showing that they are "creative" and "innovative." Similarly, choice D takes phrases straight from the text and rearranges and confuses them. The artists are described as

wanting to be "creative, innovative, individual people," not the women.

11. A
This question tests reader's vocabulary and summarization skills. This phrase, used by the author, may seem flippant and dismissive if readers focus on the word "whatever" and misinterpret it as a popular, colloquial term. In this way, choices B and C may mislead the reader to selecting one of them by including the terms "unimportant" and "stupid," respectively. Choice D is a similar misreading, but doesn't make sense when the phrase is at the beginning of the passage and the entire passage is on media messages. Choice A is literarily and contextually appropriate, and the reader can understand that the author would like to keep the introduction focused on the topic the passage is going to discuss.

12. A
This question tests a reader's inference skills. The extreme use of the word "all" in choice B suggests that every single advertising company are working to be approachable, and while this is not only unlikely, the text specifically states that "more" companies have done this, signifying that they have not all participated, even if it's a possibility that they may some day. The use of the limiting word "only" in choice C lends that answer similar problems; women are still buying from companies who do not care about this message, or those companies would not be in business, and the passage specifies that "many" women are worried about media messages, but not all. Readers may find choice D logical, especially if they are looking to make an inference, and while this may be a possibility, the passage does not suggest or discuss this happening. Choice A is correct

based on specifically because of the relation between "still working" in the answer and "will hopefully" and the extensive discussion on companies struggles, which come only with progress, in the text.

13. C
This question tests the reader's summarization skills. The entire passage is leading up to the idea that the president of the US may not have had grounds to assert his Fourteen Points when other countries had lost so much. Choice A is pretty directly inferred by the text, but it does not adequately summarize what the entire passage is trying to communicate. Choice B may also be inferred by the passage when it says that the war is "imminent," but it does not represent the entire message, either. The passage does seem to be in praise of FDR, or at least in respect of him, but it does not in any way claim that he is the smartest president, nor does this represent the many other points included. Choice C is then the obvious answer, and most directly relates to the closing sentences which it rewords.

14. C
This question tests the reader's attention to detail. The passage does state that choices A and B are true, and while those statements are in proximity to the explanation for why the war started, they are not the reason given. Choice D is a mix up of words used in the passage, which says that the largest powers were in play but not that this fact somehow started the war. The passage does make a direct statement that a domino effect started the war, supporting choice C as the correct answer.

15. A

This question tests the reader's understanding of functions in writing. Throughout the passage, it states that leaders of other nations were hesitant to accept generous or peaceful terms because of the grievances of the war, and the great loss of life was chief among these. While the passage does touch on the devastation of deadly weapons (B), the use of this raw, emotional fact serves a much larger purpose, and the focus of the passage is not the weapons. While readers may indeed consider who lost the most soldiers (C) when, so many countries were involved and the inequalities of loss are mentioned in the passage, there is no discussion of this in the passage. Choice D is related to A, but choice A is more direct and relates more to the passage.

16. B

This question tests the reader's vocabulary skills. Choice A may seem appealing to readers because it is phonetically similar to "catalyzed," but the two are not related in any other way. Choice C makes sense in context, but if plugged in to the sentence creates a redundancy that doesn't make sense. Choice D does also not make sense contextually, even if the reader may consider that funds were needed to create more weaponry, especially if it was advanced.

17. A

The correct order of ingredients is brown sugar, baking soda and chocolate chips.

18. B

Sturdy: strong, solid in structure or person. In context, Stir in chocolate chips by hand with a *sturdy* wooden spoon.

19. A

Disperse: to scatter in different directions or break up. In context, Stir until the chocolate chips and nuts are evenly *dispersed.*

20. B

You can stop stirring the nuts when they are evenly distributed. From the passage, "Stir until the chocolate chips and nuts are evenly dispersed."

21. B

Choice A is incorrect as the Monster killed Frankenstein, not the other way around. Choice B is correct, Frankenstein is dead. Choice C is incorrect - Mary Shelley is the author. Choice D is incorrect, the person is called Frankenstein.

22. C

The speaker 'suspended' from following through on his duty to destroy the monster due to curiosity and compassion. The other choices may seem reasonable, but are not explicitly given in the passage.

23. D

All the choices are correct. Frankenstein's monster destroys Frankenstein by

a. By killing Frankenstein

b. By letting himself be the monster everyone sees him as

c. By destroying everything Frankenstein loved

24. A

Superfluous means unnecessary. Looking at the context of the word as it is used in the passage:

"Your repentance," I said, "is now superfluous. If you had listened to the voice of conscience and heeded the stings of remorse before you had urged your diabolical vengeance to this extremity, Frankenstein would yet have lived."

25. B
The time limit for radar detectors is 14 days. Since you made the purchase 15 days ago, you do not qualify for the guarantee.

26. B
Since you made the purchase 10 days ago, you are covered by the guarantee. Since it is an advertised price at a different store, ABC Electric will "beat" the price by 10% of the difference, which is,

500 – 400 = 100 – difference in price

100 X 10% = $10 – 10% of the difference

The advertised lower price is $400. ABC will beat this price by 10% so they will refund $100 + 10 = $110.

27. C
The purpose of this passage is to persuade.

28. B
The correct answer can be found in the fourth sentence of the first paragraph.

Choice A is incorrect because repenting begins the day AFTER Mardi Gras. Choice C is incorrect because you can celebrate Mardi Gras without being a member of a Krewe.

Choice D is incorrect because exploration does not play any role in a modern Mardi Gras celebration.

29. A
The second sentence is the last paragraph states that Krewes are led by the Kings and Queens. Therefore, you must have to be part of a Krewe to be its King or its Queen.
Choice B is incorrect because it never states in the passage that only people from France can be Kings and Queen of Mardi Gras

Choice C is incorrect because the passage says nothing about having to speak French.

Choice D is incorrect because the passage does state that the Kings and Queens throw doubloons, which is fake money.

30. C
The first sentences of BOTH the 2nd and 3rd paragraphs mention that French explorers started this tradition in New Orleans.
Choices A, B and D are incorrect because they are just names of cities or countries listed in the 2nd paragraph.

31. B
In the final paragraph the word spectator is used to describe people who are watching the parade and catching cups, beads and doubloons.

Choices A and C are incorrect because we know the people who participate are part of Krewes. People who work the floats and parades are also part of Krewes

Choice D is incorrect because the passage makes no mention of people who do not celebrate Mardi Gras.

32. D
There is no concrete evidence of choices A, B, or C. Choice D is therefore the best answer, and the passage supports the notion that her mouth possess a special kiss that neither her daughter nor husband can attain, and in this way her mouth seems to mock them.

33. A

Choice A is the best-supported choice: The narrator notes, "Until Wendy came, her mother was the chief one," and further describes Mrs. Darling as a woman who will not compromise. Both Mr. Darling and Wendy are seemingly unable to access the full extent of Mrs. Darling's affection. The description of Mrs. Darling's mind as "like the tiny boxes, one within the other, that come from the puzzling East" suggests she is a woman with many layers, is impossible to fully understand, and to this end has even a foreign quality to her. B is incorrect as nothing about her denial of her husband or daughter appears to be accidental. Choice C's "absent-minded" descriptor could be reasonable, yet "romantic" is not in this case the same as "artistic", and there is no evidence of Mrs. Darling's artistic ability. Again, in light of Mr. Darling giving up on the elusive kiss, choice D could be reasonable, however there is nothing to suggest a serious problem is present in the matrimony. Nothing suggests Mrs. Darling is indecisive, choice E is incorrect.

Section IV - Vocabulary

34. A

Anecdote: n. A short account of an incident

35. B

Heinous: adj. shocking, terrible or wicked.

36. A

Harbinger: n. a person of thing that tells or announces the coming of someone or something

37. B

Judicious: Having, or characterized by, good judgment or sound thinking.

38. B

Ethanol: n. a colorless volatile flammable liquid C_2H_6O.

39. A

Respiratory: adj. Of, relating to, or affecting respiration or the organs of respiration.

40. B

Inherent: Naturally a part or consequence of something.

41. A

Vapid: adj. tasteless or bland.

42. C

Waif: n. homeless child or stray.

43. D

Homologous: adj. similar or identical.

44. B

Obsolete: adj. no longer in use; gone into disuse; disused or neglected.

45. A

Rankle: v. To cause irritation or deep bitterness.

46. C

Renewable

47. C

Torpid: adj. Lazy, lethargic or apathetic.

48. A

Gregarious: adj. Describing one who enjoys being in crowds and socializing.

49. B
Mutation: n. a change or alteration.

50. C
Lithe: adj. flexible or pliant.

55. A
Resent: v. to express displeasure or indignation.

56. A
Immaterial: adj. irrelevant not having substance or matter.

57. A
Impeccable: adj. perfect, no faults or errors.

58. B
Pudgy: adj. fat, plump or overweight.

59. C
Alloy: v. Mix or combine; often used of metals.

60. B
Combustible: adj. Able to catch fire and burn easily.

Section V – Math

1. B
Let XY represent the initial number, X + Y = 12, YX=XY+ 36, only b = 48 satisfies both equations.

2. A
The problem is to find the perimeter of a shape made by merging a square and a semi circle. Perimeter = 3 sides of the square + 1/2 circumference of the circle.
= (3 x 5) + ½(5 π)
= 15 + 2.5 π
Perimeter = 17.5 π cm

3. B
Let the father's age=Y, and Kate's age = X, therefore Y = 32 + X, in 5 years y = 5x, substituting for Y will be 5x = 32 + X, 5x – x = 32, 4X = 32,X = 32/8, x = 8, Kate will be 8 in 5 years time, so Kate's present age = 8 - 5 = 3.

4. A
This is a simple direct proportion problem:
If Lynn can type 1 page in p minutes,

she can type x pages in 5 minutes

Cross multiplication: x * p = 5 * 1

Then,

x = 5/p

5. A
This is an inverse ration problem.

1/x = 1/a + 1/b where a is the time Sally can paint a house, b is the time John can paint a house, x is the time Sally and John can together paint a house.

So,

1/x = 1/4 + 1/6 ... We use the least common multiple in the denominator that is 24:

1/x = 6/24 + 4/24

1/x = 10/24

x = 24/10

x = 2.4 hours.

In other words; 2 hours + 0.4 hours = 2 hours + 0.4 * 60 minutes

= 2 hours 24 minutes

6. D
First add all the numbers 62 + 18 + 39 + 13 + 16 + 37 + 25 = 210. Then divide by 7 (the number of data provided) = 210/7 = 30

7. B
Last season's ticket = X,
X + (10/100)X = 880
100x + 10x = 88000
110x = 88000
x = 88000/110
x = 800

8. B
Total Volume = Volume of large cylinder - Volume of small cylinder

Volume of a cylinder = area of base • height = $\pi r^2 * h$

Total Volume = $(\pi * 12^2 * 10) - (\pi * 6^2 * 5)$ = $1440\pi - 180\pi$

= 1260π in^3

9. A
Distance traveled by 1st train in 20 minutes = (72 km/hr × 20 minutes)/60 minutes = 24 km. Distance traveled by 2nd train in 20 minutes = (52 km/hr × 20 minutes)/60 minutes = 17.33 km. Since the trains are traveling in opposite directions, add the distances for the difference apart, 24 + 17.33 = 41.33 km.

10. B
Suppose oranges in the basket before = x
Then according to the condition
X + 8x/5 = 130
5x + 8x = 650
X = 50

11. D
We have a circle given with diameter 8 cm and a square located within the circle. We are asked to find the area of the circle for which we only need to know the length of the radius that is the half of the diameter.

Area of circle = πr^2 ... r = 8/2 = 4 cm

Area of circle = $\pi * 4^2$

= 16π cm^2 ... As we notice, the inner square has no role in this question.

12. C
In one trip around the track, he covers the distance equal to the circumference of the circular path.
Circumference of the path = 75 × π = 235.65 meters.
Distance covered in 7 rounds = 235.65 × 7 = 1650 meters.

13. B
This is an inverse proportion question. The number of employees decreases then working time will increase.

Employees	Working hours
12	7
10	x

Therefore, the equation will be
x/7 = 12/10
x = 7 * 12/10
x = 7.2

Therefore, the remaining staff will have to work, in minutes, 0.2 × 60 = 12 minutes.

14. B
The speed is 300km/hr so it will cover 5 km/minute. Therefore, the train will travel 45km in 9 minutes. Time to arrive at station B will be 9:05 pm.

15. A
The angles opposite both angles 30° & angle d are respectively equal to vertical angles.
2(30° + d) = 360°
2d = 360° - 60°
2d = 300°
d = 150°

16. A
George's average speed = 80/32/ = 25 km/hr.
Average speed for Marsha is 23 km/hr.
The distance covered by Marsha in

3.2 hrs = 3.2 X 23 = 73.6 km

So Marsha will be 80 – 73.6 = 6.4 km away from the finish when George crosses.

17. C
The length of the track = 1.2 km = 1200 meters.
John will complete 1 round in 1200/120 = 10 minutes.
Tony will complete 1 round in 1200/100 = 12 minutes.
David will complete 1 round in 1200/75 = 16 minutes.
The Least Common Multiple of these is 240. Therefore, they will be together after 240 minutes.

18. D
As 1 cm = 5 km so 12.4 cm will be = 12.4×5=62 km

19. C
Number of problems remaining = 40 – 28 = 12
Time remaining = 30 – 25 = 5 minutes = 5 X 60 = 300 seconds. Time for each remaining question = 300/12 = 25 seconds.

20. B
Perimeter of a parallelogram is the sum of the sides.

Perimeter = 2(l + b)
Perimeter = 2(3 + 10), 2 x 13
Perimeter = 26 cm

21. D
2009 X 108 is approximately 210,000. The actual number is 216,972.

22. A
The purchase price of 12 shirts when profit is 8% = 0.92 X 336 = $309.12
The purchase price of each shirt = 309.12/12 = $25.76

23. C
This is a proportionality question.
12 : 4
X : 20

4 * 5 = 20 and 12 * 5 = X
X = 60

24. D
First, convert everything to seconds.
Song A = 240 + 56 = 296 sec.
Song B = 120 + 30 = 150 sec.
Song C = 600 + 16 = 616 sec.
Total = 296 + 150 + 616 = 1062. Average will be 1062/3 = 354.
In hours, 354/60 = 5 minutes, 54 seconds.

25. B
8.50 * .4 = 3.40 + 1.30 = $4.70

26. D
We can determine the price of single rooms from the information given for the second company. 13 single rooms = 3185.

One single room = 3185 / 13 = 245
The first company paid for 6 single rooms at $245. 245 x 6 = $1470

Total amount paid for 4 double rooms by first company = $2850 - $1470 = $1380

Cost per double room = 1380 / 4 = $345

27. B
Formula for perimeter of a rectangle is 2(L + W)
p=26, so 2(L+W) = p

The length is 5 inches more than the width, so
2(w+5) + 2w = 26
2w + 10 + 2w = 26
2w + 2w = 26 - 10
4w = 18

W = 16/4 = 4 inches
L is 5 inches more than w, so L = 5 + 4 = 9 inches.

28. A
Number of mangos in the basket is 3/5 x 125 = 75
Number of ripe mangos = 2/5 x 75 = 30

29. D
Substitute the known variables, (3 x 2) + (4 x 4) x 8 =, 6 + 16 x 8, 24 x 8 = 176

30. A
2cnx = 2(4 x 5 x 3)/(2 X 5) =, 2 x 60/2 x 5 =, 120/10 = 12

31. A
First change all the terms to fractions, therefore, we get 7/2 / 14/5, to divide we need to invert the second fraction, 7/2 x 5/14, and then we cancel out to reduce to the lowest terms, 1/2 x 5/2 = 5/4, convert back to proper fraction to get 1 1/4

32. B
Substitute known variables, 2 x 9/3 + 3 x 10/5 – 2 =, 18/3 + 30/5 – 2
(6 + 6) - 2
12 - 2 = 10

33. A
First solve the fraction in each bracket separately, therefore (1/3 + 2/6) - (3/4 - 1/3) = (find common denominator) (2+2/6) – (9- 4/12) = (4/6) – (5/12) = (find common denominator again) 2/3 – 5/12 =, 8 - 5/12 = 3/12 = 1/4.

34. B
(4/5 - 3/10) + (2/3 – 3/9) =, (find a common denominator) (8-3/10) + (6-3/9) =, (5/10) + (3/9) = 1/2 + 1/3, (find a common denominator) 3+2/6 = 5/6

35. A
2 + a number divided by 7.
(2 + X) divided by 7.
(2 + X)/7

36. D
Substitute with known variables, (6 x 8) – 12 + (2 x 12) =, 48 – 12 + 24, do the additions first, 48 – (12 + 24) =, 48 – 36 = 12

37. C
Subtract the whole numbers and then subtract the fractions, therefore 3 2/3 - 1 2/8 = (3-1) (2/3 – 2/8) = find common denominator to subtract the fractions, (2) (16-6)/24 = 2 10/24, reduce to lowest terms, 2 5/12

38. A
Subtract the whole numbers and then subtract the fractions, therefore (7-4) (2/5 – 3/10) = 3 (4-3/10) = 3 1/10

39. C
-4 – 5x = 8x + 8, bring same terms to same side of the equation changing the negative or positive signs when they cross over, therefore -5x - 8x = 8 + 5, = -13x = 13, x = 1.

40. A
First, convert all the terms to fractions and then cancel out. Therefore, 7/3 x 10/7 x 3/4 = 1/3 x 10/1 x 3/4, 1/3 x 5/1 x 3/2, 1/3 x 5/1 x 3/2 = 15/6 = 2 1/2

41. B
Subtract the whole numbers and then subtract the fractions, therefore (7 - 4) (4/5 – 2/3) = 3 (12 - 10/15) = 3 2/15

42. C
12x – 8 = 3x + 10, bring same terms to same side of the equation changing the negative or positive signs when they cross over, therefore 12x - 3x = 10 + 8, 9x = 18, x = 2

43. C
(3/5 - 2/5) + (3/4 – 2/8) =, (3-2/5) + (6-2/8) =, 1/5 + 4/8 =, (find a common denominator) 8+20/40 = 28/40 = 14/20

44. D
6a + 4 = 28 + 2a, then a = , bring same terms to same side of the equation changing the negative or positive signs when they cross over, therefore 6a – 2a = 28 - 4, 4a = 24, a = 24/4 = 6

45. D
(3-1/4) – (3-2/5) =, 3/4 - 1/5 =. 15-4/20 = 11/20

46. D
6 + 9x = 12 + 7x, bring same terms to same side of the equation changing the negative or positive signs when they cross over, therefore 9x – 7x = 12 – 6, 2x = 6, x = 6/2, x = 3

47. C
First change all the terms to fractions, therefore, we get 32/5 / 16/7, to divide we need to invert the second fraction, 32/5 x 7/16, and then we cancel out to reduce to the lowest terms, 2/5 x 7/1 = 14/5, convert back to proper fraction to get 2 4/5

48. B
-6 + 7a = 9 + 4a, bring same terms to same side of the equation changing the negative or positive signs when they cross over, therefore 7a – 4a = 9 + 6 = 3a = 15, a = 15/3, a = 5

49. B
First change all the terms to fractions, therefore, we get 7/3 / 7/5, to divide we need to invert the second fraction, 7/3 x 5/7, and then we cancel out to reduce to the lowest terms, 1/3 x 5/1 = 5/3, convert back to proper fraction to get 1 2/3

50. B
First, convert all the terms to fractions and then cancel out. Therefore, 2/3 x 11/7 x 21/4 = 2/3 x 11/1 x 3/4, 1/3 x 11/1 x 3/2, 1/1 x 11/1 x 1/2 = 11/2 = 5 1/2

51. A
First change all the terms to fractions, therefore, we get 21/5 / 7/3, to divide we need to invert the second fraction, 21/5 x 3/7, and then we cancel out to reduce to the lowest terms, 3/5 x 3/1 = 9/5, convert back to proper fraction to get 1 4/5

52. B
First, convert all the terms to fractions and then cancel out. Therefore, 10/3 x 9/4 x 16/5 = 10/1 x 3/4 x 16/5, 10/1 x 3/1 x 4/5, 2/1 x 3/1 x 4/1 = 24/1 = 24

53. C
First change all the terms to fractions, therefore, we get 28/9 / 8/3, to divide we need to invert the second fraction, 28/9 x 3/8, and then we cancel out to reduce to the lowest terms, 28/9 X 3/8 = 28/3 X 1/8 = 28/24 = 14/12 = 7/6, convert back to proper fraction to get 1 1/6

54. C
+(+) becomes a positive sign and -(-) equals +, therefore -9 + (+6) – (-2) = -9 + 6 + 2 = -3 + 2 = -1

55. B (5-5) (1/2 – 3/7) = (7-6/14) = 1/14

56. D
-(-) becomes + and -(+) becomes -, therefore, -3 - (-7) - (+5) = -3 + 7 – 5, 4 - 5 = -1

57. D
First, convert all the terms to fractions and then cancel out. Therefore,

15/4 x 4/5 x 7/4 = 3/4 x 4/1 x 7/4, 3/4 x 1/1 x 7/1, 21/4 = 5 1/4

58. A
There are several ways to solve this - since a common denominator is not needed, first convert the whole numbers to fractions, add and then subtract.
So 33/5 - 24/5 = 9/5 = 1 4/5

59. B
46,227 + 101,032 = 147.259, or approximately 147,000.

60. A
√121 = 11

Section V – Language Arts

1. D
A colon informs the reader that what follows the mark proves, explains, or lists elements of what preceded the mark.

2. D
A colon informs the reader that what follows the mark proves, explains, or lists elements of what preceded the mark.

3. C
The dash is used when the speaker cannot continue.

4. B
The dash is used to show a closed range of values.

5. A
Do not use a period after Roman numerals.

6. A
A period should be used for academic degrees when abbreviated. In choice B, it should be B.S.N. For choices C and D, do not use a period for abbreviations that are accepted as the shortened form of proper names like National Aeronautics and Space Administration (NASA), and Federal Bureau of Investigation (FBI).

7. C
A period is used to end an imperative sentence, that is, at the end of a direction or a command.

8. A
North, South, East, and West are only capitalized when used as sections of the country, but not as compass directions.

9. D
The New York Times is the name of a publication so capitalized. Mottos, slogans and notices are capitalized. For example, Employees Only, or All the News That's Fit to Print.

10. B
President is not capitalized unless used with a name as in, President Obama.

11. C
The names of plays are capitalized. All words except articles are capitalized.

12. C
Capitalize words such as Mother, Father, Grandmother, Grandfather, Son, Daughter, and Sis when they are used in place of the person's name. Do not capitalize them when they follow possessive pronouns such as my, your, his, her, our, or your.

13. A
The Sahara Desert is a proper name so capitalized. The names of countries, i.e. Africa, are capitalized.

14. D
The state of Georgia is capitalized as it is a proper noun. Compass directions are not capitalized.

15. C
The names of rivers are capitalized.

16. C
Words such as college, school, department, office, division, association, and conference when they stand alone but are capitalized when they are official names.

17. D
English is capitalized because it is the name of a language. Science and math are not capitalized.

18. C
Dictator is not capitalized. President is only capitalized when used with a name, as in President Obama.

19. D
Healthful vs. Healthy. Use 'Healthy' to describe something that is of good for your health and 'healthful' refers to habits or types.

20. A
In vs. Into. 'In' a room means inside. 'Into' refers to movement or action.

21. C
Lay vs. Lie. 'Lie' requires an object and 'lay' does not. So you can lie down, (no object. and you lay a book on the floor.

22. C
Lay vs. Lie. 'Lie' requires an object and 'lay' does not. 'Laid' is the past tense of lay.

23. B
Learn vs. Teach. Learning is what students do, and teaching is what teachers do.

24. B
Lose vs. Loose. 'Lose' is to no longer have, or to lose a race. 'Loose' is not tied or able to move freely.

25. D
Persecute vs. Prosecute. To prosecute is to have a legal claim against someone and to persecute is to harass.

26. A
Precede vs. Proceed. To precede, is to go first or in front of. To proceed is to go forward.

27. C
Rise vs. Raise. 'Rise' does not require an object and raise does require an object. You have to 'raise' something.

28. A
Sit vs. Set. 'Set' requires an object – something to set down. 'Sit' is something that you do, like sit on the chair.

29. A
Stationary is the singular and plural form.

30. B

31. C
You have one son in law and two sons in law. You may have many in-laws however. Alternately, your son-in-law may own a house, so you would say, my son in law's house.

32. A
Use 'On' with vacations and holidays.

33. C
The correct spelling is summer vacation.

34. B
Taller is correct, as in taller of the two boys. Taller than is used as a comparison, as in, Richard is taller than Peter.

35. B
36. C
37. D
38. A
39. A
40. C
41. D
42. C
43. D
44. A
45. C
46. D
47. B
48. D
49. B
50. C
51. D

52. A
When referring to a person, use "who" instead of "that."

53. D
The comma separates a phrase starting with 'which.'

54. B

55. C
The subject in the first phrase, "the boy," has to agree with the subject in the second phrase, "he is."

56. C
57. B
58. A
59. B
60. A

Conclusion

CONGRATULATIONS! You have made it this far because you have applied yourself diligently to practicing for the exam and no doubt improved your potential score considerably! Getting into a good school is a huge step in a journey that might be challenging at times but will be many times more rewarding and fulfilling. That is why being prepared is so important.

Good Luck!

FREE Ebook Version

Go to http://tinyurl.com/n5g462g

Register for Free Updates and More Practice Test Questions

Register your purchase at

www.test-preparation.ca/register.html for fast and convenient access to updates, errata, free test tips and more practice test questions.

Visit us Online for more practice questions!

www.test-preparation.ca

www.study-skills.ca

www.ingramcontent.com/pod-product-compliance
Lightning Source LLC
LaVergne TN
LVHW081332060426
835513LV00014B/1258